Akka Cookbook

Make your application fast, concurrent, and reactive through exciting recipes

Héctor Veiga Ortiz

Piyush Mishra

BIRMINGHAM - MUMBAI

Akka Cookbook

First published: May 2017

Production reference: 1240517

Published by Packt Publishing Ltd.
Livery Place
35 Livery Street
Birmingham
B3 2PB, UK.
ISBN 978-1-78528-818-0

www.packtpub.com

Credits

Authors
Héctor Veiga Ortiz
Piyush Mishra

Reviewer
Steve Fosdal

Commissioning Editor
Kunal Parikh

Acquisition Editor
Chaitanya Nair

Content Development Editor
Rohit Kumar Singh

Technical Editor
Vivek Pala

Copy Editor
Stuti Shrivastava

Project Coordinator
Vaidehi Sawant

Proofreader
Safis Editing

Indexer
Francy Puthiry

Production Coordinator
Nilesh Mohite

About the Authors

Héctor Veiga Ortiz is a software engineer specializing in real-time data integration. Recently, he has focused his work on different cloud technologies (such as AWS) to develop and run scalable, resilient, and high performing applications that are able to handle high volume, real-time data in diverse protocols and formats. To accomplish this task, he has been focusing his work on messaging systems such as Akka. He has also been working on microservice architectures with frameworks such as Lightbend's Lagom. Additionally, he has a strong foundation in messaging broker knowledge, such as RabbitMQ and AMQP. Also, Héctor has a master's degree in telecommunication engineering from the Universidad Politécnica de Madrid and a master's degree in information technology and management from the Illinois Institute of Technology.

He currently works at HERE Technologies as part of the global traffic data integrations team and is actively developing scalable applications to consume data from several different sources. He heavily utilizes Akka to address the scalability and processing requirements. In the past, Héctor worked at Xaptum Technologies, a company dedicated to M2M technologies. Moreover, he has also contributed to the Akka project on a couple of occasions and is an active StackOverflow user on the `akka` tag.

Héctor has also worked as a technical reviewer on the books *RabbitMQ Cookbook* and *RabbitMQ Essentials* by Packt Publishing.

I would like to thank my family and friends for their support. I particular, I would like to acknowledge my family (my mother, Pilar; my sister, Paula; and my father, Jose Carlos), who has been supporting me from the other side of the globe. Above all, I would like to thank the love of my life, Laura. Thank you for backing me throughout this project and making my life better every single day.

Piyush Mishra is a professional with more than 4 years of experience of developing and designing fault-tolerant, scalable, distributed, highly performant systems using Scala, Akka, and Spark, and maintaining them across multiple servers. He is currently working as a software development engineer for R&D Labs at Pramati Labs.

He writes a blog on Scala, which you can find at `https://piyushmishra889.wordpress.com/`.

You can find him on LinkedIn at `https://in.linkedin.com/in/piyush1989`.

He also has presentations on Slideshare (`http://www.slideshare.net/knoldus/reactive-programming-with-scala-and-akka`), where he talks about reactive programming and applications and why we need it. He also talks about Scala, Akka, reactive applications, and their four principles.

I would like to thank my family: my father, Omkar Nath Mishra, and my wife, Laxmi, who encouraged me for writing this book. I am very thankful to Packt for the support for the entire duration of this project.

About the Reviewer

Steve Fosdal has been working in the software industry for more than a decade. He is currently focused on applying machine learning to real-time systems. His work involves using AWS, Spark, Akka, Kafka and Scala.

While getting his B.S. in physics from UW-Madison, he got interested in computational physics. His time spent working on N-body and quantum vortex simulations lead him to his current career.

He currently works as a big data software engineer at Avvo. Previously, he worked as a solution architect at Slalom and as a lead software engineer at HERE Technologies working on real-time data integration and predictive traffic.

You can find him online at http://fosdal.net.

He has also reviewed the book *Mastering RabbitMQ* by Packt Publishing.

I would like to thank my wife, Hilary, for her unbounded support for everything that I do.

www.PacktPub.com

For support files and downloads related to your book, please visit www.PacktPub.com.

Did you know that Packt offers eBook versions of every book published, with PDF and ePub files available? You can upgrade to the eBook version at www.PacktPub.comand as a print book customer, you are entitled to a discount on the eBook copy. Get in touch with us at service@packtpub.com for more details.

At www.PacktPub.com, you can also read a collection of free technical articles, sign up for a range of free newsletters and receive exclusive discounts and offers on Packt books and eBooks.

https://www.packtpub.com/mapt

Get the most in-demand software skills with Mapt. Mapt gives you full access to all Packt books and video courses, as well as industry-leading tools to help you plan your personal development and advance your career.

Why subscribe?

- Fully searchable across every book published by Packt
- Copy and paste, print, and bookmark content
- On demand and accessible via a web browser

Customer Feedback

Thanks for purchasing this Packt book. At Packt, quality is at the heart of our editorial process. To help us improve, please leave us an honest review on this book's Amazon page at `https://goo.gl/rLMAk0`.

If you'd like to join our team of regular reviewers, you can e-mail us at `customerreviews@packtpub.com`. We award our regular reviewers with free eBooks and videos in exchange for their valuable feedback. Help us be relentless in improving our products!

Table of Contents

Preface

Akka is a popular toolkit that helps develop concurrent, scalable, resilient, and reactive applications in the JVM thanks to the actor model. The toolkit has been around for some years, so we can consider it as a mature technology. Moreover, it has been successfully implemented by many companies, such as Cisco, Amazon.com, and Groupon. This book helps you understand how Akka (and all the modules around it) work and provides a set of useful recipes to easily achieve several of the most common tasks. It also includes an introductory chapter on Lagom, the latest microservices framework by Lightbend, the company behind the development of Akka.

What this book covers

Chapter 1, *Diving into Akka*, covers the basic concepts of Akka: actors, actor systems, mailboxes, and switching actor behaviors.

Chapter 2, *Supervision and Monitoring*, covers the actor life cycle, actor hierarchy, supervision, and monitoring.

Chapter 3, *Routing Messages*, covers the different types of group and pool router and how the Akka dispatcher works.

Chapter 4, *Using Futures and Agents*, covers how futures work and how well they integrate with the Akka toolkit. It also covers Akka agents.

Chapter 5, *Scheduling Actors and Other Utilities*, explains how the Akka scheduler works and contains various useful recipes about packaging, configuring, and running your Akka application.

Chapter 6, *Akka Persistence*, explains how to persist the state of an stateful actor to a variety of technologies, such as Apache Cassandra and Redis. It also covers different recovering strategies.

Chapter 7, *Remoting and Akka Clustering*, covers how to use Akka beyond a single JVM, either by using a well-known remote address or by joining a decentralized peer-to-peer-based cluster membership service.

Chapter 8, *Akka Streams*, covers the Akka Streams framework and how to integrate it with Akka and with third-party technologies.

Chapter 9, *Akka HTTP*, explains how to use Akka HTTP both on the client and server side. Also, it shows how to choose the API level depending on the use case.

Chapter 10, *Understanding Various Akka Patterns*, covers how to use different common programming patterns using Akka.

Chapter 11, *Microservices with Lagom*, introduces Lagom, the microservices framework from Lightbend. It provides information about conventions and how to create, configure, connect, and run microservices with Lagom.

What you need for this book

In this book, you will find recipes that provide examples that show the expected behavior. All code examples are written in the programming language Scala (http://www.scala-lan g.org/). Akka also provides a Java API, which we will not be covering in the examples. Despite that, the rationale behind all the recipes work the same in either Java or Scala. This book can also be used by Java developers to understand the core concepts of the different recipes.

In addition to Scala, we use sbt (http://www.scala-sbt.org/) as the build tool for the examples in the book. Sbt not only does dependency management, but also helps us run our examples.

Finally, it is recommended (but not required) to use an IDE to develop the different recipes. IntelliJ IDEA or Scala IDE are two good examples of free IDEs to develop Scala applications.

Who this book is for

This book goes through many aspects of the Akka toolkit. From easy recipes, such as *Sending messages to Actors*, to advanced topics, such as *Master Slave work pulling pattern*, its aim is to provide useful examples and explanations of how to achieve different patterns with Akka. Even if you are just starting with Akka or you have already used it in the past, these pages will provide you with a deep understanding of Akka that can be applied to new tasks not covered in this book.

Sections

In this book, you will find several headings that appear frequently (Getting ready, How to do it, How it works, There's more, and See also).

To give clear instructions on how to complete a recipe, we use these sections as follows:

Getting ready

This section tells you what to expect in the recipe, and describes how to set up any software or any preliminary settings required for the recipe.

How to do it...

This section contains the steps required to follow the recipe.

How it works...

This section usually consists of a detailed explanation of what happened in the previous section.

There's more...

This section consists of additional information about the recipe in order to make the reader more knowledgeable about the recipe.

See also

This section provides helpful links to other useful information for the recipe.

Conventions

In this book, you will find a number of text styles that distinguish between different kinds of information. Here are some examples of these styles and an explanation of their meaning.

Code words in text, database table names, folder names, filenames, file extensions, pathnames, dummy URLs, user input, and Twitter handles are shown as follows: "We create a project build definition file called `build.sbt` by executing a simple `sbt` command."

A block of code is set as follows:

```
import akka.actor.Props
import akka.actor.ActorSystem
object BehaviourAndState extends App {
  val actorSystem = ActorSystem("HelloAkka")
  // creating an actor inside the actor system
  val actor = actorSystem.actorOf(Props[SummingActor])
  // print actor path
  println(actor.path)
}
```

Any command-line input or output is written as follows:

```
sbt "runMain com.packt.chapter1.BehaviorAndState"
akka://HelloAkka/user/$a
```

New terms and **important words** are shown in bold.

Warnings or important notes appear in a box like this.

Tips and tricks appear like this.

Reader feedback

Feedback from our readers is always welcome. Let us know what you think about this book-what you liked or disliked. Reader feedback is important for us as it helps us develop titles that you will really get the most out of.

To send us general feedback, simply e-mail `feedback@packtpub.com`, and mention the book's title in the subject of your message.

If there is a topic that you have expertise in and you are interested in either writing or contributing to a book, see our author guide at `www.packtpub.com/authors`.

Customer support

Now that you are the proud owner of a Packt book, we have a number of things to help you to get the most from your purchase.

Downloading the example code

You can download the example code files for this book from your account at `http://www.packtpub.com`. If you purchased this book elsewhere, you can visit `http://www.packtpub.com/support` and register to have the files e-mailed directly to you.

You can download the code files by following these steps:

1. Log in or register to our website using your e-mail address and password.
2. Hover the mouse pointer on the **SUPPORT** tab at the top.
3. Click on **Code Downloads & Errata**.
4. Enter the name of the book in the **Search** box.
5. Select the book for which you're looking to download the code files.
6. Choose from the drop-down menu where you purchased this book from.
7. Click on **Code Download**.

You can also download the code files by clicking on the **Code Files** button on the book's webpage at the Packt Publishing website. This page can be accessed by entering the book's name in the **Search** box. Please note that you need to be logged in to your Packt account.

Once the file is downloaded, please make sure that you unzip or extract the folder using the latest version of:

- WinRAR / 7-Zip for Windows
- Zipeg / iZip / UnRarX for Mac
- 7-Zip / PeaZip for Linux

The code bundle for the book is also hosted on GitHub at `https://github.com/PacktPublishing/Akka-Cookbook`. We also have other code bundles from our rich catalog of books and videos available at `https://github.com/PacktPublishing/`. Check them out!

Errata

Although we have taken every care to ensure the accuracy of our content, mistakes do happen. If you find a mistake in one of our books-maybe a mistake in the text or the code-we would be grateful if you could report this to us. By doing so, you can save other readers from frustration and help us improve subsequent versions of this book. If you find any errata, please report them by visiting `http://www.packtpub.com/submit-errata`, selecting your book, clicking on the **Errata Submission Form** link, and entering the details of your errata. Once your errata are verified, your submission will be accepted and the errata will be uploaded to our website or added to any list of existing errata under the Errata section of that title.

To view the previously submitted errata, go to `https://www.packtpub.com/books/content/support` and enter the name of the book in the search field. The required information will appear under the **Errata** section.

Piracy

Piracy of copyrighted material on the Internet is an ongoing problem across all media. At Packt, we take the protection of our copyright and licenses very seriously. If you come across any illegal copies of our works in any form on the Internet, please provide us with the location address or website name immediately so that we can pursue a remedy.

Please contact us at `copyright@packtpub.com` with a link to the suspected pirated material.

We appreciate your help in protecting our authors and our ability to bring you valuable content.

Questions

If you have a problem with any aspect of this book, you can contact us at `questions@packtpub.com`, and we will do our best to address the problem.

1
Diving into Akka

In this chapter, we will cover the following recipes:

- Creating an Akka Scala SBT project from scratch
- Creating and understanding ActorSystem
- Defining the actor's behavior and state
- Sending messages to actors
- Asking for a result from an actor
- Communication between actors
- Creating a custom mailbox for an actor
- Prioritizing messages that an actor receives
- Creating a control-aware mailbox for an actor
- Become/unbecome behavior of an actor
- Stopping an actor

Introduction

In today's world, computer hardware is becoming cheaper and more powerful, as we have multiple cores on a single CPU chip. As cores keep on increasing, with the increasing power of hardware, we need a state of the art software framework which can use these cores efficiently.

Akka is such a framework, or you can say, a toolkit, which utilizes the hardware cores efficiently and lets you write performant applications.

As we are living in big data world, a lot of traffic comes to our servers, and we want our servers to respond in milliseconds instead of seconds. Akka is here to scale up the application as the load on it increases.

We want our application to run day and night continuously with high availability--Akka is here to build fault tolerance for our application.

We want to run our application on a cluster of multiple machines--Akka is here to scale out our application across the data center.

Can we do all of this using the Java multithreading model? Maybe.

Our assumption is that most of our readers have worked with the Java multithreading model, and they are aware of the fact that it is very difficult to write multithreaded concurrent applications. This is because we have to manage low-level details like locking an object, releasing the lock on the object, notifying, waiting for threads to join each other to complete a task, and freeing up resources that a thread holds. It is difficult for us to write multithreaded programs, because we have to focus more on thread management details instead of focusing on business logic only.

Akka is a toolkit for writing truly concurrent, fault-tolerant, distributed, and scalable applications, which can run for days, months, and years without stopping, and can heal themselves in case of failure. It is very hard to write concurrent applications using the plain Java multithreading model, which also satisfies fault-tolerant, distributed, and scalable properties. Akka provides a high-level of abstraction to build such an application that satisfy these properties.

Thus, Akka provides a basic unit of abstraction of transparent distribution called **actors**, which form the basis for writing resilient, elastic, event-driven, and responsive systems.

Let's see what is meant by these properties:

- **Resilient**: Applications that can heal themselves, which means they can recover from failure, and will always be responsive, even in case of failure like if we get errors or exceptions
- **Elastic**: A system which is responsive under varying amount of workload, that is, the system always remains responsive, irrespective of increasing or decreasing traffic, by increasing or decreasing the resources allocated to service this workload

- **Message Driven**: A system whose components are loosely coupled with each other and communicate using asynchronous message passing, and which reacts to those messages by taking an action
- **Responsive**: A system that satisfies the preceding three properties is called responsive

A system that satisfies all four properties is called a reactive system.

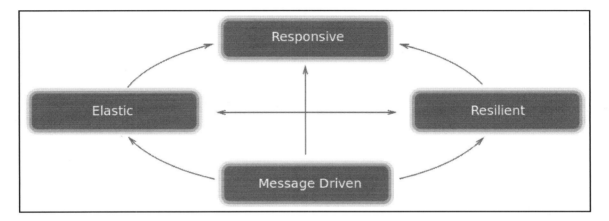

Properties of reactive system

 For more information, see Reactive manifesto (http://www.reactivemanifesto.org).

Before starting with recipes, let's take a look at the following the actor properties:

1. **State**: An actor has internal state, which is mutated sequentially as messages are processed one by one.
2. **Behavior**: An Actor reacts to messages which are sent to it by applying behavior on it.
3. **Communication**: An actor communicates with other actors by sending and receiving messages to/from them.

4. **Mailbox**: A mailbox is the queue of messages from which an actor picks up the message and processes it.

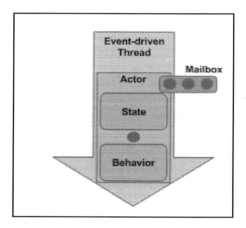

An actor's anatomy

Actors are message-driven, that is, they are passive and do nothing unless and until you send messages to them. Once you send them a message, they pick a thread from the thread pool which is also known as a dispatcher, process the message, and release the thread back to the thread pool.

Actors are also asynchronous by nature; they never block your current thread of execution, and continue to work on another thread.

Visit the Wikipedia link for an actor model (https://en.wikipedia.org/wiki/Actor_model) for details.

Let's start making recipes.

Creating an Akka Scala SBT project from scratch

Assuming that readers are Scala developers, it is obvious they have knowledge of **SBT** (**Simple Build Tool**) to build a Scala project.

Getting ready

To step through this recipe, you will need SBT installed on your machine. No other prerequisites are required.

If you don't have SBT installed on your machine, please visit the SBT manual installation page(`http://www.scala-sbt.org/release/docs/Manual-Installation.html`), and follow the instructions for the operating system you have.

SBT is used for building Scala projects as we have **Maven** for Java projects. However, both SBT and Maven are capable of building Scala, Java projects.

In this book, we will build our projects on the Ubuntu Linux operating system.

How to do it...

1. For creating an SBT project, we need to create a project directory, for example, Hello-Akka.

   Following screenshot shows the creation of the project directory:

Creating the project directory

2. Descend to the directory and run command `sbt`. We will enter into the sbt prompt mode, Now run the following commands one by one, as shown in the next screenshot:

```
set name := "Hello-Akka"
set version := "1.0"
set scalaVersion: ="2.11.7"
session save
exit
```

This will create a build file called `build.sbt` and a target to put your class files into.

3. Edit the build file, and add the Akka actor dependency as follows:

```
libraryDependencies += "com.typesafe.akka" %
  "akka-actor_2.11" % "2.4.4"
```

We can select a specific Akka actor version against a specific Scala version in the maven repository:

```
name:="Hello-Akka"

version:="1.0"

scalaVersion:="2.11.7"

libraryDependencies += "com.typesafe.akka" % "akka-actor_2.11" % "2.4.4"
~
~
~
~
~
~
~
~
~
~
                                                          1,1          All
```

Adding Akka dependency to build file

4. Run the command `sbt update`; it will download the Akka dependency. Now we have the Akka actor's capabilities in our project, and we are ready to write reactive programs.

The SBT (Simple Build tool), as the name suggests is a widely used tool for building Scala projects.

In step one, we create a project directory where we keep our source files, project build definition, and target, where class files are kept for runtime execution.

In step two, we create a project build definition file, called `build.sbt`, by executing simple `sbt` command.

In step three, we add a library dependency in the build file for the Akka actor to enable Akka capabilities.

In step four, we download the Akka dependency using the `sbt update` command, and our project is now ready for writing Akka-based applications.

This is how we can set up an Akka-based project.

Creating and understanding ActorSystem

In this small recipe, we will create and understand an ActorSystem. Since we are done with our initial setup of the `Hello-Akka` project, we don't need to make another project for it. We need to import the SBT project in an IDE like IntelliJ Idea.

Getting ready

If you are using IntelliJ Idea, then you must have Scala and the SBT plugin install on it.

 For importing an SBT Scala project in IntelliJ Idea, visit the following website: `https://www.jetbrains.com/help/idea/2016.1/getting-started-with-sbt.html?origin=old_help#import_project`.

How to do it...

It is very easy to create an ActorSystem in Akka:

1. Create a package `com.packt.chapter1` inside the `Hello-Akka src` folder. We will keep all the source code in this package.
2. Inside the package, create a file, say `HelloAkkaActorSystem.scala`, which will contain the code.
3. Create a small scala application object, `HelloAkkaActorSystem`, and create an `ActorSystem` inside it:

```
package com.packt.chapter1
Import akka.actor.ActorSystem
/**
  * Created by user
  */
object HelloAkkaActorSystem extends App {
  val actorSystem = ActorSystem("HelloAkka")
  println(actorSystem)
}
```

4. Now, run the application in IntelliJ Idea or in the console. It will print the output as follows:

```
akka://HelloAkka
```

```
piyush@ubuntu:~$ cd Hello-Akka/
piyush@ubuntu:~/Hello-Akka$ sbt "runMain com.packt.chapter1.HelloAkkaActorSystem"
Java HotSpot(TM) 64-Bit Server VM warning: ignoring option MaxPermSize=256M; support was removed in 8.0
[info] Set current project to Hello-Akka (in build file:/home/piyush/Hello-Akka/)
[info] Running com.packt.chapter1.HelloAkkaActorSystem
akka://HelloAkka
```

Downloading the Akka actor dependency

Here is a way to run a single Scala application using sbt from the console.
Descend to the application root directory, and run the following
command:
sbt "runMain com.packt.chapter1.HelloAkkaActorSystem"

How it works...

In the recipe, we create a simple Scala object creating an ActorSystem, thereafter, we run the application.

Why we need ActorSystem

In Akka, an ActorSystem is the starting point of any Akka application that we write.

Technically, an ActorSystem is a heavyweight structure per application, which allocates *n* number of threads. Thus, it is recommended to create one ActorSystem per application, until we have a reason to create another one.

ActorSystem is the home for the actors in which they live, it manages the life cycle of an actor and supervises them.On creation, an ActorSystem starts three actors:

- `/user` - The guardian actor: All user-defined actors are created as a child of the parent actor user, that is, when you create your actor in the ActorSystem, it becomes the child of the user guardian actor, and this guardian actor supervises your actors. If the guardian actor terminates, all your actors get terminated as well.
- `/system` - The system guardian: In Akka, logging is also implemented using actors. This special guardian shut downs the logged-in actors when all normal actors have terminated. It watches the user guardian actor, and upon termination of the guardian actor, it initiates its own shutdown.
- `/` - The root guardian: The root guardian is the grandparent of all the so-called top-level actors, and supervises all the top-level actors. Its purpose is to terminate the child upon any type of exception. It sets the ActorSystem status as terminated if the guardian actor is able to terminate all the child actors successfully.

For more information on ActorSystem visit:
`http://doc.akka.io/docs/akka/2.4.1/general/actor-systems.html`.

Defining the actor's behavior and state

In this recipe, we will define an actor, which will receive some messages, and apply its behavior to its state. After that, we will create that actor inside the actor system.

We will see what is meant by the terms behavior and the state of an actor.

Getting ready

To step through this recipe, we need to import the `Hello-Akka` project in any IDE, like intelliJ Idea, and ensure that SBT is installed on our machine to build and run the Scala project from the console.

How to do it...

1. Open the project `Hello-Akka` in an IDE like intelliJ Idea, and create a Scala file, `BehaviorAndState.scala`, inside the package, `com.packt.chapter1`.

2. Add an import to the top of the file: `import akka.actor.Actor`.

   Inside the file, define the actor as follows:

   ```
   class SummingActor extends Actor {
     // state inside the actor
     var sum = 0
     // behaviour which is applied on the state
     override def receive: Receive = {
       // receives message an integer
       case x: Int => sum = sum + x
       println(s"my state as sum is $sum")
       // receives default message
       case _ => println("I don't know what
         are you talking about")
     }
   }
   ```

   Here, we are not creating an actor, we are only defining the state and behavior.

3. From the previous recipe, we know that ActorSystem is the home for actors, and we know how to create an ActorSystem. Now, we will create the actor inside it.

   Add the following imports to the top of the file:

   ```
   import akka.actor.Props
   import akka.actor.ActorSystem
   object BehaviourAndState extends App {
     val actorSystem = ActorSystem("HelloAkka")
     // creating an actor inside the actor system
     val actor = actorSystem.actorOf(Props[SummingActor])
     // print actor path
     println(actor.path)
   }
   ```

4. Run the preceding application from the IDE or from the console, and it will print the actor path.

You can run the application from the console using the following command:

```
sbt "runMain com.packt.chapter1.BehaviorAndState"
akka://HelloAkka/user/$a
```

Here, HelloAkka is the ActorSystem name, user is the user guardian actor, that is, the parent actor for your actor, and $a is the name of your actor.

You can also give a name to your actor:

```
val actor = actorSystem.actorOf(Props[SummingActor],
"summingactor")
```

If you run the application again, it will print the actor name as summingactor.

The output will be as follows:

```
akka://HelloAkka/user/summingactor
```

How do we create an actor if it takes an argument in the constructor as shown in the following code:

```
class SummingActorWithConstructor(intitalSum: Int)
extends Actor {
  // state inside the actor
  var sum = 0
  // behaviour which is applied on the state
  override def receive: Receive = {
    // receives message an integer
    case x: Int => sum = intitalSum + sum + x
    println(s"my state as sum is $sum")
    // receives default message
    case _ => println("I don't know what
      are you talking about")
  }
}
```

For this, we use the following code:

```
actorSystem.actorOf(Props(classOf[
SummingActorWithConstructor], 10), "summingactor")
```

How it works...

As we know from the previous recipe, the ActorSystem is a place where the actor lives.

In the preceding application, we define the actor with its state and behavior, and then create it inside Akka using the API provided by Akka.

In case of the `summingactor`, the state is the variable `sum` and the behavior is adding of the integer to the `sum` as soon as the message arrives.

There's more...

There are some recommended practices related to creation of actors. For more details, you can check out the following link:

`http://doc.akka.io/docs/akka/current/scala/actors.html`.

Sending messages to actors

Sending messages to actors is the first step for building a Akka based application as Akka is a message driven framework, so get started

Getting ready

In this recipe, we will learn how to send messages to actors. Prerequisites are the same as the previous recipes.

How to do it...

In the previous recipe, we created an actor which calculates the sum of integers:

```
val actor = actorSystem.actorOf(Props[SummingActor],
  "summingactor")
```

Now, we will send messages as integers to the summing actor, as follows:

```
actor ! 1
```

The following will be the output:

```
My state as sum is 1
```

If we keep on sending messages inside a `while` loop, the actor will continue to calculate the sum incrementally:

```
while (true) {
  Thread.sleep(3000)
  actor ! 1
}
```

On sending messages inside a `while` loop, the following output will be displayed:

```
my state as sum is 1
my state as sum is 2
my state as sum is 3
my state as sum is 4
my state as sum is 5
```

If we send a string message `Hello`, this message will fall into the actor's default behavior case, and the output will be as follows:

```
I don't know what you are talking about
```

How it works...

Actors have methods to communicate with each other actors like tell (`!`) or ask (`?`) where the first one is fire and forget and the second returns a Future which means the response will come from that actor in the future.

As soon as you send the message to the actor, it receives the message, picks up an underlying Java thread from the thread pool, does it's work, and releases the thread. The actors never block your current thread of execution, thus, they are asynchronous by nature.

There's more...

Visit the following link to see more information on send messages:

http://doc.akka.io/docs/akka/current/scala/actors.html#Send_messages.

Asking for a result from an actor

In this recipe, we will ask the actor to give us the result that it computes. Prerequisites are the same as the previous recipes.

In the last recipe, you learnt how to send a message using the tell-and-forget pattern. In this recipe, you will learn how to get the result from an actor after it does something.

How to do it...

Let's define an actor that computes something, say, the Fibonacci of a number:

1. Create a Scala file, `FibonacciActor.scala`, in the package `com.packt.chapter1`.

2. Add import to the top of the file:

   ```
   import akka.actor.Actor
   ```

   Now we define an actor which computes the Fibonacci of a number:

   ```
   class FibonacciActor extends Actor {
     override def receive: Receive = {
       case num : Int =>
       val fibonacciNumber = fib(num)
     }
     def fib( n : Int) : Int = n match {
       case 0 | 1 => n
       case _ => fib( n-1 ) + fib( n-2 )
     }
   }
   ```

3. As of now, we have defined the actor. To send the computed result back to the sender, we have to add one more line to the actor code:

   ```
   sender ! fibonacciNumber
   ```

   Now, notice the difference:

   ```
   class FibonacciActor extends Actor {
     override def receive: Receive = {
       case num : Int =>
       val fibonacciNumber = fib(num)
       sender ! fibonacciNumber
     }
     def fib( n : Int) : Int = n match {
   ```

```
        case 0 | 1 => n
        case _ => fib( n-1 ) + fib( n-2 )
    }
}
```

Actors, by their implementation, know the default immediate sender, that is, they know who has sent them the message.

4. Create an application which asks for result from the actor.
5. Add the following imports to the top of file:

```
import akka.actor.{Props, ActorSystem}
import akka.pattern.ask
import akka.util.Timeout
import scala.concurrent.Await
import scala.concurrent.duration._
```

6. Create an object, FibonacciActorApp as follows:

```
object FibonacciActorApp extends App {
    implicit val timeout = Timeout(10 seconds)
    val actorSystem = ActorSystem("HelloAkka")
    val actor = actorSystem.actorOf(Props[FibonacciActor])
    // asking for result from actor
    val future = (actor ? 10).mapTo[Int]
    val fiboacciNumber = Await.result(future, 10 seconds)
    println(fiboacciNumber)
}
```

7. Run the preceding application in the IDE-like intelliJ Idea or from the console, and you will get the following output:

How it works...

We create an actor that computes Fibonacci number, and sends the result to the sender who sent him the message to compute the Fibonacci.

In the actor receive block, we send the Fibonacci result back to the sender. Actors, by nature, know who has sent them the message, thus we always have the sender present in the context of the receive block.

When you send a message to the actor using a question mark (?), it returns a future promising that you will get the result when the operation would be completed.

We will learn about futures in later chapters.

There's more...

To know more about sending messages to actors, go to the following link:

`http://doc.akka.io/docs/akka/current/scala/actors.html#Send_messages.`

Communication between actors

In an Akka-based application, there are many actors and they will have some way to communicate among themselves..

In this recipe, you will learn how two actors communicate with each other. For this, we need to import the same project, `Hello-Akka`, in our IDE. Prerequisites are the same as in the previous recipes.

Getting ready

To step through this recipe we will import the `Hello-Akka` project in our IDE and other prerequisites are same as before.

How to do it...

We will create the following two actors here:

- `QueryActor`: Sends a message to `RandomNumberGenerator` to generate a random number
- `RandomNumberGeneratorActor`: Sends the generated random number to the `QueryActor`

The following are the steps for creating the actors:

1. Create a Scala file, `Communication.scala`, in the package `com.packt.chapter1`.
2. Create an object, `Messages`, which will contain the messages to be sent to the actors for communicating with each other.

3. Add import to the top of the file:

```
import akka.actor.ActorRef
```

After adding the import add the code that follows:

```
object Messages {
  case class Done(randomNumber: Int)
  case object GiveMeRandomNumber
  case class Start(actorRef: ActorRef)
}
```

4. Define `RandomNumberGeneratorActor`, which generates a random number and sends it back to the sender.

5. Add the two imports given next to the top of the file:

```
import akka.actor.Actor
import scala.util.Random._
```

Now add the code that follows:

```
class RandomNumberGeneratorActor extends Actor {
  import Messages._
  override def receive: Receive = {
    case GiveMeRandomNumber =>
    println("received a message to
      generate a random integer")
    val randomNumber = nextInt
    sender ! Done(randomNumber)
  }
}
```

6. Create a `queryActor`, which sends messages to `RandomNumberGeneratorActor` and receives the random number:

```
class QueryActor extends Actor {
  import Messages._
  override def receive: Receive = {
    case Start(actorRef) => println(s"send me the next
      random number")
    actorRef ! GiveMeRandomNumber
    case Done(randomNumber) =>
    println(s"received a random number $randomNumber")
  }
}
```

7. Create an application object, `Communication`, to see the output:

```
object Communication extends App {
  import Messages._
  val actorSystem = ActorSystem("HelloAkka")
  val randomNumberGenerator =
   actorSystem.actorOf(Props[RandomNumberGeneratorActor],
  "randomNumberGeneratorActor")
  val queryActor = actorSystem.actorOf(Props[QueryActor],
   "queryActor")
  queryActor ! Start(randomNumberGenerator)
}
```

8. Now run the application in the IDE or from the console, and the output will be displayed as follows:

```
send me the next random number
received a message to generate a random integer
received a random number 841431704
```

How it works...

In step two, we see there is message object, which contains messages to be sent to the actors. Actors will use these messages for communication.

In step three, we define `RandomNumberGeneratorActor`, which receives the message `GiveMeRandomNumber`, and sends it to the sender as follows:

```
sender ! Done(randomNumber)
```

In step four, we define `QueryActor`, which actually sends the message to `RandomNumberGenerator`, and receives the result in case of `Done`.

In step five, we create a test application to see the execution flow of the whole message.

There's more...

In the following recipes, we will see how actors implement the master-slave work pulling pattern.

Creating a custom mailbox for an actor

In this recipe, you will learn how to create a custom mailbox for an actor. As you're already aware, in Akka, each actor has its own mailbox-like queue from which it picks up the messages one by one, and processes them. There are some custom mailbox implementations provided by Akka, such as PriorityMailbox and controlAwareMailbox, other than the default mailbox.

There might be a situation when you want to control the way the actor picks up the message or anything else. We will create an actor mailbox that will accept messages from actors of a particular name.

Getting ready

To step through this recipe, we need to import our Hello-Akka project in the IDE-like intelliJ Idea. Prerequisites are the same as those in the previous recipes.

How to do it...

1. Create a Scala file, say CustomMailbox.scala, in package com.packt.chapter1.

   Add the following required imports to the top of the file:

   ```
   import java.util.concurrent.ConcurrentLinkedQueue
   import akka.actor.{Props, Actor,
       ActorSystem,ActorRef}
   import akka.dispatch.{ MailboxType,
       ProducesMessageQueue,
       Envelope, MessageQueue}
   import com.typesafe.config.Config
   ```

2. Define a MyMessageQueue, which extends trait MessageQueue and implementing methods:

   ```
   class MyMessageQueue extends MessageQueue {
     private final val queue = new
       ConcurrentLinkedQueue[Envelope]()
     // these should be implemented; queue used as example
     def enqueue(receiver: ActorRef, handle: Envelope): Unit =
       {
         if(handle.sender.path.name == "MyActor") {
   ```

```
    handle.sender !  "Hey dude, How are you?, I Know your
      name,processing your request"
      queue.offer(handle)
    }
    else handle.sender ! "I don't talk to strangers, I
    can't process your request"
  }
  def dequeue(): Envelope = queue.poll
  def numberOfMessages: Int = queue.size
  def hasMessages: Boolean = !queue.isEmpty
  def cleanUp(owner: ActorRef, deadLetters: MessageQueue) {
    while (hasMessages) {
      deadLetters.enqueue(owner, dequeue())
    }
  }
}
```

3. Let's provide a custom mailbox implementation, which uses the preceding MessageQueue:

```
class MyUnboundedMailbox extends MailboxType
 with ProducesMessageQueue[MyMessageQueue] {
  def this(settings: ActorSystem.Settings,
  config: Config) = { this()
  }
  // The create method is called to create the MessageQueue
  final override def create(owner: Option[ActorRef], system::
  Option[ActorSystem]):MessageQueue = new MyMessageQueue()
}
```

4. Create an application.conf file and put the below configuration. An application.conf file is used to configure Akka application properties and it resides in the project's resource directory.

```
custom-dispatcher {
  mailbox-requirement =
    "com.packt.chapter1.MyMessageQueue"
}
akka.actor.mailbox.requirements {
  "com.packt.chapter1.MyMessageQueue" = custom-dispatcher-
    mailbox
}
custom-dispatcher-mailbox {
  mailbox-type = "com.packt.chapter1.MyUnboundedMailbox"
}
```

5. Now define an actor that would use the preceding configuration, say, `MySpecialActor`. It's special, because it would talk to the actor whom it knows, and say hello to that actor only:

```
class MySpecialActor extends Actor {
  override def receive: Receive = {
    case msg: String => println(s"msg is $msg" )
  }
}
```

6. Define an actor who will try to talk to the special actor:

```
class MyActor extends Actor {
  override def receive: Receive = {
    case (msg: String, actorRef: ActorRef) => actorRef !
     msg
    case msg => println(msg)
  }
}
```

7. Create a test application, `CustomMailbox`, as follows:

```
object CustomMailbox extends App  {
  val actorSystem = ActorSystem("HelloAkka")
  val actor =
   actorSystem.actorOf(Props[MySpecialActor].withDispatcher
   ("custom-dispatcher"))
  val actor1 = actorSystem.actorOf(Props[MyActor],"xyz")
  val actor2 =
   actorSystem.actorOf(Props[MyActor],"MyActor")
  actor1 !  ("hello", actor)
  actor2 !  ("hello", actor)
}
```

8. Run the application in the IDE or from the console, and you will get the following output:

```
I don't talk to strangers, I can't process your request
Hey dude, How are you?, I Know your name,processing your request
msg is hello
```

How it works...

As you know, a mailbox uses a message queue, and we need to provide a custom implementation for the queue.

In step two, we define a class, `MyMessageQueue`, which extends the trait `MessageQueue` and the implementing methods.

We want our actor to receive messages from only those actors whose name is `MyActor`, and not from any other actor.

To achieve the aforementioned functionality, we implement the `enqueue` method, and specify that the message should be enqueued if sender name is `MyActor`, otherwise ignore the message.

In this case, we used `ConcurrentLinkedQueue` as the underlying data structure for the queue.

However, it is up to us which data structure we pick for enqueing and removing messages. Changing the data structure may also change the processing order of messages.

In step three, we define the custom mailbox using `MyMessageQueue`.

In step four, we configure the preceding mailbox with a `custom-dispatcher` in `application.conf`.

In step five and six, we define `MySpecialActor`, which will use the custom mailbox when we create it with the `custom-dispatcher`. `MyActor` is the actor which tries to communicate with `MySpecialActor`.

In step seven, we have two instances of `MyActor`, `actor1` and `actor2`, which send messages to `MySpecialActor`.

Since `MySpecialActor` talks to only those Actors whose name is `MyActor`, it does not process messages from `MyActor` whose name is `xyz`, as you can see in the output.

Prioritizing messages that an actor receives

There are situations when you want your actor to process some particular messages first, and then move on to others. This means you want to give priority to some messages over others.

For such scenarios, Akka has comes up with priority mailbox, which lets you prioritize messages.

Getting ready

To step through this recipe, we need to import our `Hello-Akka` project in IDE-like IntelliJ Idea. Prerequisites are the same as those in previous recipes.

How to do it...

1. Create a Scala file named `PriorityMailBox.scala` in package `comi.packt.chapter1`.
2. Create an actor called `MyPriorityActor` as follows:

```
class MyPriorityActor extends Actor {
  def receive: PartialFunction[Any, Unit] = {
    // Int Messages
    case x: Int => println(x)
    // String Messages
    case x: String => println(x)
    // Long messages
    case x: Long => println(x)
    // other messages
    case x => println(x)
  }
}
```

3. To prioritize the messages, create a priority mailbox as follows:

```
class MyPriorityActorMailbox(settings:
  ActorSystem.Settings, config: Config) extends
  UnboundedPriorityMailbox (
  // Create a new PriorityGenerator,
    lower prio means more important
    PriorityGenerator {
      // Int Messages
      case x: Int => 1
      // String Messages
      case x: String => 0
      // Long messages
      case x: Long => 2
      // other messages
      case _ => 3
})
```

4. Add this configuration to `application.conf`:

```
prio-dispatcher {
  mailbox-type =
    "com.packt.chapter1..MyPriorityActorMailbox"
}
```

5. Create an application, `PriorityMailBoxApp`, as shown in the following code:

```
object PriorityMailBoxApp extends App {
   val actorSystem = ActorSystem("HelloAkka")
   val myPriorityActor =
   actorSystem.actorOf(Props[MyPriorityActor].withDispatcher
("prio-dispatcher"))
   myPriorityActor ! 6.0
   myPriorityActor ! 1
   myPriorityActor ! 5.0
   myPriorityActor ! 3
   myPriorityActor ! "Hello"
   myPriorityActor ! 5
   myPriorityActor ! "I am priority actor"
   myPriorityActor ! "I process string messages first,then
     integer, long and others"
}
```

6. Run the application in IDE or from the console. The following output will be displayed:

```
Hello
I process string messages first,then integer, long and others
I am priority actor
1
3
5
6.0
5.0
```

How it works...

In step two, we just define an actor which processes `Int`, `Long`, `String`, and other messages.

In step four, we configure a `prio-dispatcher` with this `MyPriorityActorMailbox`.

In step five, we create an actor which will use the `prio-dispatcher`.

In step six, as we can see in the output, the string messages are processed first, because they were given highest priority.

Creating a control-aware mailbox for an actor

There are some situations when you want your actor to process a certain message first before any other message, at any point of time. This means that you can tell an actor to do some particular work before doing any other job.

Getting ready

To step through this recipe, we need to import our Hello-Akka project in IDE-like IntelliJ Idea. Prerequisites are the same as those of the previous recipes.

How to do it...

1. Create a file, ControlAwareMailbox.scala, in package com.packt.chapter1.
2. Add the following imports to the top of the file:

```
import akka.dispatch.ControlMessage
import akka.actor.{Props, Actor, ActorSystem}
```

3. Create a control message case object as follows:

```
case object MyControlMessage extends ControlMessage
```

4. Define an actor:

```
class Logger extends Actor {
  def receive = {
    case MyControlMessage => println("Oh, I have to process
      Control message first")
    case x => println(x.toString)
  }
}
```

5. Add the following configuration to `application.conf`:

```
control-aware-dispatcher {
 mailbox-type =
   "akka.dispatch.UnboundedControlAwareMailbox"
 //Other dispatcher configuration goes here
}
```

6. Create a test application in which we can send a message to the preceding application, and it will process the control message first:

```
object ControlAwareMailbox extends App {
  val actorSystem = ActorSystem("HelloAkka")
  val actor =
   actorSystem.actorOf(Props[Logger].withDispatcher(
  "control-aware-dispatcher"))
  actor ! "hello"
  actor ! "how are"
  actor ! "you?"
  actor ! MyControlMessage
}
```

7. Run the application in IDE or from the console. You will get the following output:

```
Oh, I have to process Control message first
hello
how are
you?
```

How it works...

In step three, we create an object, MyControlMessage, which extends the ControlMessage.

ControlMessage is a trait. The message which extends this trait will be handled on priority by ControlAwareMailbox. ControlAwareMailbox maintains two queues to allow messages that extend ControlMessage to be delivered with priority.

In step four, we create an actor which will handle ControlMessage.

In step five, we configure the control-aware-dispatcher in application.conf.

In step six. we create the actor with `control-aware-dispatcher`.

In step seven, we are able to see in the output that the actor processed `ControlMessage` `first`.

Become/unbecome behavior of an actor

In some situations, we want our actor to change its behavior based on its state. This means that there are cases where an actor receives a message, and if its state changes or transitions, it changes the way further messages should be handled.

Thus, using become/unbecome, we can hot swap the actor functionality at runtime.

Getting ready

To step through this recipe, we need to import the `Hello-Akka` project in the IDE-like IntelliJ Idea. Prerequisites are the same as those in previous recipes.

How to do it...

1. Create a file named `BecomeUnbecome.scala` in package `com.packt.chapter1`.
2. Add the following imports to the top of the file:

   ```scala
   import akka.actor.{Props, ActorSystem, Actor}
   ```

3. Define an actor which changes its behavior based on whether the state is `true` or `false`, as shown in the following code:

   ```scala
   class BecomeUnBecomeActor extends Actor {
     def receive: Receive = {
       case true => context.become(isStateTrue)
       case false => context.become(isStateFalse)
       case _ => println("don't know what you want to say !! ")
     }
     def isStateTrue: Receive  = {
       case msg : String => println(s"$msg")
       case false => context.become(isStateFalse)
     }
     def isStateFalse: Receive  = {
       case msg : Int => println(s"$msg")
   ```

```
        case true =>   context.become(isStateTrue)
    }
}
```

4. Create a test application, `BecomeUnBecomeApp`, as follows:

```
object BecomeUnBecomeApp extends App {
  val actorSystem = ActorSystem("HelloAkka")
  val becomeUnBecome =
   actorSystem.actorOf(Props[BecomeUnBecomeActor])
  becomeUnBecome ! true
  becomeUnBecome ! "Hello how are you?"
  becomeUnBecome ! false
  becomeUnBecome ! 1100
  becomeUnBecome ! true
  becomeUnBecome ! "What do u do?"
}
```

5. Run the application in an IDE like IntelliJ Idea or from the console; the output will be as follows:

```
Hello how are you?
1100
What do u do?
```

How it works...

In step two, we define an actor, which changes its state to handle string and integer values.

If the state is `true`, we set the behavior as `context.become(isStateTrue)`, and it starts handling string messages. If the state is `false`, we set the behavior as `context.become(isStateFalse)`, and it starts handling integer messages.

In step four, we create the actor and send it to see if the output matches the functionality.

Stopping an actor

It is obvious that an actor has to be shut down gracefully after it has processed all the messages or on application shutdown.

Getting ready

To step through this recipe, we need import the `Hello-Akka` project in an IDE like IntelliJ Idea. Prerequisites are the same as those in previous recipes.

How to do it...

1. Create a file, `Shutdown.scala`, in package `com.packt.chapter1`.
2. Add the following imports to the top of file:

   ```
   import akka.actor.{PoisonPill, Props, ActorSystem, Actor}
   ```

3. Create a case object, `Stop`, as the message:

   ```
   case object Stop
   ```

4. Define an actor, `ShutdownActor`, as follows:

   ```
   class ShutdownActor extends Actor {
     override def receive: Receive = {
       case msg:String => println(s"$msg")
       case Stop => context.stop(self)
     }
   }
   ```

5. There are two ways we can stop the actor:

   - Using `PoisonPill`
   - Using `context.self(actorRef)`

   Create an actor and send it a message as shown in the following code:

   ```
   object ShutdownApp extends App{
     val actorSystem = ActorSystem("HelloAkka")
     val shutdownActor1 =
      actorSystem.actorOf(Props[ShutdownActor],
      "shutdownActor1")
     shutdownActor1 ! "hello"
     shutdownActor1 ! PoisonPill
     shutdownActor1 ! "Are you there?"
     val shutdownActor2 =
      actorSystem.actorOf(Props[ShutdownActor],
      "shutdownActor2")
     shutdownActor2 ! "hello"
   ```

```
        shutdownActor2 ! Stop
        shutdownActor2 ! "Are you there?"
    }
```

6. Run the preceding application, and you will get the following output:

```
hello
hello
[INFO] [05/22/2016 20:39:53.137] [HelloAkka-akka.actor.default-
dispatcher-4] [akka://HelloAkka/user/shutdownActor1] Message
[java.lang.String] from Actor[akka://HelloAkka/deadLetters] to
Actor[akka://HelloAkka/user/shutdownActor1#417818231] was not
delivered. [1] dead letters encountered.
[INFO] [05/22/2016 20:39:53.138] [HelloAkka-
akka.actor.default-dispatcher-4]
[akka://HelloAkka/user/shutdownActor2] Message
[java.lang.String] from Actor[akka://HelloAkka/deadLetters]
to Actor[akka://HelloAkka/user/shutdownActor2#788021817] was
not delivered. [2] dead letters encountered.
```

How it works...

In step three, we create a `Stop` message. Upon receiving this message, the actor will stop using `context.stop(self)`.

In step four, we define an actor which handles the `Stop` message.

In step five, we create two actors of the same class, `shutdownActor1` and `shutdownActor2`. We shut down `shutdownActor1` using `PoisonPill` and `shutdownActor2` using `context.stop(self)`.

`PoisonPill` and `context.stop(self)` are the two ways to kill an actor. `PoisonPill` is the inbuilt message that is handled after all the messages that were already queued in the mailbox.

`Context.stop` is basically used for an ordered shutdown of actors when you want the child actors to stop first, then the parent actor, followed by the ActorSystem to stop top-level actors.

2

Supervision and Monitoring

In this chapter, we will cover the following recipes:

- Creating child actors of a parent actor
- Overriding the life cycle hooks of an actor
- Sending messages to actors and collecting responses
- Understanding `OneForOneStrategy` for actors
- Understanding `AllForOneStrategy` for actors
- Monitoring an actor life cycle using DeathWatch

Introduction

In the previous chapter, you learned about some basic and advanced things about Akka actors. In this chapter, you will learn about supervision and monitoring of Akka actors.

Using supervision and monitoring, we can write fault-tolerant systems, which can run continuously for days, months, and years without stopping. Let's see what is meant by fault tolerance.

What is fault tolerance?

Fault tolerance is a property of systems that are intended to be always responsive rather than failing completely in case of a failure. Such systems are known as fault tolerance systems or resilient systems.

In simple words, a fault-tolerant system is one which is destined to continue as more or less fully operational, with perhaps a reduction in throughput or an increase in response time because of partial failure of its components.

Even if a components fails, the whole system never gets shut down; instead, it remains operational and responsive with just a decreased throughput.

Similarly, while designing a distributed system, we need to care about what would happen if one or more it's components go down. So, the system design should itself be such that the system is able to take appropriate action to resolve the issue.

Before designing such a system, we need to keep the following things in mind:

- **Breaking the system into components**: While designing a fault-tolerant system, the first requirement is to break the system into parts, that is, components which are each responsible for some functionality. Certain failure in one component of the system should not interfere with the other parts of the system, and should not bring cascading failures in the system.
- **Focus on the important components of the system**: There are some parts that are important for a system to have. Such parts should run without interference from the failing parts to avoid inaccurate results.
- **Backup of important components**: It is recommended to have a backup of components so that in case of failure, similar components can ensure the high availability of the system.

In general, the following are some of the ways to build fault tolerance for systems:

- **Duplication**: The purpose of duplication is to run multiple identical instances of system components so that if a failure occurs, other instances will be available to process the request
- **Replication**: The purpose of replication is to provide multiple identical instances of the components (hardware and software) and to send a direct request to all of them one of the results is then chosen from among them based on them
- **Isolation**: The purpose of isolation is to keep the components running in different processes, and communicate through passing of messages to ensure isolation of concerns and loose coupling between them. This means that one should not be affected because of another's failure

- **Delegation**: The purpose of delegation is to hand over the processing responsibility of a task to another component so that the delegating component can perform other processing, or optionally observe the progress of the delegated task in case additional action, such as handling failure or reporting progress, is required

What is a component?

All of us know what a module is in software architecture. A module is a piece of a software that contains a particular functionality to do a certain task. We cannot say that a component is synonymous with module. Instead, a component is a self-contained, isolated, and encapsulated entity, which means that it does not affect other components. Different components can use the same module , but their own behavior is a module of its own. Asynchronous message passing is a way to build a communication layer between them.

Microservices rely on component-based architecture. Microservices are small, independent, decoupled processes running in isolation from each other to build a complex system. We can scale each component/microservice according to workload.

How Akka fits in between all of them?

Akka as a toolkit provides a way to build fault tolerance for applications.

- The Akka supervisor actor can resume, stop, restart, or terminate the execution of the supervised actor, thus providing a way for fault isolation
- Akka provides parent-child model actor, so we can build a tree-like hierarchical structure of our application
- We can create a duplicate actor in case of failure, and replace the faulty one using supervisor strategies
- Akka actors, as components, have a life cycle-you can start, stop, restart and kill them, that is, you can destroy an actor after it has done some work, or if it fails
- Asynchronous message passing allows us to put a boundary between two actors so as to separate the concerns of the different components

Akka is built keeping the aforementioned things in mind. It uses the **letitcrash** model to build fault-tolerant applications.

Akka lets actors crash and separate business logic from error/exception handling logic. It uses the delegation model to delegate the responsibility of error/exception handling to the supervisor of the actor.

Let's see the building blocks of the letitcrash model in the following recipes.

Creating child actors of a parent actor

In this recipe, we will learn how to create child actors of an actor. Akka follows a tree-like hierarchy to create actors and it is also the recommended practice.

By following such practices, we can handle failures in actors as the parent can take care of it. Lets see how to do it.

Getting ready

We need to import the `Hello-Akka` project in the IDE of our choice. The Akka actor dependency that we added in `build.sbt` is sufficient for most of the recipes in this chapter, so we will skip the *Getting ready* section in our further recipes.

How to do it...

1. Create a file named `ParentChild.scala` in package `com.packt.chapter2`.
2. Add the following imports to the top of the file:

    ```
    import akka.actor.{ActorSystem, Props, Actor}
    ```

3. Create messages for sending to actors.

    ```
    case object CreateChild
    case class Greet(msg: String)
    ```

4. Define a child actor as follows:

    ```
    class ChildActor extends Actor {
      def receive = {
        case Greet(msg) => println(s"My
    ```

```
        parent[${self.path.parent}] greeted to
        me [${self.path}] $msg")
    }
}
```

5. Define a parent actor as follows, and create a child actor in its context:

```
class ParentActor extends Actor {
  def receive = {
    case CreateChild  =>
    val child = context.actorOf(Props[ChildActor], "child")
    child ! Greet("Hello Child")
  }
}
```

6. Create an application object as shown next:

```
object ParentChild extends App {
  val actorSystem = ActorSystem("Supervision")
  val parent = actorSystem.actorOf(Props[ParentActor],
  "parent")
  parent ! CreateChild
}
```

7. Run the preceding application, and you will get the following output:

```
My parent[akka://Supervision/user/parent] greeted to me
[akka://Supervision/user/parent/child] Hello Child
```

How it works...

In this recipe, we created a child actor, which receives a message, Greet, from the parent actor. We see the parent actor create a child actor using context.actorOf. This method creates a child actor under the parent actor. We can see the path of the actor in the output clearly.

Overriding the life cycle hooks of an actor

Since we are talking about supervision and monitoring of actors, you should understand the life cycle hooks of an actor. In this recipe, you will learn how to override the life cycle hooks of an actor when it starts, stops, prestarts, and postrestarts.

How to do it...

1. Create a file called `ActorLifeCycle.scala` in package `com.packt.chapter2`.
2. Add the following imports to the top of the file:

```
import akka.actor._
import akka.actor.SupervisorStrategy._
import akka.util.Timeout
import scala.concurrent.Await
import scala.concurrent.duration._
import akka.pattern.ask
```

3. Create the following messages to be sent to the actors:

```
case object Error
case class StopActor(actorRef: ActorRef)
```

4. Create an actor as follows, and override the life cycle methods:

```
class LifeCycleActor extends Actor {
  var sum = 1
  override def preRestart(reason: Throwable, message:
   Option[Any]): Unit = {
    println(s"sum in preRestart is $sum")
  }
  override def preStart(): Unit = println(
    s"sum in preStart is $sum")
  def receive = {
    case Error => throw new ArithmeticException()
    case _ => println("default msg")
  }
  override def postStop(): Unit = {
    println(s"sum in postStop is  ${sum * 3}")
  }
  override def postRestart(reason: Throwable): Unit = {
    sum = sum * 2
    println(s"sum in postRestart is $sum")
  }
}
```

5. Create a supervisor actor as follows:

```
class Supervisor extends Actor {
  override val supervisorStrategy =
  OneForOneStrategy(maxNrOfRetries = 10,
    withinTimeRange = 1 minute)
```

```
  {
    case _: ArithmeticException => Restart
    case t =>
    super.supervisorStrategy.decider.applyOrElse(t, (_:
     Any) => Escalate)
  }
  def receive = {
    case (props: Props, name: String) =>
    sender ! context.actorOf(props, name)
    case StopActor(actorRef) => context.stop(actorRef)
  }
}
```

6. Create a test application as shown next, and run the application.

```
object ActorLifeCycle extends App {
  implicit val timeout = Timeout(2 seconds)
  val actorSystem = ActorSystem("Supervision")
  val supervisor = actorSystem.actorOf(Props[Supervisor],
   "supervisor")
  val childFuture = supervisor ? (Props(new
   LifeCycleActor),
   "LifeCycleActor")
  val child = Await.result(childFuture.mapTo[ActorRef], 2
   seconds)
  child ! Error
  Thread.sleep(1000)
  supervisor ! StopActor(child)
}
```

7. Create another test application as follows, and run it.

```
object ActorLifeCycle extends App {
  implicit val timeout = Timeout(2 seconds)
  val actorSystem = ActorSystem("Supervision")
  val supervisor = actorSystem.actorOf(Props[Supervisor],
   "supervisor")
  val childFuture = supervisor ? (Props(new
   LifeCycleActor), "LifeCycleActor")
  val child = Await.result(childFuture.mapTo[ActorRef], 2
   seconds)
  child ! Error
  Thread.sleep(1000)
  supervisor ! StopActor(child)
}
```

On running the preceding test application, you will get the following output:

```
sum in preStart is 1
sum in preRestart is 1
sum in postRestart is 2
[ERROR] [07/01/2016 00:49:57.568] [Supervision-
akka.actor.default-dispatcher-5]
[akka://Supervision/user/supervisor/LifeCycleActor] null
java.lang.ArithmeticException at
com.packt.chapter2.LifeCycleActor$
$anonfun$receive$2.applyOrElse(ActorLifeCycle.scala:51)
sum in postStop is  6
```

How it works...

In this preceding recipe, we create an actor, which maintains sum as a state, and we modify its life cycle hooks. We create this actor under the parent supervisor, which handles the ArthimaticException in the child actor. Let's see what happens in life cycle hooks.

When an actor starts, it calls the preStart method, so we see the following output:

"sum in preStart is 1".

When an actor throws an exception, it sends a message to the supervisor, and the supervisor handles the failure by restarting that actor. It clears out the accumulated state of the actor, and creates a fresh new actor, means, it then restores the last value assigned to the state of old actor to the preRestart value.

After that postRestart method is called, and whenever the actor stops, the supervisor calls the postStop.

Sending messages to actors and collecting responses

In this recipe, you will learn how a parent sends messages to its child, and collects responses from them.

To step through this recipe, we need to import the Hello-Akka project in the IDE.

How to do it...

1. Create a file, `SendMesagesToChilds.scala`, in package `com.packt.chapter2`.
2. Add the following imports to the top of the file:

```
import akka.actor.{ Props, ActorSystem, Actor, ActorRef }
```

3. Create messages to be sent to the actors as follows:

```
case class DoubleValue(x: Int)
case object CreateChild
case object Send
case class Response(x: Int)
```

4. Define a child actor. It doubles the value sent to it.

```
class DoubleActor extends Actor {
  def receive = {
    case DoubleValue(number) =>
    println(s"${self.path.name} Got the number $number")
    sender ! Response(number * 2)
  }
}
```

5. Define a parent actor. It creates child actors in its context, sends messages to them, and collects responses from them.

```
class ParentActor extends Actor {
  val random = new scala.util.Random
  var childs =
   scala.collection.mutable.ListBuffer[ActorRef]()
  def receive = {
    case CreateChild =>
    childs ++= List(context.actorOf(Props[DoubleActor]))
    case Send =>
    println(s"Sending messages to child")
    childs.zipWithIndex map { case (child, value) =>
    child ! DoubleValue(random.nextInt(10)) }
  case Response(x) => println(s"Parent: Response
   from child $
  {sender.path.name} is $x")
  }
}
```

6. Create a test application as follows, and run it:

```
object SendMessagesToChild extends App {
  val actorSystem = ActorSystem("Hello-Akka")
  val parent =
   actorSystem.actorOf(Props[ParentActor], "parent")
  parent ! CreateChild
  parent ! CreateChild
  parent ! CreateChild
  parent ! Send
}
```

On running the preceding test application, you will get the following output:

```
$b Got the number 6
$a Got the number 5
$c Got the number 8
Parent: Response from child $a is 10
Parent: Response from child $b is 12
Parent: Response from child $c is 16
```

How it works...

In this last recipe, we create a child actor called DoubleActor, which doubles the value it gets. We also create a parent actor, which creates a child actor when it receives a CreateChild message, and maintains it in the list.

When the parent actor receives the message Send, it sends a random number to the child, and the child, in turn, sends a response to the parent.

Understanding OneForOneStrategy for actors

In this recipe, you will learn about OneForOneStrategy to implement the let it crash model.

The OneForOneStrategy class is applied when we want to supervise the child actors in such a way that only the failed child would be restarted, resumed, or escalated, not it's siblings. If we don't specify any supervisor strategy, then the default would be OneForOneStrategy. Let's understand it.

The OneForOneStrategy class is useful when actors are not dependent on each other, they are each responsible for a single task, and failure of one actor does not affect another.

To step through this recipe, we need to import the Hello-Akka project in IDE.

How to do it...

1. Create a file, SupervisorStrategy.scala, in package com.packt.chapter2.
2. Add the following import to the top of the file:

```
import akka.actor.SupervisorStrategy.{Escalate,
  Restart, Resume, Stop}
import akka.actor.{Actor, ActorSystem,
  OneForOneStrategy, Props}
```

3. Define two actors as shown next. The first one is Printer, and the second one is IntAdder. Both are independent of each other.

```
class Printer extends Actor {
  override def preRestart(reason: Throwable, message:
   Option[Any]): Unit = {
    println("Printer : I am restarting because of
     ArithmeticException")
  }
  def receive = {
    case msg: String => println(s"Printer $msg")
    case msg: Int => 1 / 0
  }
}
  class IntAdder extends Actor {
  var x = 0
  def receive = {
    case msg: Int => x = x + msg
    println(s"IntAdder : sum is $x")
    case msg: String => throw new IllegalArgumentException
  }
  override def postStop = {
    println("IntAdder :I am getting stopped
      because I got a string message")
  }
}
```

4. Define a supervisor. This supervisor specifies `OneForOneStrategy` for its children.

```
class SupervisorStrategy extends Actor {
  import scala.concurrent.duration._
  override val supervisorStrategy =
  OneForOneStrategy(maxNrOfRetries = 10, withinTimeRange =
   1 minute)
  {
    case _: ArithmeticException => Restart
    case _: NullPointerException => Resume
    case _: IllegalArgumentException => Stop
    case _: Exception => Escalate
  }
  val printer = context.actorOf(Props[Printer])
  val intAdder = context.actorOf(Props[IntAdder])
  def receive = {
    case "Start" =>  printer ! "Hello printer"
    printer ! 10
    intAdder ! 10
    intAdder ! 10
    intAdder ! "Hello int adder"
  }
}
```

5. Create a test application as follows:

```
object SupervisorStrategyApp extends App {
  val actorSystem = ActorSystem("Supervision")
  actorSystem.actorOf(Props[SupervisorStrategy]) !
   "Start"
}
```

6. Run the application, and you will get the following output:

```
Printer Hello printer
IntAdder : sum is 10
IntAdder : sum is 20
Printer : I am restarting because of ArithmeticException
IntAdder :I am getting stopped because I got a string message
[ERROR] [07/08/2016 23:34:12.414] [Supervision-
akka.actor.default-
dispatcher-5] [akka://Supervision/user/$a/$a] / by zero
java.lang.ArithmeticException: / by zero
[ERROR] [07/08/2016 23:34:12.422] [Supervision-
akka.actor.default-
dispatcher-5] [akka://Supervision/user/$a/$b] null
```

```
java.lang.IllegalArgumentException
```

How it works...

In the preceding recipe, we create two actors, IntAdder and Printer, under the same supervisor. Since the supervisor specifies OneForOneStrategy for its children, we see that only the child that fails is restarted by the supervisor, not the others.

Understanding AllForOneStrategy for actors

In this recipe, we will learn about AllForOneStrategy for child actors.

AllForOneStrategy implies that in case of failure of any one actor under a supervisor, the strategy will be applied to all the children under supervision.

To step through this recipe, we need to import Hello-Akka project in IDE.

How to do it...

1. Let's create a scala file, AllForOneStrategy.scala, in package com.packt.chapter2.

2. Add the following imports to the top of the file:

```
import akka.actor.SupervisorStrategy.{Escalate,
  Stop, Resume, Restart}
import akka.actor._
import scala.concurrent.duration._
```

3. Create messages as case classes.

```
case class Add(a: Int, b: Int)
case class Sub(a: Int, b: Int)
case class Div(a: Int, b: Int)
```

4. Let's create a calculator actor as follows:

```
class Calculator(printer: ActorRef) extends Actor {
  override def preRestart(reason: Throwable,
  message: Option[Any]): Unit = {
    println("Calculator : I am restarting because of
```

```
        ArithmeticException")
    }
    def receive = {
      case Add(a, b) => printer ! s"sum is ${a + b}"
      case Sub(a, b) => printer ! s"diff is ${a - b}"
      case Div(a, b) => printer ! s"div is ${a / b}
    }
}
```

5. Create a `ResultPrinter` actor.

```
class ResultPrinter extends Actor {
  override def preRestart(reason: Throwable, message:
   Option[Any]): Unit = {
    println("Printer : I am restarting as well")
  }
  def receive = {
    case msg => println(msg)
  }
}
```

6. Create a supervisor actor with `AllForOneStrategy` as follows:

```
class AllForOneStrategySupervisor extends Actor {
  override val supervisorStrategy =
  AllForOneStrategy(maxNrOfRetries = 10, withinTimeRange =
   1 seconds)
  {
    case _: ArithmeticException => Restart
    case _: NullPointerException => Resume
    case _: IllegalArgumentException => Stop
    case _: Exception => Escalate
  }
  val printer = context.actorOf(Props[ResultPrinter])
  val calculator =
   context.actorOf(Props(classOf[Calculator], printer))
  def receive = {
    case "Start" => calculator ! Add(10, 12)
    calculator ! Sub(12, 10)
    calculator ! Div(5, 2)
    calculator ! Div(5, 0)
  }
}
```

7. Create a test application.

```
object AllForOneStrategyApp extends App {
  val system = ActorSystem("Hello-Akka")
```

```
val supervisor =
  system.actorOf(Props[AllForOneStrategySupervisor],
  "supervisor")
  supervisor ! "Start"
}
```

8. Now run this application, and you will get the following output:

```
sum is 22
diff is 2
div is 2
Calculator : I am restarting because of ArithmeticException
Printer : I am restarting as well
[ERROR] [08/03/2016 23:54:55.796] [Hello-
Akka-akka.actor.default-dispatcher-3]
[akka://Hello-Akka/user/supervisor/$b] / by zero
java.lang.ArithmeticException: / by zero
```

How it works...

In this preceding recipe, we create two child actors, Calculator and ResultPrinter, under the supervision of the the AllForOneStrategy Supervisor. These actors are closely related in the sense that the result of any operation carried out by Calculator are sent to ResultPrinter to print.

When an exception occurs in Calculator, both the actors are restarted because of AllForOneStrategy.

Monitoring an actor life cycle using DeathWatch

In some scenarios, it becomes necessary to check continuously whether a particular service is running or not. In this recipe, we will learn how to monitor an actor.

To step through this recipe, you need to import the Hello-Akka project.

How to do it...

1. Let's create a file, `DeathWatch.scala`, in package `com.packt.chapter2`.
2. Add the following imports to the top of the file:

```
import akka.actor.{Actor, ActorSystem, Props,
  Terminated}
```

3. Create the following case objects as messages:

```
case object Service
case object Kill
```

4. Define a service actor, which would be monitored.

```
class ServiceActor extends Actor {
  def receive = {
    case Service => println("I provide a special service")
  }
}
```

5. Create an actor, which would be creating `ServiceActor` as its child.

```
class DeathWatchActor extends Actor {
  val child = context.actorOf(Props[ServiceActor],
   "serviceActor")
  context.watch(child)
  def receive = {
    case Service => child ! Service
    case Kill =>
    context.stop(child)
    case Terminated(`child`) => println("The service actor
     has terminated and no longer available")
  }
}
```

6. Create a test application, `DeathWatchApp`, as follows:

```
object DeathWatchApp extends App {
  val actorSystem = ActorSystem("Supervision")
  val deathWatchActor =
   actorSystem.actorOf(Props[DeathWatchActor])
  deathWatchActor ! Service
  deathWatchActor ! Service
  Thread.sleep(1000)
  deathWatchActor ! Kill
```

```
    deathWatchActor ! Service
}
```

7. When you run the preceding application, the output would be as follows:

```
I provide a special service
I provide a special service
The service actor has terminated and no longer available
[INFO] [08/08/2016 23:07:38.564] [Supervision-
akka.actor.default-dispatcher-4]
[akka://Supervision/user/$a/serviceActor] Message
[com.packt.chapter2.Service$] from
Actor[akka://Supervision/user/$a#269717766] to
Actor[akka://Supervision/user/$a/serviceActor#-172722412]
was not delivered. [1] dead letters encountered. This
logging can be turned off or adjusted with configuration
settings 'akka.log-dead-letters' and 'akka.log-dead-letters-
during-shutdown'.
```

How it works...

In this preceding recipe, we created a service actor. This service actor will be monitored by DeathWatchActor, which registers the service actor for monitoring the usage of context.watch. However, we can unwatch the actor using context.unwatch.

In the output, we see that the service actor sends the terminated message on termination.

3
Routing Messages

In this chapter, we will cover the following recipes:

- Creating a `SmallestMailboxPool` of actors
- Creating a `BalancingPool` of actors
- Creating a `RoundRobinPool` of actors
- Creating a `BroadcastPool` of actors
- Creating a `ScatterGatherFirstCompletedPool` of actors
- Creating a `ConsistentHashingPool` of actors
- Creating a `TailChoppingPool` of actors
- Creating a `RandomPool` of actors
- Sending specially handled messages to routers
- Creating a dynamically resizable pool of actors

Introduction

In the previous chapter, we learned some basic and advanced things about Akka fault tolerance and supervision for actors. In this chapter, we will learn how messages are routed to multiple actors via routers.

Where to use routers

In some situations, we may need a specific type of message routing mechanism for a specific requirement. Some of these situations are listed as follows:

- We want to send messages to the actor that is less busy among other actors of the same type, that is, to the actor with lowest number of messages
- We may want to send messages in a round-robin order to actors, that is, send messages one by one to all actors in a loop
- We may want to send a single message to all the actors in the group
- We may want to redistribute the work among actors automatically with the help of some mechanism

All of the following recipes are very simple:just one line of code, which specifies the type of router, does all the work.

Creating a SmallestMailboxPool of actors

In this recipe, you will learn how to create a `SmallestMailboxPool` or group for actors. `SmallestMailboxPool` is a pool of actors, and resembles the property whereby messages will globally be delivered to the actor with the least number of messages in its mailbox.

Getting ready

To step through this recipe, you will have to import the `Hello-Akka` project in an IDE such as IntelliJ Idea, and create a package called `chapter3`.

How to do it...

1. Create a Scala file, `Smallestmailbox.scala`, in the package `com.packt.chapter3`.
2. Add the following imports at the top of the file:

```
import akka.actor.{Props, ActorSystem, Actor}
import akka.routing.SmallestMailboxPool
```

3. Let's define an actor as follows:

```
class SmallestmailboxActor extends Actor {
  override def receive = {
    case msg: String => println(s" I am ${self.path.name}")
    case _ => println(s" I don't understand the message")
  }
}
```

4. Let's create a test application:

```
object Smallestmailbox extends App {
  val actorSystem = ActorSystem("Hello-Akka")
  val router =
   actorSystem.actorOf(SmallestMailboxPool(5).props
   (Props[SmallestmailboxActor]))
  for (i <- 1 to 5) {
    router ! s"Hello $i"
  }
}
```

5. Run the preceding application; you will see the following output:

```
I am $a
I am $d
I am $c
I am $b
I am $e
```

How it works...

We used `akka.routing.SmallestMailboxPool` to implement the `SmallestMailboxPool` of five actors. In the application, we sent five messages to the actor. Each message goes to a different actor.

To verify that the message goes to the smallest mailbox actor, we have to implement a custom mailbox to track which actor has the smallest number of messages in its mailbox, and send some more messages to the router.

Creating a BalancingPool of actors

A `BalancingPool` tries to redistribute the work among the actors for performance improvement. In the `BalancingPool`, all actors share the same mailbox.

Getting ready

Just import the Hello-Akka project in the IDE; other prerequisites are the same as before.

How to do it...

1. Create a Scala file, Balancingpool.scala, in the package com.packt.chapter3.

2. Add the following imports at the top of the file:

```
import akka.actor.{Props, ActorSystem, Actor}
import akka.routing.BalancingPool
```

3. Define a simple actor as an example:

```
class BalancingPoolActor extends Actor {
  override def receive = {
    case msg: String => println(s" I am ${self.path.name}")
    case _ => println(s" I don't understand the message")
..}
}
```

4. Create a simple test application as follows:

```
object balancingpool extends App {
  val actorSystem = ActorSystem("Hello-Akka")
  val router =
   actorSystem.actorOf(BalancingPool(5).props
   (Props[RoundRobinPoolActor]))
  for (i <- 1 to 5) {
    router ! s"Hello $i"
  }
}
```

5. Run the application, and you will see the following output:

```
I am $a
I am $d
I am $c
I am $e
I am $b
```

How it works...

In the preceding recipe, we created a BalancingPool of actors. To verify that the BalancingPool works, we will have to send more messages to the router, and we check the performance of the application with an increasing load.

A SmallestMailboxPool is better, since we always know that the new message will go to the actor who is least busy.

Creating a RoundRobinPool of actors

In this recipe, you will learn how to create a RoundRobinPool for actors. A RoundRobinPool is a group of the same type of actors and resembles the property whereby messages are delivered one by one to all the actors in the loop. In RoundRobinPool, all the actors share the same mailbox.

Getting ready

To step through this recipe, you will have to import the Hello-Akka project in the IDE.

How to do it...

1. Create a Scala file, RoundRobin.scala, in the package com.packt.chapter3.
2. Add the following imports to the top of the file:

```
import akka.actor.{Props, ActorSystem, Actor}
import akka.routing.RoundRobinPool
```

3. Let's define an actor as follows:

```scala
class RoundRobinPoolActor extends Actor {
  override def receive = {
    case msg: String => println(s" I am ${self.path.name}")
    case _ => println(s" I don't understand the message")
  }
}
```

4. Let's create a test application:

```
object RoundRobinPoolApp extends App {
  val actorSystem = ActorSystem("Hello-Akka")
  val router =
   actorSystem.actorOf(RoundRobinPool(5).props
   (Props[RoundRobinPoolActor]))
  for (i <- 1 to 5) {
    router ! s"Hello $i"
  }
}
```

5. Run the preceding application, and you will see the following output:

```
I am $a
I am $b
I am $e
I am $d
I am $c
```

How it works...

We used `akka.routing.RoundRobinPool` to implement a `RoundRobinPool` of five actors. In the application, we sent five messages to the actor. Each goes to a different actor, one by one, in a loop.

So after every five messages, the new message goes to the first actor in the loop. However, you would see the output is different: actor e processed the message before actor d and c did. This is because actor e got the thread for execution earlier than d or c.

Creating a BroadcastPool of actors

In some situations, we may want to send the same message to all the actors. Here is a `BroadcastPool` that lets us do so. It can be used when we want to send a common command to all the actors to do the same work.

Getting ready

Just import the `Hello-Akka` project in the IDE; the other prerequisites are the same as before.

How to do it...

1. Create a Scala file, `Broadcastpool.scala`, in the package `com.packt.chapter3`.

2. Add the following imports to the top of the file:

```
import akka.actor.{Props, ActorSystem, Actor}
import akka.routing.BroadcastPool
```

3. Define a simple actor as an example:

```
class BroadcastPoolActor extends Actor {
  override def receive = {
    case msg: String => println(s" $msg, I am
    ${self.path.name}")
    case _ => println(s" I don't understand the message")
  }
}
```

4. Create a simple test application as follows:

```
object Broadcastpool extends App {
  val actorSystem = ActorSystem("Hello-Akka")
  val router =
   actorSystem.actorOf(BroadcastPool(5).props
   (Props[BroadcastPoolActor]))
  router ! "hello"
}
```

5. Run the application, and the output will be as follows:

```
hello, I am $b
hello, I am $e
hello, I am $c
hello, I am $a
hello, I am $d
```

How it works...

In the preceding recipe, we created a `BroadcastPool` of actors. We sent a message, `hello`, to the router, and it sent the same message to all the actors under it.

Creating a ScatterGatherFirstCompletedPool of actors

In this recipe, we will learn about the `ScatterGatherFirstCompletedPool` of actors. Eponymously it sends the same message to all the actors, waits for the actor who first completes the work, and sends a response to it. It then discards replied from the other actors.

Getting ready

1. Create a Scala file, `ScatterGatherFirstCompletedpool.scala`, in the package `com.packt.chapter3`.

2. Add the following imports at the top of the file:

```
import akka.actor.{Actor, ActorSystem, Props}
import akka.pattern.ask
import akka.routing.ScatterGatherFirstCompletedPool
import akka.util.Timeout
import scala.concurrent.Await
import scala.concurrent.duration
```

3. Create an example actor as follows:

```
class ScatterGatherFirstCompletedPoolActor extends Actor {
  override def receive = {
    case msg: String => sender ! "I say hello back to you"
    case _ => println(s" I don't understand the message")
  }
}
```

4. Create a test application as follows:

```
object ScatterGatherFirstCompletedpool extends App {
  implicit val timeout = Timeout(10 seconds)
  val actorSystem = ActorSystem("Hello-Akka")
  val router =
   actorSystem.actorOf(ScatterGatherFirstCompletedPool(5,
   within = 10.seconds).
  props(Props[ScatterGatherFirstCompletedPoolActor]))
  println(Await.result((router ? "hello").mapTo[String], 10
   seconds))
}
```

5. Run the preceding application, and the output is as follows:

```
I say hello back to you
```

How it works...

ScatterGatherFirstCompletedPool has a property whereby it sends the same message to all the routee actors, but waits for the first reply from any of them, and then discards the other replies.

For this, we created an actor, and then created a ScatterGatherFirstCompletedPool of actors.

Since it waits for the the actors' reply, we use future to get the response-Situations where you have many machines and want to send the work to the machine that responds quickly.

Creating a TailChoppingPool of actors.

In this recipe, we will learn about the TailChoppingPool of actors. TailChoppingPool first sends the message to one, randomly picked, routee, and then, after a small delay, to a second routee (picked randomly from the remaining routees), and so on. It waits for the first reply it receives, and forwards it back to the original sender. Other replies are discarded.

Getting ready

1. Create a Scala file, TailChoppingpool.scala, in the package com.packt.chapter3.

2. Add the following imports at the top of the file:

```
import akka.actor.{Actor, ActorSystem, Props}
import akka.pattern.ask
import akka.routing.TailChoppingPool
import akka.util.Timeout
import scala.concurrent.Await
import scala.concurrent.duration
```

3. Create an example actor as follows:

```
class TailChoppingActor extends Actor {
  override def receive = {
      case msg: String => sender ! "I say hello back to you"
    case _ => println(s" I don't understand the message")
  }
}
```

4. Create a test application as follows:

```
object ScatterGatherFirstCompletedpool extends App {
  implicit val timeout = Timeout(10 seconds)
  val actorSystem = ActorSystem("Hello-Akka")
  val router = actorSystem.actorOf(TailChoppingPool(5,
   within = 10.seconds,interval = 20.millis).
  props(Props[TailChoppingActor]))
  println(Await.result((router ? "hello").mapTo[String], 10
   seconds))
}
```

5. Run the preceding application, and the output would be as follows:

```
I say hello back to you
```

How it works...

Unlike `ScatterGatherFirstCompletedPool`, `TailChoopingPool` randomly picks a routee and sends a message to it, waits for the reply, and after an interval picks a random routee from amongst all of them, and sends a message to it. That's why we call it TailChopping.

Creating a ConsistentHashingPool of actors

In this recipe, you will learn about the `ConsistentHashingPool` of actors. A `ConsistentHashingPool` uses consistent hashing to send message to actors.

The idea behind `ConsistentHashingPool` is that it always forwards a message with the same key to the same actor based on the sent message.

Consistent caching is used for a distributed cache across multiple nodes. It gives us flexibility regarding what is cached and where, for faster results.

Getting ready

To step through this recipe, you need to import a Scala project in our IDE such as IntelliJ Idea. Before we go through the recipe, however, you are required to understand consistent hashing.

For consistent hashing, refer to the following Wikipedia link:
`https://en.wikipedia.org/wiki/Consistent_hashing`.

There are three ways to define the data to use for the consistent hash key:

- You can define `hashMapping` of the router to map incoming messages to their consistent hash key. This makes the decision transparent for the sender.
- The messages may implement `akka.routing.ConsistentHashingRouter.ConsistentHashable`. The key is part of the message, and it's convenient to define it together with the message definition.
- The messages can be wrapped in `akka.routing.ConsistentHashingRouter.ConsistentHashableEnvelop` to define what data to use for the consistent hash key. The sender knows the key to use.

How to do it...

1. Create a Scala file, `ConsistantHashingpool.scala`, in the package `com.packt.chapter3`.

2. Add the following imports to the top of the file:

```
import akka.actor.{Actor, ActorSystem, Props}
import akka.routing.ConsistentHashingPool
import akka.routing.ConsistentHashingRouter.{
ConsistentHashMapping, ConsistentHashable,
  ConsistentHashableEnvelope}
import akka.util.Timeout
import scala.concurrent.duration._
```

3. Create the following messages to be sent to the actor.

```
case class Evict(key: String)
case class Get(key: String) extends ConsistentHashable {
  override def consistentHashKey: Any = key
}
```

```
case class Entry(key: String, value: String)
```

4. Let's define an actor as follows for caching purposes:

```
class Cache extends Actor {
  var cache = Map.empty[String, String]
  def receive = {
   case Entry(key, value) =>
    println(s" ${self.path.name} adding key $key")
    cache += (key -> value)
    case Get(key) =>
    println(s" ${self.path.name} fetching key $key")
    sender() ! cache.get(key)
    case Evict(key)  =>
    println(s" ${self.path.name} removing key $key")
    cache -= key
  }
}
```

5. Create a test application as follows:

```
object ConsistantHashingpool extends App {
  val actorSystem = ActorSystem("Hello-Akka")
  def hashMapping: ConsistentHashMapping = {
    case Evict(key) => key
  }
  val cache =
  actorSystem.actorOf(ConsistentHashingPool(10, hashMapping
   = hashMapping).
  props(Props[Cache]), name = "cache")
  cache ! ConsistentHashableEnvelope(
  message = Entry("hello", "HELLO"), hashKey = "hello")
  cache ! ConsistentHashableEnvelope(
  message = Entry("hi", "HI"), hashKey = "hi")
  cache ! Get("hello")
  cache ! Get("hi")
  cache ! Evict("hi")
}
```

6. Run the above application; the output is as follows:

```
$e adding key hi
$d adding key hello
$d fetching key hello
$e fetching key hi
$e removing key hi
```

How it works...

So we have implemented a `ConsistentHashingPool` of actors. For this, we first created the message that implements the `ConsistentHashable` trait. And then we defined an actor that maintains a map for caching. In the test application, we create an application in which we create a `ConsistentHashingPool` of actors. We can see in the output that the actor always return the same key and value which they have received for insertion in the cache.

Creating a RandomPool of actors

A random pool of actors does nothing more than send messages to a randomly picked routee among a list of routees. It is useful when you don't care which routee picks up the message and does the work for you, and it may be the case that you end up sending the message to the busiest actor.

Getting ready

All prerequisites are the same as in previous recipes; just import the `Hello-Akka` project and start.

How to do it...

1. Create a Scala file, `RandomPool.scala`, in `com.packt.chapter3`.

2. Add the following import to the top of the file:

```
import akka.actor.{Props, ActorSystem, Actor}
import akka.routing.RandomPool
```

3. Define an actor as follows:

```
class RandomPoolActor extends Actor {
  override def receive = {
    case msg: String => println(s" I am ${self.path.name}")
    case _ => println(s" I don't understand the message")
  }
}
```

4. Create a test application as follows:

```
object RandomPoolApp extends App {
  val actorSystem = ActorSystem("Hello-Akka")
  val router =
   actorSystem.actorOf(RandomPool(5).props
   (Props[RandomPoolActor]))
  for (i <- 1 to 5) {
    router ! s"Hello $i"
  }
}
```

5. Run the preceding application, and the output will be as follows:

```
I am $b
I am $c
I am $b
I am $c
I am $e
```

How it works...

For the preceding recipe, we have to do nothing except import the RandomPool class and make a pool of actors as we did in the test application.

Sending specially handled messages to routers

There are some kinds of message that are specially handled by actors. They have a special behavior. These messages are mostly used for handling management of the actors.

The following are the different types of message:

- Broadcast messages
- PoisonPill messages
- Kill messages
- Management messages such as AddRoutee, RemoveRoutee, and so on

Getting ready

We will limit our recipe to the `Broadcast`, `PoisonPill`, and `Kill` messages. All prerequisites are the same as earlier.

How to do it...

1. Create a Scala file, `SpeciallyHandled.scala`, in the package `com.packt.chapter3`.

2. Add the following import to the top of the file:

```
import akka.actor.{PoisonPill, Props, ActorSystem, Actor}
import akka.routing.{Broadcast, RandomPool}
```

3. Add the following case object message sent to the actor:

```
case object Handle
```

4. Define an actor as follows:

```
class SpeciallyHandledActor extends Actor {
  override def receive = {
    case Handle => println(s"${self.path.name} says hello")
  }
}
```

5. Create a test application as follows:

```
object SpeciallyHandled extends App {
  val actorSystem = ActorSystem("Hello-Akka")
  val router =
   actorSystem.actorOf(RandomPool(5).props
   (Props[SpeciallyHand
   ledActor]))
  router! Broadcast(Handle)
  router ! Broadcast(PoisonPill)
  router! Handle
}
```

6. Run the preceding application, and the output will be as follows:

```
$b says hello
$a says hello
$c says hello
```

```
$e says hello
$d says hello
```

In the last line of the output, you will see the "message not delivered" error.

How it works...

As you have seen in the output, the same message can be sent to all the actors by wrapping the `Handle` message into the `Broadcast` envelope. After that, we sent `PoisonPill`, which is a specially handled message in the `Broadcast` envelope, to kill all the actors under the router.

There is another one: the `Kill` message. When sent to the router, it throws an `ActorKilledException` and fails. It is then resumed, restarted, or terminated, depending on how it is supervised.

Creating a dynamically resizable pool of actors

There are situations when we want a variable number of actors under the router to handle the increasing and decreasing number of requests. The following is a recipe for such situations:

Getting ready

To step through this recipe, we need to import the `Hello-Akka` project. All prerequisites are the same as before.

How to do it...

1. Create a Scala file, `ResizablePool.scala`, in the package `com.packt.chapter3`.

2. Add the following import to the top of the file:

```
import akka.actor.{Props, Actor, ActorSystem}
import akka.routing.{RoundRobinPool, DefaultResizer}
```

3. Create a case object as the message to be sent to the actor:

```
case object Load
```

4. Define a dummy actor as follows:

```
class LoadActor extends Actor {
  def receive = {
    case Load => println("Handing loads of requests")
  }
}
```

5. Create a test application as follows:

```
object ResizablePool extends App {
  val system = ActorSystem("Hello-Akka")
  val resizer = DefaultResizer(lowerBound = 2,
    upperBound = 15)
  val router = system.actorOf(RoundRobinPool(5,
  Some(resizer)).props(Props[LoadActor]))
}
```

Run the preceding application, and the output will be as follows:

```
Handing loads of requests
```

It is up to the reader to make the actor compute some numbers like Fibonacci, and cross-verify whether the throughput increases with an increase in requests.

4
Using Futures and Agents

In this chapter, we will cover the following recipes:

- Using a future directly for a simple operation
- Using futures with actors
- Using futures inside actors
- Using for-comprehensions for futures
- Handling callback on futures
- Creating a simple parallel application using futures
- Reducing a sequence of futures
- Reading and updating agents
- Composing agents monadically

Introduction

In the last chapter, we learned how to route messages to actors, and in this chapter, we will learn about **futures**.

Futures are used to perform an operation in other threads for concurrency and parallel execution. They contain the result of the concurrent operation and can be accessed synchronously, by blocking the current thread of execution, or asynchronously, (non-blocking) by handling the callback on a future.

Futures require `ExecutionContext`, which is backed by a thread pool to execute callbacks and other operations.

So, more or less, futures are used to execute operations on other threads concurrently.

Using a future directly for a simple operation

As an introductory example, we will see how to use a future just for a simple operation: we will add two integers and use a future to run this operation asynchronously.

Getting ready

To step through this recipe, we will need to import the `Hello-Akka` project; all other prerequisites are the same as before.

How to do it...

For this recipe, we will need to perform the following steps:

1. Create a file, such as `AddFuture.scala`, in the `com.packt.chapter4` package.
2. Add the following imports to the top of the file:

```
import scala.concurrent.duration._
import scala.concurrent.{Await, Future}
import scala.concurrent.ExecutionContext.Implicits.global
```

3. Create a test application, as follows:

```
object AddFuture extends App {
  val future = Future(1+2).mapTo[Int]
  val sum = Await.result(future, 10 seconds)
  println(s"Future Result $sum")
}
```

How it works...

In the preceding recipe, we computed the sum of two numbers by wrapping it in a future. We mapped the result to `Int` as we were expecting `sum`. We imported `scala.concurrent.ExecutionContext.Implicits.global` to execute the future. Here, we are using the `Await` pattern to block the current thread to retrieve the result.

After you run the preceding application, you will see the following result:

```
Future Result 3
```

Using futures with actors

In this recipe, we will see how to use a future with an actor, and how to retrieve the result of a computation done by a future.

Getting ready

Just import the Hello-Akka project, and the other prerequisites are the same as earlier.

How to do it...

The following are the steps to use a future with an actor and to retrieve a result of the computation:

1. Create a scala file, FutureWithActor.scala, in the com.packt.chapter4 package.
2. Add the following imports to the top of the file:

```
import akka.actor.{Actor, ActorSystem, Props}
import akka.pattern.ask
import akka.util.Timeout
import scala.concurrent.Await
import scala.concurrent.duration._
```

3. Create an actor that calculates the sum of two integers and sends it back to the sender, as shown in the following code snippet:

```
class ComputationActor extends Actor {
  def receive = {
    case (a: Int, b: Int) => sender ! (a + b)
  }
}
```

4. Create the sample test application, as follows:

```
object FutureWithScala extends App {
  implicit val timeout = Timeout(10 seconds)
  val actorSystem = ActorSystem("Hello-Akka")
  val computationActor =
    actorSystem.actorOf(Props[ComputationActor])
  val future = (computationActor ? (2,3) ).mapTo[Int]
  val sum = Await.result(future, 10 seconds)
  println(s"Future Result $sum")
```

```
        }
```

Run the application, and the output will be as shown in the next section.

How it works...

We have created an actor that calculates the sum, and we are using a ? mark to send the message to the actor and return a `future` validator. Here, we don't need `Executioncontext` explicitly as it is provided by the actor system itself.

After you run the preceding application, its output will be as follows:

```
Future Result 5
```

Using futures inside actors

We will learn how to use a future inside an actor to schedule an operation asynchronously to another thread.

Getting ready

All the prerequisites are the same as earlier; just import the `Hello-Akka` project in the IDE.

How to do it...

The following are the steps to use future inside the actor:

1. Create a scala file, say `FutureInsideActor.scala`, in the `com.packt.chapter4` package.
2. Add the following import to the top of the file:

```
import akka.actor.{Props, ActorSystem, Actor}
import scala.concurrent.{Await, Future}
import scala.concurrent.duration._
```

3. Create an actor that uses a future inside, as shown in the following code snippet:

```scala
class FutureActor extends Actor {
  import context.dispatcher
  def receive = {
    case (a:Int, b:Int) => val f = Future(a+b)
    (Await.result(f, 10 seconds))
  }
}
```

4. Create a test application, as follows:

```scala
object FutureInsideActor extends App {
  val actorSystem = ActorSystem("Hello-Akka")
  val fActor = actorSystem.actorOf(Props[FutureActor])
  fActor !(10, 20)
}
```

How it works...

In this recipe, we are using future as we have used it in other places. The only difference is that we got `ExecutionContext` by importing `context.dispatcher` inside the actor, which is a default disptacher in Akka.

Here, we are using `Await.result` to retrieve a result from the future, and it blocks the thread inside the actor, which is not recommended. Instead, we should use a callback function, such as `onComplete`.

After you run the preceding application, its output will be as follows:

```
Future result is 30
```

Using for-comprehensions for futures

In this small recipe, we will see how to use for comprehensions to iterate over futures as we do with Scala collections. As a future is a monad, like a list in Scala, we can operate on it in the same way as we operate on a list. It is also a way of composing futures.

Getting ready

All the prerequisites are the same as before; just import the `Hello-Akka` project in the IDE.

How to do it...

1. Create a Scala file, `ForComprehensions.scala`, in the `com.packt.chapter4` package.
2. Add the following imports to the top of the file:

```
import scala.concurrent.duration._
import scala.concurrent.{Await, Future}
import scala.concurrent.ExecutionContext.Implicits.global
```

3. Create a test application, as follows:

```
object ForComprehensions extends App {
  val futureA = Future(20 + 20)
  val futureB = Future(30 + 30)
  val finalFuture: Future[Int] = for {
    a <- futureA
    b <- futureB
    } yield a + b
  println("Future result is " + Await.result(finalFuture, 1
  seconds))
}
```

How it works...

In the preceding application, we are creating two futures that add integers, and we are using for-comprehensions to iterate over both the futures. Here, we are not blocking on individual futures. Instead, we are creating a final future out of them and waiting (blocking) on it for a result.

After you run the preceding application, the result will be as follows:

```
Future result is 100
```

Handling callback on futures

In this recipe, you will learn how to handle future responses with callback functions; it is also known as asynchronous handling of futures. Using the callback function, we don't block the current thread for response from a future.

Getting ready

To step through this recipe, we will need to import the `Hello-Akka` project in the IDE, and the rest of the prerequisites are same as earlier.

How to do it...

1. Create a scala file, `callback.scala`, in the `com.packt.chapter4` package.
2. Add the following import to the top of the file:

```
import scala.concurrent.ExecutionContext.Implicits.global
import scala.concurrent.Future
import scala.util.{Failure, Success}
```

3. Create a Scala application, as follows:

```
object Callback extends App {
  val future = Future(1 + 2).mapTo[Int]
  future onComplete {
    case Success(result) => println(s"result is $result")
    case Failure(fail) => fail.printStackTrace()
    }
  println("Executed before callback")
}
```

How it works...

In the preceding application, we created a future that just adds two integers; here, we used the callback function, `onComplete`. In the `onComplete` function, we handled two cases, which could either be `Success` or `failure`. It handled the future asynchronously, as we see in the output that `println` executed before the future completed.

After you run the preceding application, you will get the following output:

```
Executed before callback
result is 3
```

Creating a simple parallel application using futures

In this recipe, we will create an application that will compute the result in parallel. You will learn how independent operations can be parallelized, which will reduce the running time of a program.

Getting ready

To step through this recipe, we need to import the `Hello-Akka` project in the IDE. The rest of the prerequisites are the same as before.

How to do it...

1. Create a simple scala file, say `Parallel.scala`, in the `com.packt.chapter4` package.
2. Add the following imports to the top of the file:

```
import scala.concurrent.ExecutionContext.Implicits.global
import scala.concurrent.{Await, Future}
```

3. Create a Scala object, as shown in the following code snippet, which calculates a Fibonacci number:

```
object Fib {
  def fib(n: Int): Int = {
    def fib_tail(n: Int, a: Int, b: Int): Int = n match {
      case 0 => a
      case _ => fib_tail(n - 1, b, a + b)
    }
    fib_tail(n, 0, 1)
  }
}
```

4. Create a simple test application, `Parallel`, as follows:

```
object Parallel extends App {
  import Fib._
  val t1 = System.currentTimeMillis
  val sum = fib(100) + fib(100) + fib(100)
  println(s"sum is $sum time taken in sequential
   computation $
  {System.currentTimeMillis - t1 / 1000.0}")
  val t2 = System.currentTimeMillis
  val future1 = Future(fib(100))
  val future2 = Future(fib(100))
  val future3 = Future(fib(100))

  val future = for {
    x <- future1
    y <- future2
    z <- future3
  } yield (x + y + z)
  future onSuccess {
    case sum =>
    val endTime = ((System.currentTimeMillis - t2) /
     1000.0)
    println(s"sum is $sum time taken in parallel computation
    $endTime seconds")
  }
  Thread.sleep(5000)
}
```

How it works...

In the preceding recipe's output, we clearly see the parallel computation time is way less than the sequential implementation.

We just created the future of a Fibonacci number and composed it using for-comprehensions; we also call back on the final future rather than blocking each of them, thus we will get parallel computation capabilities from future.

After you run the preceding application, its output will be as follows:

```
sum is 1354645321 time taken in sequential computation 1.477588591743776E12
sum is 1354645321 time taken in parallel computation  0.131 seconds
```

Reducing a sequence of futures

We know how to compose futures of different types using for-comprehensions, but in this recipe, we will learn how to compose a sequence of futures of the same type.

Getting ready

Import the `Hello-Akka` project in the IDE. The other prerequisites are the same as earlier.

How to do it...

1. Create a scala file, `RedcuingFutures`, in the `com.packt.chapter4` package.
2. Add the following imports to the top of the file:

```
import akka.util.Timeout
import scala.concurrent.duration._
import scala.concurrent.{Await, Future}
import scala.concurrent.ExecutionContext.Implicits.global
```

3. Create a simple application, as follows:

```
object ReducingFutures extends App {
  val timeout = Timeout(10 seconds)
  val listOfFutures = (1 to 10).map(Future(_))
  val finalFuture = Future.reduce(listOfFutures)(_ + _)
  println(s"sum of numbers from 1 to 10 is $
  {Await.result(finalFuture, 10
  seconds)}")
}
```

How it works...

In this recipe, we created futures of numbers from 1 to 10 and obtained a list of futures; thereafter, we reduced the futures using the `Future.reduce` method, which takes a sequence of futures and a function to reduce them all, as we usually do with lists.

After you run the preceding application, you will get the following output:

```
sum of numbers from 1 to 10 is 55
```

Reading and updating agents

Agents are used to provide shared access to storage locations. They provide independent, asynchronous change of individual locations. Agents are bound to a single storage location for their lifetime and only allow mutation of that location (to a new state) to occur as a result of an action. Actions are functions (with, optionally, additional arguments) that are asynchronously applied to an agent's state and whose return value becomes the Agent's new state.

While updates to Agents are asynchronous, the state of an Agent is always immediately available for reading by any thread using get or apply without any messages.

Getting ready

Before we go through this recipe, we will need to download the `akka-agent` dependency in our project. For this, we will need to add the following dependency to the project's `build.sbt`:

```
libraryDependencies += "com.typesafe.akka" % "akka-agent_2.11" % "2.4.4"
```

Now, open the terminal in Linux or command prompt in Windows and go to the project directory and run an `sbt update` command. This will download the jar dependency for us.

Now, import the `Hello-Akka` project in the IDE.

How to do it...

1. Create a Scala file, `Agent.scala`, in the `com.packt.chapter4` package.
2. Add the following imports to the top of the file:

```
import akka.agent.Agent
import akka.util.Timeout
import scala.concurrent.ExecutionContext.Implicits.global
import scala.concurrent.duration._
import scala.concurrent.{Await, Future}
```

3. Create a test application, as follows:

```
object AgentApp extends App {
  val timeout = Timeout(10 seconds)
  val agent = Agent(5)
```

```
val result = agent.get
println(s"Result is now $result")
val f1: Future[Int] = agent alter 7
println(s"Result after sending a value ${Await.result(f1,
  10 seconds)}")
val f2: Future[Int] = agent alter (_ + 3)
println(s"Result after sending a function
  ${Await.result(f2, 10
seconds)}")
}
```

Run the application and output would be shown in the next section.

How it works...

In the preceding application, we are creating a simple agent whose initial value is 5. You can read the agent value using the get method. We can send a value or function to the agent using the alter function that returns the future. Thus, we can retrieve the result from the future. The first value was 5, then we send the 7 to the agent, it updated the result to 7; thereafter, we send a function to the agent that increments the current value by 3, and we got 10.

After you run the preceding application, its output will be as follows:

```
Result is now 5
Result after sending a value 7
Result after sending a function 10
```

Composing agents monadically

Like futures, we can also compose future using for-comprehensions. In this recipe, we will see how we can do this.

Getting ready

We have already downloaded the akka-agent dependency in the project, so we will need to just import the project into the IDE.

How to do it..

1. Create a scala file, `AgentComposition.scala`, in the `com.packt.chapter4` package.

2. Add the following imports to the top of the file:

```
import akka.agent.Agent
import scala.concurrent.ExecutionContext.Implicits.global
```

3. Create a test application, as follows:

```
object AgentComposition extends App {
  val agent1 = Agent("Hello, ")
  val agent2 = Agent("World")
  val finalAgent = for {
    value1 <- agent1
    value2 <- agent2  }  yield value1 + value2
  println(finalAgent.get)
}
```

How it works...

It is the same as when we composed futures using for-comprehensions. We can also use the `map` and `flatMap` methods on agents as well.

After running the preceding application, its output will be as follows:

```
Hello world
```

5

Scheduling Actors and Other Utilities

In this chapter, we will cover the following recipes:

- Scheduling an operation at a specified interval
- Scheduling an actor's operation at a specified interval
- Canceling a scheduled operation of the actor
- Creating a circuit breaker to avoid cascading failure
- How to introduce logging with actors
- Writing unit test for actors
- Packaging and deploying the Akka standalone application
- Packaging and deploying Akka application inside a Docker container
- Configuring Akka applications

Introduction

In the previous chapters, you learned about supervision, routing of messages, futures, and so on. In this chapter, you will learn how can we schedule an operation to be run at the specified interval, scheduling actors, logging, testing, and how to deploy the Akka application. These recipes are not related and have their own context and meaning. We can think of these recipes as utilities.

Scheduling an operation at a specified interval

There are some situations where we want an operation to occur at a specified time or occur repeatedly after an interval. This is like a cron job. Let's go through the recipe.

Getting ready

To step through this recipe, we need to import our Hello-Akka project into the IDE and create a com.packt.chapter5 package in which we will put all the code.

How to do it...

1. Let's create a file, say, ScheduleOperation.scala in the com.packt.chapter5 package.

2. Add the following imports to the top of the file:

```
import akka.actor.ActorSystem
import scala.concurrent.duration._
```

3. Create a test application, as follows, in which we create an actor system and schedule the operation:

```
object ScheduleOperation extends App {
val system = ActorSystem("Hello-Akka")
import system.dispatcher
system.scheduler.scheduleOnce(10 seconds)
  { println(s"Sum of (1 + 2) is ${1 + 2}")
  }
system.scheduler.schedule(11 seconds, 2 seconds) {
 println(s"Hello, Sorry for disturbing you every 2 seconds")
 }
}
```

How it works...

If you run the preceding application, you will see the output as follows:

```
Sum of (1 +2) is 3 Hello, Sorry for disturbing you in every 2 seconds
Hello, Sorry for disturbing you in every 2 seconds Hello, Sorry for
disturbing you in every 2 seconds ....... and so on
```

Going through the code, we see that there are two methods in system.scheduler, that is, scheduleOnce and schedule. In the scheduleOnce method, we schedule the operation in such a way that it happens after a specified seed time but not repeatedly; in our case, it is 10 seconds. In the schedule method, we have scheduled the operation every 2 seconds, and it starts after the specified seed interval; in our case, the seed interval is 11 seconds.

Scheduling an actor's operation at a specified interval

Scheduling an actor is the same as we scheduling the simple operation. There are cases where we want an actor to do some after some work repeatedly after an interval of time.

Getting ready

Just import the Hello-Akka project in the IDE; no other prerequisites are required.

How to do it...

1. Create a file, say, ScheduleActor.scala in the com.packt.chapter5 package.
2. Add the following imports to the top of the file:

```
import akka.actor.{Actor, Props, ActorSystem}
import scala.concurrent.duration._
```

3. Create a simple actor, as follows, that adds two random integers:

```
class RandomIntAdder extends Actor {
  val r = scala.util.Random
  def receive = {
    case "tick" =>
```

```
val randomInta = r.nextInt(10)
val randomIntb = r.nextInt(10)
println(s"sum of $randomInta and $randomIntb is
${randomInta + randomIntb}")

      }
   }
```

4. Create a test application, as follows, in which we schedule the actor:

```
object ScheduleActor extends App {
  val system = ActorSystem("Hello-Akka")
  import system.dispatcher
  val actor = system.actorOf(Props[RandomIntAdder])
  system.scheduler.scheduleOnce(10 seconds, actor, "tick")
  system.scheduler.schedule(11 seconds, 2 seconds, actor,
  "tick")
}
```

How it works...

We will see the following output by running the application, and it will appear after a delay of 10 seconds and every 11 seconds:

```
sum of 6 and 1 is 7
sum of 7 and 0 is 7
sum of 5 and 1 is 6
sum of 4 and 3 is 7
sum of 2 and 5 is 7
```

So, we can schedule the actor in the same way as we scheduled the operation earlier. It is up to us which way we choose to implement the functionality. We can implement our own scheduler.

 To implement your own scheduler in Akka, visit http://doc.akka.io/do cs/akka/current/java/scheduler.html for reference.

Canceling a scheduled operation of the actor

By now, we know how to schedule the actor, but it is also necessary to cancel the scheduler if it has reached a certain condition. For this, we will have to maintain a state if the scheduler has run enough times to achieve the desired result.

Getting ready

Import the `Hello-Akka` project in the IDE; the other prerequisites are the same as earlier.

How to do it...

1. Create a file, say, `CancelOperation.scala`, in the `com.packt.chapter5` package.

2. Add the following import to the top of the file:

```
import akka.actor.{Cancellable, Props, ActorSystem, Actor}
import scala.concurrent.duration._
```

3. Define an actor, as follows. It will not compile, as it is referencing the `Scheduler` object:

```
class CancelOperation extends Actor {
  var i = 10
  def receive = {
    case "tick" => {
      println(s"Hi, Do you know i do the same task again and
      again")
      i = i - 1
      if (i == 0) Scheduler.cancellable.cancel()
    }
  }
}
```

4. Create a simple test application, as follows:

```
object Scheduler extends App {
  val system = ActorSystem("Hello-Akka")
  import system.dispatcher
  val actor = system.actorOf(Props[CancelOperation])
  val cancellable: Cancellable = system.scheduler.schedule(0
  seconds, 2 seconds, actor, "tick")
}
```

How it works...

If we run the preceding application, we will see the following output 10 times:

```
Hi, Do you know i do the same task again and again
```

So when we create the scheduler, it can be assigned to the `Cancellable` interface type, which exposes the cancel method. Thus, we can cancel the scheduler. In our case, we canceled the scheduler when it ran 10 times.

Creating a circuit breaker to avoid cascading failure

In an Akka distributed system, we are expected to write a lot of services in the form of actors who do their work asynchronously. In such an application, there are chances that some services would be under a huge load and might fail anytime. So there would be chances that if a service depends on a particular service and if that particular service fails, then there would be propagation of failure in the services that are calling that particular service. Thus, we need a mechanism to avoid calling those services if they are failing or unresponsive and stop serving further requests.

To deal with such a scenario, Akka provides a circuit breaker.

Getting ready

To step through this recipe, import the `Hello-Akka` project in the IDE; other prerequisites are the same as earlier. In this recipe, we will create a dummy database and fetch records from it. We will use the circuit breaker to see how it blocks further requests if there is a delay in serving requests more than a specified number of times in the circuit breaker.

How to do it…

1. Create a scala file, say, `CircuitBreaker.scala`, in the `com.packt.chapter5` package.

2. Add the following imports to the top of the file:

    ```scala
    import akka.actor.{Actor, ActorSystem, Props}
    import akka.pattern.{CircuitBreaker, ask}
    import akka.util.Timeout
    import scala.concurrent.duration._
    ```

3. Add some case classes to hold the data:

    ```scala
    case class FetchRecord(recordID: Int)
    case class Person(name: String, age: Int)
    ```

4. Create a dummy DB, as follows, in which we have created a Scala map to hold some `Person` records:

    ```scala
    object DB {
      val data = Map(1 -> Person("John", 21), 2 -> Person("Peter",
      30), 3 ->
      Person("James", 40), 4 -> Person("Alice", 25), 5 ->
      Person("Henry", 26),
      6 -> Person("Jackson", 48))
    }
    ```

5. Create an actor, as follows, who fetches records mapped to the record ID:

    ```scala
    class DBActor extends Actor {
      def receive = {
        case FetchRecord(recordID) =>
          if (recordID >= 3 && recordID <= 5)
            Thread.sleep(3000)
          else sender ! DB.data.get(recordID)
      }
    }
    ```

6. Create a circuit breaker, as follows, with the timeout configuration:

    ```scala
    val breaker =
      new CircuitBreaker(system.scheduler,
        maxFailures = 3,
        callTimeout = 1 seconds,
        resetTimeout = 2 seconds).
        onOpen(println("===========State is open============")).
    ```

```
        onClose(println("===========State is closed============")
    )
```

7. Create a test application, as follows, and use the circuit breaker inside it:

```
object CircuitBreakerApp extends App {

  val system = ActorSystem("hello-Akka")
  implicit val ec = system.dispatcher
  implicit val timeout = Timeout(3 seconds)

  val breaker =
    new CircuitBreaker(system.scheduler,
      maxFailures = 3,
      callTimeout = 1 seconds,
      resetTimeout = 2 seconds).
      onOpen(println("===========State is open=============")).
      onClose(println("=========State is closed===========")
      )

  val db = system.actorOf(Props[DBActor], "DBActor")

  (1 to 10).map(recordId => {
    Thread.sleep(3000)
    val askFuture = breaker.withCircuitBreaker(db ?
    FetchRecord(recordId))
    askFuture.map(record => s"Record is: $record and RecordID
    $recordId").recover({
      case fail => "Failed with: " + fail.toString
    }).foreach(x => println(x))
  })
```

How it works...

If we run the preceding application, then we will see the following output:

```
Record is:
Some(Person(John,21)) and RecordID 1 Record is:
Some(Person(Peter,30)) and RecordID 2 Failed with:
akka.pattern.CircuitBreaker$$anon$1:
Circuit Breaker Timed out. Failed with:
akka.pattern.CircuitBreaker$$anon$1:
Circuit Breaker Timed out. Failed with:
akka.pattern.CircuitBreaker$$anon$1: Circuit Breaker Timed out.
=============State is open===============
Failed with: akka.pattern.CircuitBreakerOpenException: Circuit Breaker is
```

```
open; calls are failing fast
=============State is closed==============
Record is:
None and RecordID 7 Record is:
None and RecordID 8 Record is:
None and RecordID 9 Record is:
None and RecordID 10
```

On examining the preceding output, you will see that we got a three-time failure for the record ID (3 ,4 ,5). As per the configuration of the circuit breaker, it blocks further requests after maximum failure; that why we see State is open and there is no output for record ID 6 because the circuit breaker has reset the time to 2 seconds; after the reset interval, it starts working normally.

How to introduce logging with actors

Logging is the best way to debug an application for errors and information. In this recipe, we will look at how to introduce logging with actors. There are third-party libraries that provide logging to an application, such as sl4jLogger. In Akka, logging is not tied to a particular API, but we will go with ActorLogging, provided by Akka.

Getting ready

To step through this recipe, we do not require any other API dependencies; just import the Hello-Akka project in the IDE.

How to do it...

1. Create a file, say, Logging.scala, in the com.packt.chapter5 package.
2. Add the following import to the file:

   ```
   import akka.actor.{Props, ActorSystem, ActorLogging, Actor}
   ```

3. Create an actor, as follows, that uses logging:

   ```
   class LoggingActor extends Actor with ActorLogging {
     def receive = {
       case (a: Int, b: Int) => {
         log.info(s"sum of $a and $b is ${a + b}")
       }
   ```

```
    case msg => log.warning(s"i don't know what are you talking
    about : msg")
  }
}
```

4. Create a test application, as follows:

```
object Logging extends App {
  val system = ActorSystem("hello-Akka")
  val actor = system.actorOf(Props[LoggingActor], "SumActor")
  actor !(10, 12)
  actor ! "Hello !!"
  system.terminate()
}
```

How it works...

We will see the following output if we run the application:

```
[INFO] [12/12/2016 23:06:06.478]
[hello-Akka-akka.actor.default-dispatcher-6]
[akka://hello-Akka/user/SumActor]
sum of 10 and 12 is 22
[WARN] [12/12/2016 23:06:06.480]
[hello-Akka-akka.actor.default-dispatcher-6]
[akka://hello-Akka/user/SumActor]
i don't know what are you talking about:
Hello !!
```

We can configure the logging level to debug, inform, or warn in the application config.

 For more information, visit http://doc.akka.io/docs/akka/2.4.14/sca
la/logging.html#logging-of-dead-letters.

Writing unit test for actors

When we develop an Akka application, we should write an automated test for our actors to check whether they are working as expected. Since the actor model is different as they are asynchronous in nature, we have a different view of how we will perform unit tests on them.

Getting ready

First of all, we will add the `akka-testkit` dependency to our application's `build.sbt`. So, add the following dependency to `build.sbt`:

```
libraryDependencies += "com.typesafe.akka" % "akka-testkit_2.11" % "2.4.4"

libraryDependencies += "org.scalatest" % "scalatest_2.11" % "3.0.1"
```

Now move to the project root directory and run the `sbt update` command; it will download the preceding dependencies. Now import the `Hello-Akka` project in the IDE.

How to do it...

1. Create a `com.packt.chapter5` package in the `src/test/scala` project folder.
2. Create a Scala file, say, `Testing.scala`, in the `com.packt.chapter5` package.
3. Add the following import to the top of the file:

```
import akka.actor.{Actor, ActorSystem, Props}
import akka.testkit.{ImplicitSender, TestKit}
import org.scalatest.{BeforeAndAfterAll, Matchers,
WordSpecLike}
```

4. Let's create an actor who simply returns a sum of two integers:

```
class SumActor extends Actor {
  def receive = {
    case (a: Int, b: Int) => sender ! (a + b)
  }
}
```

5. Create a specification test class, as follows:

```
class TestSpec() extends TestKit(ActorSystem("TestSpec")) with
ImplicitSender with WordSpecLike with Matchers with
BeforeAndAfterAll {

  override def afterAll {
    TestKit.shutdownActorSystem(system)
  }

  "Sum actor" must {

    "send back sum of two integers" in {
```

```
            val sumActor = system.actorOf(Props[SumActor])
            sumActor !(10, 12)
            expectMsg(22)
        }
      }
    }
```

How it works...

If we run the preceding application, we will see that the entire test has passed with a green light. We can run the test from command line, as follows:

```
sbt "test-only com.packt.chapter5.TestSpec"
```

Thus, Akka provides its own testing framework to test the actor. There are a lot of testing techniques, which can not be covered in one recipe. For more information, visit the documentation at http://doc.akka.io/docs/akka/current/scala/testing.html.

Packaging and deploying the Akka standalone application

After developing any application, we package it as a distribution/assembly to run on any platform. In this trick, you will learn how to package an Akka application into a distribution and how to deploy it to run as a standalone application.

Getting ready

We will use the SBT assembly plugin to package the application into a fat jar. Just import the Hello-Akka project into the IDE. We are assuming that you have a working knowledge of SBT and its assembly plugin.

How to do it...

1. For every SBT project, we have an assembly.sbt file in the project's project folder. If the file is not present, then we create one.

2. Add the SBT assembly plugin dependency in the file:

```
addSbtPlugin("com.eed3si9n" % "sbt-assembly" % "0.14.3")
```

3. Now go to the project root directory and run the `sbt update` command from the command line and it will download the plugin dependency jar.

4. Now go to the project root directory and run the `sbt assembly` command to package the jar. It will package the code along with the project dependencies.

5. Now we can run any recipe, as follows:

```
java -cp assemblyPath fullyQualifiedClassName
java -cp /user-directory/Hello-Akka/target/scala-2.11/Hello-Akka-
assembly-1.0.jar
com.packt.chapter5.ScheduleActor
```

How it works...

Sbt assembly enables us to package the application into a fat jar.

For more information, visit `https://github.com/sbt/sbt-assembly`.

Packaging and deploying Akka application inside a Docker container

In this recipe, you will learn how to run our Akka application inside a docker container. This is done assuming that most of you are familiar with docker and have a working installation of docker on your Linux machine. Docker is an application container engine. The focus of this recipe is to run the application inside docker.

For more information on how to install docker, visit `https://www.digita locean.com/community/tutorials/how-to-install-and-use-docker-o n-ubuntu-16-04`.

Getting ready

In the previous recipe, you learned how to package the Akka application into an assembly jar. It is recommended that you go through that recipe, *Packaging and deploying the Akka standalone application*. We will use this assembly jar while building a docker image.

How to do it...

1. First of all, ensure that docker is properly installed on your machine. Run the following command to check the version:

   ```
   sudo docker version
   ```

   If the preceding command fails, then visit the installation pages listed earlier.

2. Assuming we are inside the `Hello-Akka` project, create a directory inside the `Hello-Akka` project, say, `dockerApp`, where we will keep our Docker file and other stuff.

3. Now create a folder inside `dockerApp`, say, `docker`, where we will copy our application assembly jar.

4. Create a bash script, say, `dockerize.sh`, inside the `dockerApp` directory and place the following commands inside it:

   ```
   #!/bin/bash
   echo "====================Removing target before making
   assembly================================="
   rm -fr ../target && rm -fr docker/*
   echo "====================Entering to Hello-Akka directory and
   creating assembly================"
   cd ../ && sbt assembly
   echo "====================Coming back to dockerApp
   directory==================================="
   cd - echo "====================Copying application jar to
   docker folder============================="
   sudo cp ../target/scala-2.11/Hello-Akka-assembly-1.0.jar
   docker/
   echo "====================Building docker
   image==============================================="
   sudo docker build -t akkaapp .
   echo "====================Running docker
   container============================================="
   sudo docker run akkaapp
   ```

5. Create a docker file, say, `Dockerfile`, inside the `dockerApp` directory and place the following commands inside it:

```
FROM java:8
COPY docker/Hello-Akka-assembly-1.0.jar Hello-Akka-assembly-
1.0.jar
RUN java -cp Hello-Akka-assembly-1.0.jar
com.packt.chapter5.ScheduleActor
```

6. Run the `dockerize` script; it will create the assembly jar, build the docker image, and run the docker container.

How it works...

To understand this recipe, we must have a running installation of docker. We can check with the command used in step one. After that, we create a bash script that assembles the application and builds a docker image. In order to create a docker image, we always have a `Dockerfile` in which we place the commands to run the application.

Configurating Akka applications

There are many properties that need to be set in the Akka application, either programmatically or via configuration. Configuration is the recommended approach to set the properties in the Akka application.

Getting ready

To step through this recipe, we just need to import the `Hello-Akka` project; other prerequisites are the same as earlier. By default, configuration is read from application.conf, but it can be read from any `.conf` file. Usually, we put all conf files in the project resources folder.

How to do it...

1. Create a conf file, say, `akka.conf`, in the project's `src/main/resources` folder.

2. For example, add the following properties to `akka.conf`:

```
myactor {
  actorname=actor1
  actorsystem=hell-akka
}
```

3. Create an `ActorWithConfig.scala` file in the `com.packt.chapter5` package.
4. Add the following import to the top of the file:

```
import akka.actor.{Props, Actor, ActorSystem}
import com.typesafe.config.Config
import com.typesafe.config.ConfigFactory
```

5. Define an actor:

```
class MyActor extends Actor {
  def receive = {
    case msg: String => println(msg)
  }
}
```

6. Create an application, as follows, in which we read the configuration:

```
object ActorWithConfig extends App {
  val config: Config = ConfigFactory.load("akka.conf")
  val actorsystem =
  ActorSystem(config.getString("myactor.actorsystem"))
  val actorName = config.getString("myactor.actorname")
  val actor = actorsystem.actorOf(Props[MyActor], actorName)
  println(actor.path)
}
```

How it works...

We will see the following output if we run the preceding application:

```
akka://hello-akka/user/actor1
```

Here, in the output, we see that the actor path comprises the values provided in `akka.conf`. Reading configuration is not limited to this recipe; it is just a starting point. Visit the complete documentation at http://doc.akka.io/docs/akka/snapshot/general /configuration.html.

6
Akka Persistence

We will cover the following recipes in this chapter:

- Preparing an actor for persistence
- Recovering the state of an actor
- Safely shutting down a persistent actor
- Reducing recovery time using snapshots
- Creating a persistence FSM model
- Persisting the state to LevelDB
- Persisting the state to Cassandra
- Persisting the state to Redis
- Understanding event sourcing
- Handling failure in event sourcing
- Using persistence query
- Persistence query for LevelDB

Introduction

Another useful module in the Akka ecosystem is Akka persistence. In some use cases, the state held by stateful actors is essential for your application to behave correctly. This kind of application cannot afford to lose that state. This could happen if the actor holding the state gets restarted; it is migrated to a different node in a cluster, or your JVM crashes. Akka persistence comes in handy with this task: it provides a mechanism to save the state and be able to recover it. Unlike traditional approaches, Akka persistence uses event sourcing to achieve this task. In the event sourcing world, we never store the actual state but an ordered set of events that happened in the actor to achieve that particular state. This way, we have a log of events that we can use to restore the state of an actor when required. Also, this technique provides a way of understanding how an actor reached its current state since we can analyze and replay each event. In this chapter, we will cover how to make your actors persistent and how to use different data stores to persist these events.

Preparing an actor for persistence

Before we take a look at Akka persistence, let's review the terminology and architectures used in it:

- `PersistentActor`: A stateful actor that persists events to the journal. When a persistent actor is started or restarted, journaled messages are replayed to that actor so that it can recover the internal state from these messages.
- `AsyncWriteJournal`: A journal keeps an ordered collection of events that can be sent to a persistent actor. An application can control which messages are journaled and which are received by the persistent actor without being journaled. The data store behind the journal is configurable and needs to be decided depending on the needs. By default, Akka persistence comes with a LevelDB journal plugin (which uses the local filesystem and is not replicated).
- `AtLeastOnceDelivery`: A messaging delivery mechanism that ensures at-least-once delivery semantics to destinations.
- **Snapshot store**: A snapshot store persists snapshots of a persistent actor's. Snapshots are used to speed up recovery time from the journal. The data store behind the snapshot store is configurable (the same as the journal) and uses the local filesystem as the default.

In this recipe, we will look at how to enable persistence for your actors using the default journal LevelDB.

Getting ready

In order to work with Akka persistence, we need to download the Akka persistence dependencies in our project. For that, we need to add the following lines to your `build.sbt` file:

```
libraryDependencies += "com.typesafe.akka" % "akka-persistence_2.11" %
"2.4.17"
libraryDependencies += "org.iq80.leveldb"  % "leveldb" % "0.7"
```

Once that is ready, make sure that you run `sbt update`.

How to do it...

For this recipe, we need to perform the following steps:

1. First, let's set up a package where we will add all our classes. Create a package named `com.packt.chapter6` inside `src/main/scala`.

2. Then let's create the required classes to store our events and keep our state. Create a file named `SamplePersistenceModel.scala` inside the `com.packt.chapter6` package with the following content:

```scala
package com.packt.chapter6

sealed trait UserAction
case object Add extends UserAction
case object Remove extends UserAction
case class UserUpdate(userId: String, action: UserAction)

sealed trait Event
case class AddUserEvent(userId: String) extends Event
case class RemoveUserEvent(userId: String) extends Event

case class ActiveUsers(users: Set[String] = Set.empty[String])
{
  def update(evt: Event) = evt match {
    case AddUserEvent(userId) => copy(users + userId)
    case RemoveUserEvent(userId) => copy(users.filterNot(_ ==
    userId))
  }
  override def toString = s"$users"
}
```

3. Afterward, let's create our persistent actor. Create a file named
   `SamplePersistenceActor.scala` inside the `com.packt.chapter6` package.
   The code should look like this:

```
package com.packt.chapter6

import akka.persistence.{PersistentActor, SnapshotOffer}

class SamplePersistenceActor extends PersistentActor {
  override val persistenceId = "unique-id-1"
  var state = ActiveUsers()
 def updateState(event: Event) = state = state.update(event)

  val receiveRecover: Receive = {
    case evt: Event => updateState(evt)
    case SnapshotOffer(_, snapshot: ActiveUsers) => state =
    snapshot
  }

  val receiveCommand: Receive = {
    case UserUpdate(userId, Add) =>
    persist(AddUserEvent(userId))(updateState)
    case UserUpdate(userId, Remove) =>
    persist(RemoveUserEvent(userId))(updateState)
    case "snap"  => saveSnapshot(state)
    case "print" => println(state)
  }
}
```

4. We also need to configure our journal and snapshot data stores. For this example,
   we will be using LevelDB for the journal. These configurations need to be set in
   `reference.conf`. Create a file named `reference.conf` inside
   `src/main/resource`. The content will be as follows:

```
akka.persistence.journal.plugin =
"akka.persistence.journal.leveldb"
akka.persistence.snapshot-store.plugin =
"akka.persistence.snapshot-store.local"

akka.persistence.journal.leveldb.dir = "target/sample/journal"
akka.persistence.snapshot-store.local.dir =
"target/sample/snapshots"

akka.persistence.journal.leveldb.native = false
```

5. Now let's create an app to test our actor. Create a file named
   SamplePersistenceApp.scala inside the com.packt.chapter6 package with
   the following code:

```scala
package com.packt.chapter6

import akka.actor.{ActorSystem, Props}

object SamplePersistenceApp extends App {
 val system = ActorSystem("example")
 val persistentActor1 =
 system.actorOf(Props[SamplePersistenceActor])
 persistentActor1 ! UserUpdate("foo", Add)
 persistentActor1 ! UserUpdate("baz", Add)
 persistentActor1 ! "snap"
 persistentActor1 ! "print"
 persistentActor1 ! UserUpdate("baz", Remove)
 persistentActor1 ! "print"
 Thread.sleep(2000)
 system.stop(persistentActor1)
 val persistentActor2 =
 system.actorOf(Props[SamplePersistenceActor])
 persistentActor2 ! "print"
 Thread.sleep(2000)
 system.terminate()
}
```

6. Once all code is ready, let's run our code either in IntelliJ or the command line
   and analyze the output:

```
hveiga$ sbt "runMain com.packt.chapter6.SamplePersistenceApp"
[info] Running com.packt.chapter6.SamplePersistenceApp
Set(foo, baz)
Set(foo)
Set(foo)
[success] Total time: 8 s, completed Apr 6, 2017 2:20:12 PM
```

How it works...

In this recipe, we covered how to create a persistent actor. To achieve that, we need to mix in the PersistentActor trait. Our scenario simulates an actor that holds information about active users. To begin, we need to define events, commands, and state. State is the class that represents the current state of the actor and what we want to be able to recover. In our case, we have ActiveUsers. Events represent the changes happening to the state, in our case, AddUser and RemoveUser. Commands represent the regular messages sent to the actor, in our case, UserUpdate. Each persistent actor needs to define a persistenceId, a receiveRecover, and a receiveCommand behavior. The persistence ID needs to be an identifier that uniquely identifies your actor in your whole system, including your data store. This ID is used to be able to recover the state and we need to ensure it doesn't change across different actor incarnations. The receive command behavior is the regular behavior of your actor, where you will persist the changes in the state. Finally, the receive recover behavior is used to replay the events or snapshot to reach the latest state.

In our particular scenario, we can see that we are storing two types of event: AddUser and RemoveUser. Every time we receive a UserUpdate command in our receiveCommand behavior, we call persist to record the change in the journal. It's worth mentioning that your command does not directly update your state. When we call persist, we need to provide the event and the function that will update it. We use the updateState function for this purpose. This same function is also used when recovering the state in the receiveRecover behavior. The other concept being used in this example is snapshot. While this persist operation happens atomically, it is also possible to store multiple of them at once using persistAll(). Moreover, there are asynchronous versions of these methods that provide the same functionality but without blocking. A snapshot is a copy of the state and allows you to reduce the recovery time. In our case, we call saveSnapshot when the actor receives a snap command. When recovering the state from the data store, Akka persistence will first check for snapshots and then for saved events. This way, it will ensure the fastest recovery time. When we run the application, we can see that when stop our actor and create a new incarnation of it, the state is recovered. You will learn more about recovery in a later recipe called *Handling failure in event sourcing*.

Recovering the state of an actor

Persistent actors recover the state based on their persistence ID. This ID needs to unique for a given persistent actor and within the data store. It is required to ensure the consistency of the journal when we persist events and when we recover. Each time a persistent actor is created, Akka persistence checks the journal and the snapshot stores for events and snapshots, respectively. The default behavior is to apply the latest snapshot and replay the missing events afterward. However, this behavior can be modified to our needs, as we will see in this recipe. In this recipe, we will show and explain what the different recovery strategies in Akka persistence are.

Getting ready

To step through this recipe, we need to import the `hello-Akka` project in the IDE; other prerequisites are the same as earlier as we have downloaded the `akka-persistence` dependency. For this recipe, we will use the LevelDB plugin.

How to do it...

For this recipe, we need to perform the following steps:

1. First, let's create the classes for events and commands. Create a file named `FriendModel.scala` inside the `com.packt.chapter6` package with the following content:

```
package com.packt.chapter6

case class AddFriend(friend: Friend)
case class RemoveFriend(friend: Friend)
case class Friend(id: String)
sealed trait FriendEvent
case class FriendAdded(friend: Friend) extends FriendEvent
case class FriendRemoved(friend: Friend) extends FriendEvent

case class FriendState(friends: Vector[Friend] =
Vector.empty[Friend]) {
  def update(evt: FriendEvent) = evt match {
    case FriendAdded(friend) => copy(friends :+ friend)
    case FriendRemoved(friend) => copy(friends.filterNot(_ ==
    friend))
  }
  override def toString = friends.mkString(",")
```

}

2. Second, let's create the actor that will keep a list of friends. This list will change over time when adding and removing friends. Create a file named `FriendActor.scala` inside the `com.packt.chapter6` package with the following code:

```scala
package com.packt.chapter6

import akka.actor.{ActorLogging, Props}
import akka.persistence.{PersistentActor, Recovery,
RecoveryCompleted, SnapshotOffer}

object FriendActor {
  def props(friendId: String, recovery: Recovery) = Props(new
  FriendActor(friendId, recovery))
}

class FriendActor(friendId: String, r: Recovery) extends
PersistentActor with ActorLogging {
  override val persistenceId = friendId
  override val recovery = r
  var state = FriendState()
 def updateState(event: FriendEvent) = state =
 state.update(event)

  val receiveRecover: Receive = {
    case evt: FriendEvent =>
      log.info(s"Replaying event: $evt")
      updateState(evt)
    case SnapshotOffer(_, recoveredState : FriendState) =>
      log.info(s"Snapshot offered: $recoveredState")
      state = recoveredState
    case RecoveryCompleted => log.info(s"Recovery completed.
    Current state: $state")
  }

  val receiveCommand: Receive = {
    case AddFriend(friend) => persist(FriendAdded(friend))
    (updateState)
    case RemoveFriend(friend) => persist(FriendRemoved(friend))
    (updateState)
    case "snap" => saveSnapshot(state)
    case "print" => log.info(s"Current state: $state")
  }
}
```

3. Afterward, let's create a set of small apps to demonstrate the different recovery options. To begin, create a file named `FriendApp.scala` inside the `com.packt.chapter6` package. The first app will send some add and remove friend messages to create the journal and a snapshot:

```
package com.packt.chapter6

import akka.actor.ActorSystem
import akka.persistence.{Recovery, SnapshotSelectionCriteria}

object FriendApp extends App {
  val system = ActorSystem("test")
  val hector = system.actorOf(FriendActor.props("Hector",
  Recovery()))
  hector ! AddFriend(Friend("Laura"))
  hector ! AddFriend(Friend("Nancy"))
  hector ! AddFriend(Friend("Oliver"))
  hector ! AddFriend(Friend("Steve"))
  hector ! "snap"
  hector ! RemoveFriend(Friend("Oliver"))
  hector ! "print"
  Thread.sleep(2000)
  system.terminate()
}
```

4. In the same file, add the following code to demonstrate the default behavior of recovery:

```
object FriendRecoveryDefault extends App {
  val system = ActorSystem("test")
  val hector = system.actorOf(FriendActor.props("Hector",
  Recovery()))
  hector ! "print"
  Thread.sleep(2000)
  system.terminate()
}
```

5. In the same file, add the following code to demonstrate how to not recover from snapshots and only from events:

```
object FriendRecoveryOnlyEvents extends App {
  val system = ActorSystem("test")
  val recovery = Recovery(fromSnapshot =
  SnapshotSelectionCriteria.None)
  val hector = system.actorOf(FriendActor.props("Hector",
  recovery))
  hector ! "print"
```

```
    Thread.sleep(2000)
    system.terminate()
}
```

6. In the same file, add the following code to demonstrate how to place a limit up to which event is to be recovered:

```
object FriendRecoveryEventsSequence extends App {
    val system = ActorSystem("test")
    val recovery = Recovery(fromSnapshot =
    SnapshotSelectionCriteria.None, toSequenceNr = 2)
    val hector = system.actorOf(FriendActor.props("Hector",
    recovery))
    Thread.sleep(2000)
    system.terminate()
}
```

7. In the same file, add the following code to demonstrate how to limit how many events to replay:

```
object FriendRecoveryEventsReplay extends App {
    val system = ActorSystem("test")
    val recovery = Recovery(fromSnapshot =
    SnapshotSelectionCriteria.None, replayMax = 3)
    val hector = system.actorOf(FriendActor.props("Hector",
    recovery))
    Thread.sleep(2000)
    system.terminate()
}
```

8. Ensure that the following values are present in the reference.conf file that lives in src/main/resources:

```
akka.persistence.journal.plugin =
"akka.persistence.journal.leveldb"
akka.persistence.snapshot-store.plugin = .
"akka.persistence.snapshot-store.local"
akka.persistence.journal.leveldb.dir = "target/friend/journal"
akka.persistence.snapshot-store.local.dir =
"target/friend/snapshots"
```

9. After all code is ready, let's run it in either IntelliJ or the command line and analyze the output:

```
hveiga$ sbt "runMain com.packt.chapter6.FriendApp"
[INFO] [akka://test/user/$a] Recovery completed. Current state:
[INFO] [akka://test/user/$a] Current state:
```

```
Friend(Laura),Friend(Nancy),Friend(Steve)
...
hveiga$ sbt "runMain com.packt.chapter6.FriendRecoveryDefault"
[INFO] [akka://test/user/$a] Snapshot offered:
Friend(Laura),Friend(Nancy),Friend(Oliver),Friend(Steve)
[INFO] [akka://test/user/$a] Replaying event:
FriendRemoved(Friend(Oliver))
[INFO] [akka://test/user/$a] Recovery completed. Current state:
Friend(Laura),Friend(Nancy),Friend(Steve)
[INFO] [akka://test/user/$a] Current state:
Friend(Laura),Friend(Nancy),Friend(Steve)
...
hveiga$ sbt "runMain com.packt.chapter6.FriendRecoveryOnlyEvents"
[INFO] [akka://test/user/$a] Replaying event:
FriendAdded(Friend(Laura))
[INFO] [akka://test/user/$a] Replaying event:
FriendAdded(Friend(Nancy))
[INFO] [akka://test/user/$a] Replaying event:
FriendAdded(Friend(Oliver))
[INFO] [akka://test/user/$a] Replaying event:
FriendAdded(Friend(Steve))
[INFO] [akka://test/user/$a] Replaying event:
FriendRemoved(Friend(Oliver))
[INFO] [akka://test/user/$a] Recovery completed. Current state:
Friend(Laura),Friend(Nancy),Friend(Steve)
[INFO] [akka://test/user/$a] Current state:
Friend(Laura),Friend(Nancy),Friend(Steve)
...
hveiga$ sbt "runMain
com.packt.chapter6.FriendRecoveryEventsSequence"
[INFO] [akka://test/user/$a] Replaying event:
FriendAdded(Friend(Laura))
[INFO] [akka://test/user/$a] Replaying event:
FriendAdded(Friend(Nancy))
[INFO] [akka://test/user/$a] Recovery completed. Current state:
Friend(Laura),Friend(Nancy)
...
hveiga$ sbt "runMain
com.packt.chapter6.FriendRecoveryEventsReplay"
[INFO] [akka://test/user/$a] Replaying event:
FriendAdded(Friend(Laura))
[INFO] [akka://test/user/$a] Replaying event:
FriendAdded(Friend(Nancy))
[INFO] [akka://test/user/$a] Replaying event:
FriendAdded(Friend(Oliver))
[INFO] [akka://test/user/$a] Recovery completed. Current state:
Friend(Laura),Friend(Nancy),Friend(Oliver)
```

How it works...

In this recipe, we covered the different recovery options Akka persistence provides when handling failure. To demonstrate this, we have created a small actor `FriendActor` that keeps a list of friends. When creating the actor, we need to provide a `Recovery` object. It is this object where we can customize how we want the recovery to happen. In the first app, we are adding four friends, taking a snapshot, and removing one of the friends. All these events get persisted for the `Hector` ID. After running this app, we create four different apps.

When we run `FriendRecoveryDefault`, we see how recovery occurs by default. Based on the output, we can see that it first takes the snapshot and then it replays the event of removing `Oliver` since the snapshot was taken before that event happened. By default, Akka persistence will take the latest snapshot and replay the events from that point in time. When we run `FriendRecoveryOnlyEvents`, we provide `fromSnapshot = SnapshotSelectionCriteria.None` in the recovery object. This tells persistence to not use any snapshot, and we can see in the logs that all events are replayed. When we run `FriendRecoveryEventsSequence`, we provide a `toSequenceNr` value of 2. This means that up to two events will get replayed. That is why we only see the addition of Laura and Nancy as friends. Finally, when we run `FriendRecoveryEventsReplay`, we provide a `replayMax` value of 3. This means that only three events will get replayed, as we can see in the logs. In complicated scenarios, it is possible to play with the values of `toSequenceNr` and `replayMax` to just replay the events required instead of all events persisted in the journal.

Safely shutting down a persistent actor

Shutting down an actor is often achieved by sending a `PoisonPill` message to it. This allows the previous messages in the mailbox to get processed by the actor before it is stopped. Although this is totally correct for regular actors, it can turn into unexpected behaviors when using a persistent actor. Incoming commands are stashed while the persistent actor is awaiting confirmation from the journal that events have been stored when calling `persist()`. The incoming commands will be drained from the Actor's mailbox and put into its internal stash while awaiting the confirmation (thus, before calling the `persist` handlers). Therefore, the persistent actor may receive and (auto) handle the `PoisonPill` message before it processes the other messages, causing a premature (and maybe unexpected) shutdown of the actor. In this recipe, we will look at how we should correctly shut down a persistent actor.

Getting ready

To step through this recipe, we need to import the hello-Akka project in the IDE; other prerequisites are the same as earlier, as we have downloaded the akka-persistence dependency. We will make use of the SamplePersistenceActor class developed in the previous recipe, *Preparing an actor for persistence*.

How to do it...

For this recipe, we need to perform the following steps:

1. First, let's create an explicit object to shut down our persistent actors. Inside the SamplePersistenceModel.scala file, add the following object at the end:

   ```
   case object ShutdownPersistentActor
   ```

2. Second, let's modify our actor to handle this object. Update the receiveCommand function inside our the SamplePersistenceActor class to look like the following snippet. Also, add a postStop hook:

   ```
   val receiveCommand: Receive = {
     case UserUpdate(userId, Add) => persist(AddUserEvent(userId))
     (updateState)
     case UserUpdate(userId, Remove) =>
     persist(RemoveUserEvent(userId))(updateState)
     case "snap"  => saveSnapshot(state)
     case "print" => println(state)
     case ShutdownPersistentActor => context.stop(self)
   }

   override def postStop() = println(s"Stopping [${self.path}]")
   ```

3. Create a file named SafePersistenceActorShutdownApp.scala inside the com.packt.chapter6 package with the following content:

   ```
   package com.packt.chapter6

   import akka.actor.{ActorSystem, PoisonPill, Props}

   object SafePersistenceActorShutdownApp extends App {
     val system = ActorSystem("safe-shutdown")
     val persistentActor1 =
     system.actorOf(Props[SamplePersistenceActor])
     val persistentActor2 =
   ```

```
system.actorOf(Props[SamplePersistenceActor])

persistentActor1 ! UserUpdate("foo", Add)
persistentActor1 ! UserUpdate("foo", Add)
persistentActor1 ! PoisonPill
persistentActor2 ! UserUpdate("foo", Add)
persistentActor2 ! UserUpdate("foo", Add)
persistentActor2 ! ShutdownPersistentActor
}
```

4. Once all the code is ready, let's run our application either in IntelliJ or the command line:

```
hveiga$ sbt clean
[success] Total time: 0 s, completed
hveiga$ sbt "runMain
com.packt.chapter6.SafePersistenceActorShutdownApp"
[info] Running com.packt.chapter6.SafePersistenceActorShutdownApp
Stopping [akka://safe-shutdown/user/$a]
[INFO] [akka://safe-shutdown/user/$a] Message
[com.packt.chapter6.UserUpdate] from Actor[akka://safe-
shutdown/deadLetters] to Actor[akka://safe-
shutdown/user/$a#1801050022] was not delivered. (...)
[INFO] [akka://safe-shutdown/user/$a] Message
[com.packt.chapter6.UserUpdate] from Actor[akka://safe-
shutdown/deadLetters] to Actor[akka://safe-
shutdown/user/$a#1801050022] was not delivered. (...)
Stopping [akka://safe-shutdown/user/$b]
```

How it works...

In this recipe, you have learned that we need to create an explicit object to shut down our persistent actors instead of using the PoisonPill object that we normally use for regular actors. We created ShutdownPersistentActor for this purpose. We can check the behavior of PoisonPill and the custom message separately by looking at the output generated by SafePersistenceActorShutdownApp. When shutting down with PoisonPill, we can see the Stopping [akka://safe-shutdown/user/$a] message first and then two info logs advertising that our UserUpdate message didn't get received by the actor. When shutting down with ShutdownPersistentActor, we simply see Stopping [akka://safe-shutdown/user/$b], indicating that the two messages have been received by the actor before stopping it.

Reducing recovery time using snapshots

As we have mentioned in the introduction, Akka persistence uses event sourcing to persist the state of an actor. Event sourcing is a technique to store the changes to the state instead of the state itself. This way, we can have a sequence of what happened. This mechanism is great and has some advantages over the traditional approach, but it might be overkill when you have millions of events to persist and replay when recovering. That is why Akka persistence allows you to take snapshots of our current state to speed up the recovery time. Persistent actors can save snapshots of the internal state by calling the `saveSnapShot` method. If saving a snapshot succeeds, the persistent actor receives a `SaveSnapshotSuccess` message; otherwise, they receive a `SaveSnapshotFailure` message.

Getting ready

To step through this recipe, we need to import the `hello-Akka` project in the IDE; other prerequisites are the same as earlier as we have downloaded the `akka-persistence` dependency. We will make use of the classes we created in the first recipe, *Preparing an actor for persistence*.

How to do it...

For this recipe, we need to perform the following steps:

1. First, let's create a new actor to showcase all the snapshot capabilities. Create a file named SnapshotActor.scala inside the com.packt.chapter6 package. The code should look like this:

```scala
package com.packt.chapter6

import akka.actor.ActorLogging
import akka.persistence._

class SnapshotActor extends PersistentActor with ActorLogging {
  override val persistenceId = "ss-id-1"
  var state = ActiveUsers()
  def updateState(event: Event) = state = state.update(event)

  val receiveRecover: Receive = {
    case evt: Event => updateState(evt)
    case SnapshotOffer(metadata, snapshot: ActiveUsers) =>
```

```
          state = snapshot
          case RecoveryCompleted => log.info(s"Recovery completed.
    Current state: [$state]")
      }

      val receiveCommand: Receive = {
        case UserUpdate(userId, Add) =>
        persist(AddUserEvent(userId))(updateState)
        case UserUpdate(userId, Remove) =>
        persist(RemoveUserEvent(userId))(updateState)
        case "snap" => saveSnapshot(state)
        case SaveSnapshotSuccess(metadata)       =>
        log.info(s"Snapshot success [$metadata]")
        case SaveSnapshotFailure(metadata, e) =>
        log.warning(s"Snapshot failure [$metadata] Reason: [$e]")
      }

      override def postStop() = log.info("Stopping")
      override def recovery =
      Recovery(SnapshotSelectionCriteria.Latest)
    }
```

2. Second, let's create a small app to test our new actor. Create a file named SnapshotApp.scala inside the com.packt.chapter6 package. The content will be as follows:

```
package com.packt.chapter6

import akka.actor.{ActorSystem, Props}

object SnapshotApp extends App {
  val system = ActorSystem("snapshot")
  val persistentActor1 = system.actorOf(Props[SnapshotActor])
  persistentActor1 ! UserUpdate("user1", Add)
  persistentActor1 ! UserUpdate("user2", Add)
  persistentActor1 ! "snap"
  Thread.sleep(2000)
  system.stop(persistentActor1)
  val persistentActor2 = system.actorOf(Props[SnapshotActor])
  Thread.sleep(2000)
  system.terminate()
}
```

3. Once all the code is ready, let's run it either in IntelliJ or the command line:

```
hveiga$ sbt clean
[success] Total time: 0 s, completed Apr 6, 2017 8:27:06 PM
hveiga$ sbt "runMain com.packt.chapter6.SnapshotApp"
[info] Running com.packt.chapter6.SnapshotApp
[INFO] [akka://snapshot/user/$a] Recovery completed. Current
state: [Set()]
[INFO] [akka://snapshot/user/$a] Snapshot success
[SnapshotMetadata(ss-id-1,2,1491528436556)]
[INFO] [akka://snapshot/user/$a] Stopping
[INFO] [akka://snapshot/user/$b] Recovery completed. Current
state: [Set(user1, user2)]
[INFO] [akka://snapshot/user/$b] Stopping
[success] Total time: 10 s
```

How it works...

In this recipe, we covered how to use snapshots with our persistent actor. We have seen that snapshots dramatically help reduce the recovery time for our persistent actors. To demonstrate this, we have created a new actor, SnapshotActor. Every time this actor receives a snap command, it will call saveSnapshot(state) to save a current version of the state. This operation can either be successful, or it can fail. If it succeeds, your actor will receive a SaveSnapshotSuccess message with a metadata object that contains the persistence ID, the sequence number of your snapshot, and a timestamp. If it fails, your actor will receive a SaveSnapshotFailure message with some metadata and a reason why it failed. We can see an example of the save snapshot succeeding in the logs.

On the other hand, when recovering the state from a snapshot, your actor will receive a SnapshotOffer message to update the current state in the receiveRecover behavior. This message contains an instance of your state as well as some metadata. Once the recovery process is complete, your actor will receive a RecoveryCompleted message to indicate that. We can see the recovery process happening in our app when we stop our actor and create a new incarnation of it. The state gets recovered and we see this in the logs: Recovery completed. Current state: [Set(user1, user2)]. Even if we take a snapshot of the state, events will still be stored to the journal. We might want to remove some old events in the journal once we have taken a snapshot. We can achieve this using the deleteMessages method, where you need to provide a sequence number. All messages with a sequence number less than the number provided will be removed. Similar behavior happens when we call deleteSnapshot. We also need to give a sequence number to this method. All snapshots with a sequence number less than the given one will be erased.

Creating a persistence FSM model

FSM stands for finite-state machine. Akka provides the functionality to easily create an FSM within an actor. To learn more about FSM and Akka, take a look at the *Finite-state machine* recipe in `Chapter 10`, *Understanding Various Akka Patterns*. From this point, we will assume you have some basic knowledge of Akka FSM. Akka persistence also you to make your FSM persistent. When our FSM changes from one state to another, the change gets persisted, and therefore it's possible to restart our FSM with the latest state.

In this recipe, we will look at how to integrate persistence in your Akka FSM application using a countdown latch as an example. A countdown latch is a synchronization primitive that allows one or more threads to wait until a certain number of operations are completed on other threads. In this example, we will persist the number of operations to be able to restore in case of failure.

Getting ready

To step through this recipe, we need to import the `hello-Akka` project in the IDE; other prerequisites are the same as earlier as we have downloaded the `akka-persistence` dependency.

How to do it...

For this recipe, we need to perform the following steps:

1. First, let's create the model classes for our countdown latch. Create a file named `PersistentFSMModel.scala` inside the `com.packt.chapter6` package. The content should look like this:

   ```scala
   package com.packt.chapter6

   import akka.persistence.fsm.PersistentFSM.FSMState

   sealed trait CountDownLatchState extends FSMState
   case object Closed extends CountDownLatchState { val identifier
   = "Closed" }
   case object Open extends CountDownLatchState { val identifier =
   "Open" }

   case class Count(n: Int = -1)
   ```

```
sealed trait Command
case class Initialize(count: Int) extends Command
case object Mark extends Command

sealed trait DomainEvent
case object LatchDownOpen extends DomainEvent
case class LatchDownClosed(remaining: Int) extends DomainEvent
```

2. Second, let's create the actual FSM actor where we will define the states and what to do depending on the commands. Create a file named PersistentFSMActor.scala inside the com.packt.chapter6 package. The code should look like this:

```
package com.packt.chapter6

import akka.actor.{ActorLogging, Props}
import akka.persistence.fsm.PersistentFSM
import scala.reflect.ClassTag

class PersistentFSMActor(_persistenceId: String)(implicit val
domainEventClassTag: ClassTag[DomainEvent])
extends PersistentFSM[CountDownLatchState,Count,DomainEvent]
with ActorLogging {

  startWith(Closed, Count())
  when(Closed) {
    case Event(Initialize(count), _) =>
      log.info(s"Initializing countdown latch with count
      $count")
      stay applying LatchDownClosed(count)
    case Event(Mark, Count(n)) if n != 0 =>
      log.info(s"Still $n to open gate.")
      stay applying LatchDownClosed(n)
    case Event(Mark, _) =>
      log.info(s"Gate open.")
      goto(Open) applying LatchDownOpen
  }
  when(Open) {
    case Event(Initialize(count), _) => goto(Closed) applying
LatchDownClosed(count)
  }

  override def preStart() = log.info("Starting.")
  override def postStop() = log.info("Stopping.")
  override val persistenceId = _persistenceId
  override def applyEvent(event: DomainEvent, countdown: Count)
  = event match {
```

```
      case LatchDownClosed(i) => Count(i-1)
      case LatchDownOpen => Count()
    }
  }
```

3. In the same file, let's create a handy object for our `Props` method:

```
object PersistentFSMActor {
  def props(persistenceId: String) = Props(new
PersistentFSMActor(persistenceId))
}
```

4. Afterward, let's create a small app to test the code and demonstrate that we can recover from a failure. This time, we will simulate the failure by stopping the actor and creating a new one with the same persistence ID. Create a file named `PersistentFSMApp.scala` inside the `com.packt.chapter6` package with the following content:

```
package com.packt.chapter6

import akka.actor.ActorSystem

object PersistentFSMApp extends App {
  val system = ActorSystem("test")
  val actor1 = createActor("uid1")
  actor1 ! Initialize(4)
  actor1 ! Mark
  actor1 ! Mark
  Thread.sleep(2000)
  system.stop(actor1)
  val actor2 = createActor("uid1")
  actor2 ! Mark
  actor2 ! Mark

  def createActor(id: String) =
system.actorOf(PersistentFSMActor.props(id))
}
```

5. Once all code is ready, let's run it to test it out either in IntelliJ or the command line:

```
hveiga$ sbt "runMain com.packt.chapter6.PersistentFSMApp"
[info] Running com.packt.chapter6.PersistentFSMApp
[INFO] [akka://test/user/$a] Starting.
[INFO] [akka://test/user/$a] Initializing countdown latch with
count 4
[INFO] [akka://test/user/$a] Still 3 to open gate.
```

```
[INFO] [akka://test/user/$a] Still 2 to open gate.
[INFO] [akka://test/user/$a] Stopping.
[INFO] [akka://test/user/$b] Starting.
[INFO] [akka://test/user/$b] Still 1 to open gate.
[INFO] [akka://test/user/$b] Gate open.
```

How it works...

In this recipe, we covered how to integrate persistence into the FSM Akka module. To achieve this, first, we need to define our classes for the FSM: states, data, commands, and events. States are the different states in which your FSM can be at a given time. In our case, these states are Open and Close. Both extend CountDownLatchState, which is the type we provide to PersistentFSM in our actor. Data represents some additional information in the current state of your FSM. In our case, we are using Count to know how many operations left until the latch is done. Commands represent messages you send to your FSM actor. In our case, we only have two: Initialize and Mark. The Initialize message starts the countdown latch with a given count. The Mark message is used to signal that an operation is done and the count should be decremented. Lastly, events represent the persistence events that will be persisted in the journal.

For each state, we need to define a behavior. We do that by providing implementations to the *when* method. This behavior needs to define what the next state is and which event we will be applying to record this change in the journal. We use goto to move to a different state or stay to keep the FSM in the current state. The last piece to explain is the applyEvent method. The applyEvent method is used to update the data of the current state. This happens when we call applying in our behaviors. In addition, the same method is used when replaying the events from the journal to recover the data for a given persistent actor. When we create our actor, we initialize our countdown latch to 4. We send two Mark messages and then we stop the actor from simulating some failure. When we instantiate the actor with the same persistence ID again, it recovers the state from the journal. Consequently, when we send the next two Mark messages, it picks up the count from when it was and ends up logging Gate open since we sent a total of four Mark messages.

It is important to mention that this feature is still marked as experimental and the APIs might change in the future.

Persisting the state to LevelDB

Akka persistence defines the mechanism to store the state of your actors by storing either a sequence of events or complete snapshots. However, Akka persistence does not impose which underlying technology to use as the data store for them. Akka persistence basically acts as the API. A simple solution to understand how Akka persistence works is LevelDB. LevelDB stores events in the local filesystem, and it is not a replicated journal. That is why it is not recommended that you use LevelDB in a production environment.

In this recipe, we will review how to define which underlying technology we want for persistence, in this case, LevelDB. LevelDB provides a plugin for the journal, but not for snapshots. That is why we will not talk about snapshots in this recipe.

Getting ready

To step through this recipe, we need to import the `hello-Akka` project in the IDE; other prerequisites are the same as earlier as we have downloaded the `akka-persistence` dependency.

How to do it...

For this recipe, we need to perform the following steps:

1. First, we need to bring in the required dependencies. Open `build.sbt` and make sure that these lines are present:

   ```
   libraryDependencies += "org.iq80.leveldb"  % "leveldb" % "0.7"
   libraryDependencies += "org.fusesource.leveldbjni"   %
   "leveldbjni-all"   % "1.8"
   ```

2. Run `sbt compile` to ensure `sbt` refreshes the dependencies.

3. Then, we need to configure the plugin in our `reference.conf` file. Create a file named `reference.conf` inside `src/main/resources` and put the following configuration in it:

   ```
   akka.persistence.journal.plugin =
   "akka.persistence.journal.leveldb"
   akka.persistence.journal.leveldb {
     dir = "target/sample/journal"
     native = false
   }
   ```

How it works…

In this recipe, we covered how to configure our application to use LevelDB as our Akka persistence journal plugin. For that, we need to bring in the required dependencies and configure the `akka.persistence.journal.plugin` property inside `reference.conf`. This ensures that all your persistent actors will be using LevelDB as the storage plugin. Since LevelDB uses the local filesystem to store the events, we need to provide an explicit location in the `akka.persistence.journal.leveldb` property. In our case, when we run our actors, we will see some binary files under `target/sample/journal`, which LevelDB uses to handle and store all events. The `native` property can be set to `true` for using Native LevelDB (via JNI) or to `false` for using LevelDB Java port.

One important detail to point out is the possibility of forcing given persistent actors to use specific plugins for journals and snapshots that are different from those defined in `reference.conf`. This allows some flexibility if you want to use different storage plugins for different actors. It can be done by overriding `journalPluginId`, `snapshotPluginId`, or both in the persistent actors:

```
trait GivenActorWithSpecificPlugins extends PersistentActor {
  override val persistenceId = "some-id"
  // Absolute path to the journal plugin configuration entry in the
  `reference.conf`.
  override def journalPluginId = "some-journal-plugin-id"
  // Absolute path to the snapshot store plugin configuration entry in the
  `reference.conf`.
  override def snapshotPluginId = "some-snapshot-plugin-id"
}
```

The LevelDB plugin can be also used as a shared journal plugin so that multiple actor systems can share the same journal. Even if this is not recommended since it might become a single point of failure, it can be achieved using the persistence plugin proxy. Unfortunately, all the required steps to implement this are out of the scope of this recipe. Visit this link to learn more about it: `http://doc.akka.io/docs/akka/current/scala/persistence.html#persistence-plugin-proxy`

Persisting the state to Cassandra

Another option as a storage plugin for Akka persistence is Apache Cassandra. Apache Cassandra is a popular, highly available, failure-tolerant, scalable database used by many successful companies, such as Apple and Netflix. The Akka ecosystem provides a plugin to use Apache Cassandra as your storage plugin for both journal and snapshots. In this recipe, we will review how to bring the required dependencies, define Apache Cassandra as your desired plugin for journal and snapshots, and run a small app to test it out.

Getting ready

To step through this recipe, we need to import the `hello-Akka` project in the IDE; other prerequisites are the same as earlier as we have downloaded the `akka-persistence` dependency. We will need an Apache Cassandra instance to test this recipe. For convenience, we will assume that we have one instance running in the default port `9042`. In this recipe, we will have an actor that will hold the latest value of a stock, and it will use Akka persistence to store its state every time there is a change.

 To install Apache Cassandra, follow the steps in the official documentation
at `http://cassandra.apache.org/doc/latest/getting_started/installing.html`.

How to do it...

For this recipe, we need to perform the following steps:

1. First, we need to bring in the required dependencies. Open `build.sbt` and make sure that these lines are present:

   ```
   libraryDependencies += "com.typesafe.akka" %% "akka-
   persistence-cassandra" % "0.25.1"
   ```

2. Afterward, make sure that you run `sbt compile`.

3. Let's begin creating the case classes to define the commands and the events. Create a file named `StockPersistenceModel.scala` inside the `com.packt.chapter6` package. This file should contain the following:

   ```
   package com.packt.chapter6
   ```

```
case class ValueUpdate(newValue: Double)
case class StockValue(value: Double, timestamp: Long =
System.currentTimeMillis())
case class ValueAppended(stockValue: StockValue)

case class StockHistory(values: Vector[StockValue] =
Vector.empty[StockValue]) {
  def update(evt: ValueAppended) = copy(values :+
  evt.stockValue)
  override def toString = s"$values"
}
```

4. After this, let's define our persistent actor. Create a file named StockPersistenceActor.scala inside the com.packt.chapter6 package. The code would look like this:

```
package com.packt.chapter6

import akka.actor.{ActorLogging, Props}
import akka.persistence.{PersistentActor, RecoveryCompleted}

object StockPersistenceActor {
  def props(stockId: String) = Props(new
StockPersistenceActor(stockId))
}

class StockPersistenceActor(stockId: String) extends
PersistentActor with ActorLogging {
  override val persistenceId = stockId
  var state = StockHistory()
  def updateState(event: ValueAppended) = state =
  state.update(event)

  val receiveRecover: Receive = {
    case evt: ValueAppended => updateState(evt)
    case RecoveryCompleted => log.info(s"Recovery completed.
    Current state: $state")
  }

  val receiveCommand: Receive = {
    case ValueUpdate(value) =>
    persist(ValueAppended(StockValue(value)))(updateState)
    case "print" => log.info(s"Current state: $state")
  }
}
```

5. Let's create a small app to test it out. Create a file named
   `StockPersistenceApp.scala` inside the `com.packt.chapter6` package. The
   content should be as follows:

```scala
package com.packt.chapter6

trait AkkaHelper {
  lazy val system = akka.actor.ActorSystem("example")
  lazy val teslaStockActor =
  system.actorOf(StockPersistenceActor.props("TLSA"))
}

object StockApp extends App with AkkaHelper {
  teslaStockActor ! ValueUpdate(305.12)
  teslaStockActor ! ValueUpdate(305.15)
  teslaStockActor ! "print"
  Thread.sleep(5000)
  system.terminate()
}

object StockRecoveryApp extends App with AkkaHelper {
  teslaStockActor ! ValueUpdate(305.20)
  teslaStockActor ! "print"
  Thread.sleep(2000)
  system.terminate()
}
```

6. Finally, let's create our configuration file to let Akka persistence know we want to
   use the Cassandra plugin. Create a file named `application-cassandra.conf`
   inside `src/main/resources` with this configuration:

```
akka.persistence.journal.plugin = "cassandra-journal"
akka.persistence.snapshot-store.plugin = "cassandra-snapshot-
store"
```

7. Once all the code is ready, let's run both apps and see the result. Make sure you
   have Cassandra running locally in port `9042`:

```
hveiga$ sbt -Dconfig.resource=application-cassandra.conf "runMain
com.packt.chapter6.StockApp"
[info] Running com.packt.chapter6.StockApp
[INFO] [akka://example/user/$a] Recovery completed. Current
state: Vector()
[INFO] [akka://example/user/$a] Current state:
Vector(StockValue(305.12,1492276972404),
StockValue(305.15,1492276972542))
[success] Total time: 14 s, completed Apr 15, 2017 12:22:59 PM
```

```
hveiga$ sbt -Dconfig.resource=application-cassandra.conf "runMain
com.packt.chapter6.StockRecoveryApp"
[info] Running com.packt.chapter6.StockRecoveryApp
[INFO] [akka://example/user/$a] Recovery completed. Current
state: Vector(StockValue(305.12,1492276972404),
StockValue(305.15,1492276972542))
[INFO] [akka://example/user/$a] Current state:
Vector(StockValue(305.12,1492276972404),
StockValue(305.15,1492276972542),
StockValue(305.2,1492276998372))
[success] Total time: 6 s, completed Apr 15, 2017 12:23:22 PM
```

How it works...

In this recipe, we covered how to configure our app to use the Cassandra plugin. First, we need to ensure we have the right dependencies, and for that, we use sbt to bring them. Then, we need to configure akka.persistence.journal.plugin to cassandra-journal and akka.persistence.snapshot-store.plugin to cassandra-snapshot-store. We do that in application-cassandra.conf. We use this file when we run our apps by adding -Dconfig.resource in the sbt command.

We can see from the output how this example is working. To start with, we do not have any state stored, so we see Recevery completed. Current state: Vector(). Then, we send two ValueUpdate messages and a print message. Then, we verify that the state now contains both values. When we run our second app, StockRecoveryApp, we can see at the beginning how the actor updated its state through recovery, and this state matches the one printed earlier. At this point, your actor is fully functional again and we can continue to process new messages.

The akka-persistence-cassandra module is able to do both journaling and snapshots. It also has the functionality to run Akka persistence query, which allows developers to browse the different stored events. You will learn more about persistence query in a later recipe called *Using persistence query*.

Persisting the state to Redis

Redis is a popular in-memory data store. It supports multiple data structures that allow developers to use it as a database, cache, or even a message broker. Redis also supports replication, transactions, and some other useful features that makes it attractive to use it as our data store for Akka persistence. In this recipe, we will review how to bring in the required dependencies, define Redis as your desired plugin for journal and snapshots, and run a small app to test it out.

Getting ready

To step through this recipe, we need to import the `hello-Akka` project in the IDE; other prerequisites are the same as earlier as we have downloaded the `akka-persistence` dependency. We will need a Redis instance to test this recipe. For convenience, we will assume we have one instance running on the default port `6379`. In this recipe, we are going to make use of the classes defined in the previous recipe, *Persisting state to Cassandra*.

To install Redis, follow the steps in the official documentation: `https://re dis.io/download`.

How to do it...

For this recipe, we need to perform the following steps:

1. First, we need to bring in the required dependencies. Open `build.sbt` and make sure that these lines are present:

   ```
   resolvers += Resolver.jcenterRepo
   libraryDependencies += "com.hootsuite" %% "akka-persistence-
   redis" % "0.6.0"
   ```

2. Afterward, make sure that you run `sbt compile`.

3. Then, let's create our configuration file to let Akka persistence know we want to use the Redis plugin. Create a file named `application-redis.conf` inside `src/main/resources` with this configuration:

   ```
   akka.persistence.journal.plugin = "akka-persistence-
   redis.journal"
   ```

```
akka.persistence.snapshot-store.plugin = "akka-persistence-
redis.snapshot"

redis {
  host = "localhost"
  port = 6379
  db = 1
}
```

4. Once all the code is ready, let's run both apps and see the result. Make sure you have Redis running locally in port 6379:

```
hveiga$ sbt -Dconfig.resource=application-redis.conf "runMain
com.packt.chapter6.StockApp"
[info] Running com.packt.chapter6.StockApp
[INFO] [akka://example/user/RedisClient-$a] Connect to
localhost/127.0.0.1:6379
[INFO] [akka://example/user/$a] Recovery completed. Current
state: Vector()
[INFO] [akka://example/user/$a] Current state:
Vector(StockValue(305.12,1492278134212),
StockValue(305.15,1492278134607))
[INFO] [akka://example/user/RedisClient-$a] RedisWorkerIO stop
[success] Total time: 6 s, completed Apr 15, 2017 12:42:18 PM
hveiga$ sbt -Dconfig.resource=application-redis.conf "runMain
com.packt.chapter6.StockRecoveryApp"
[info] Running com.packt.chapter6.StockRecoveryApp
[INFO] [akka://example/user/RedisClient-$a] Connect to
localhost/127.0.0.1:6379
[INFO] [akka://example/user/$a] Recovery completed. Current
state: Vector(StockValue(305.12,1492278134212),
StockValue(305.15,1492278134607))
[INFO] [akka://example/user/$a] Current state:
Vector(StockValue(305.12,1492278134212),
StockValue(305.15,1492278134607),
StockValue(305.2,1492278156167))
[INFO] [akka://example/user/RedisClient-$b] RedisWorkerIO stop
[success] Total time: 3 s, completed Apr 15, 2017 12:42:37 PM
```

How it works...

In this recipe, we covered how to configure our app to use the Redis plugin. First, we need to ensure we have the right dependencies, and for that, we use `sbt` to bring them. Then, we need to configure `akka.persistence.journal.plugin` to `akka-persistence-redis.journal` and `akka.persistence.snapshot-store.plugin` to `akka-persistence-redis.snapshot`. We do that in `application-redis.conf`. We use this file when we run our apps by adding `-Dconfig.resource` in the `sbt` command.

From the output, we can see how this example is working. To start with, we do not have any state stored, so we see `Recovery completed. Current state: Vector()`. Then, we send two `ValueUpdate` messages and a `print` message. Then, we verify that the state now contains both values. When we run our second app, `StockRecoveryApp`, we can see at the beginning how the actor updated its state through recovery and this state matches with the one printed earlier. At this point, your actor is fully functional again and we can continue to process new messages. This behavior is exactly the same as the one we just reviewed when using Apache Cassandra and its plugin. This is actually the power of Akka persistence, where it should not matter what the underlying data store is; the behavior with the different plugins should be the same.

Understanding event sourcing

As we have been discussing through this whole chapter, event sourcing is the technique used by Akka persistence. Event sourcing is a pattern to store the state of entities where instead of persisting the actual state at a given time, you persist the changes happening to that particular entity. These changes are known as events. In this recipe, we will review the advantages of event sourcing and how this mechanism can be a better fit for distributed application.

Getting ready

There are no prerequisites for this recipe.

How to do it...

For this recipe, we will list the steps on how event sourcing works with Akka:

1. Once we create a persistent actor, recovery triggers. Akka persistence checks whether there are either events in the journal or snapshots in the snapshot store for the given persistence ID.

2. If it finds events in the journal, it proceeds to replay those events to update the state accordingly. If your actor receives other messages while doing this, they get `stashed` to be processed once the recovery has been completed.

3. If it finds a snapshot in the snapshot store, it proceeds to update the state accordingly. If your actor receives other messages while doing this, they get stashed to be processed once the recovery has been completed.

4. Once your actor has recovered, it is ready to receive new messages.

5. Every message (also known as a command) received by your actor that modifies the state needs to be recorded. We accomplish this by creating an event that represents that particular change. We call `persist()` and provide a handler for the event. The `persist()` method will make sure that your event gets appended to the journal and will execute the handler that will update the state of your actor. This action happens atomically.

6. If there is a failure while persisting, the actor will unconditionally be stopped since consistency cannot be guaranteed anymore.

This pattern has some advantages compared to the traditional CRUD operations:

1. Event sourcing allows the use of data stores with only append and read functionalities. Since there is no need to update the already persisted events, we can select very diverse technologies for this purpose. While CRUD is usually tied to databases (either SQL or NoSQL), event sourcing can work with technologies such as Apache Kafka.

2. It decouples the process of updating the state from the operations required to apply these actions.

3. It provides visibility of how your state is being updated since you can replay the events to understand every step. We will discuss this more in the next recipe, *Handling failure with event sourcing*.

How it works...

In this recipe, we reviewed how event sourcing works in Akka and what the advantages of using this pattern are. The Akka team recommends this approach to store actor state as a fast and clean way of being able to recover from failures.

There are a few tips and considerations we also need to understand about event sourcing in general:

- **There is no standard approach**: Currently, there is no specific way or tool to implement event source.
- **Add a timestamp**: In case of running multiple instances, your store might become invalid if the stored events are not in order. This can be easily solved by adding a timestamp to every event. Akka persistence already saves events with timestamps.
- **Recovery time might be long**: If the size of the journal becomes large, it might take some time to recover your state by replaying all those stored events. If this is an issue in your system, snapshots can alleviate and speed up the recovery time.

In the last chapter of this book, `Chapter 11`, *Microservices with Lagom*, we will see how Lagom also uses event sourcing and CQRS to persist entities when you have stateful microservices.

Handling failure in event sourcing

Failure is a regular thing in computer science. Systems crash. Hardware stops working. There are always some out-of-control variables that we cannot predict. However, we can assume failure will happen eventually and take some actions to deal with it. Akka persistence was designed to help ease the recovery from a failure when your actors need to maintain a state and cannot simply be restarted to start from fresh. In this recipe, we will review what happens to persistent actors when something goes wrong.

Getting ready

There are no prerequisites for this recipe.

How to do it...

The following scenarios can happen when using event sourcing and persistent actors:

- **Cannot recover events from the journal**: When creating a new persistent actor, the journal might not be available. Therefore, your actor cannot check whether it needs to recover its state. At this point, Akka persistence decides that it cannot continue, executes the onRecoveryFailure callback, and stops the actor unconditionally.

- **Cannot persist events to the journal**: When you have a running persistent actor, the journal might become unavailable at any given time. At this point, Akka persistence cannot persist more events and then cannot ensure that consistency will be maintained in your persistent actor. Akka persistence decides that it cannot continue, executes the onPersistFailure callback, and stops the actor unconditionally.

- **Cannot delete messages from the journal**: When you have a running persisting actor, the journal might become unavailable at any given time. At this point, Akka persistence cannot delete events from the journal. The actor receives a DeleteMessagesFailure message and continues running. Having a failure when deleting messages is not as critical as when persisting; since the consistency is still maintained, your actor does not need to be stopped.

How it works...

In this recipe, we covered the different scenarios where your persistence actors can fail. Akka persistence needs to ensure consistency. That explains why it is strict about stopping an actor unconditionally when persist() or any of the variants do not work. We discovered that it also provides two methods to know what the state of recovery is: recoveryRunning and recoveryFinished. Both return a Boolean value. You can use them to check whether the recovery phase is completed or is still getting executed. Moreover, it provides two callbacks, onRecoveryFailure and onPersistFailure, to allow the developers some logic before unconditionally stopping the actor since it was not possible to recover or persist an event.

It is advisable that you use `BackoffSupervisor` when your persistence actor is stopped. If the problem with the journal is network- or load-related, it's good to not overwhelm with a frequent restart but use an exponential backoff strategy to let the journal become responsive again. An example of this is as follows:

```
val childProps = Props[SomePersistentActor]
val props = BackoffSupervisor.props(
 Backoff.onStop(
 childProps,
 childName = "someActor",
 minBackoff = 5 seconds,
 maxBackoff = 30 seconds,
 randomFactor = 0.3))
context.actorOf(props, name = "someSupervisor")
```

Using persistence query

Akka persistence query is a helper module in the Akka persistence ecosystem that gives visibility into the journal events. Akka persistence query provides means to run asynchronous queries against the journal by using Akka Streams. Akka persistence query defines a set of predefined queries to analyze the log of events. Akka persistence query has a very loose API on purpose, so it is common to find different journal plugins with slightly different implementations. In this recipe, we will review the different predefined queries and see what each query is used for.

Getting ready

This recipe does not have any prerequisites. However before going through this recipe, it is required to understand what event adapters are in the Akka persistence context. Event adapters help to detach the data model from the domain model completely. This might be helpful in scenario where your data model evolves over time or you want to use a different format when storing the events in the journal. Event adapters are also used for tagging. In some scenarios, it might desirable to add some metadata to the events we are storing. Akka persistence provides a case class called `Tagged` to accomplish this task where you can provide your event and a set of tags. To add these tags to your events, you need to write your own event adapter by extending `WriteEventAdapter`. A small example of a tagging event adapter is as follows:

```
import akka.persistence.journal.WriteEventAdapter
import akka.persistence.journal.Tagged
```

```
class MyTaggingEventAdapter(tags: Set[String]) extends WriteEventAdapter {
  override def toJournal(event: Any): Any = Tagged(event, tags)
  override def manifest(event: Any): String = ""
}
```

How to do it...

For this recipe, we are going to review all predefined queries:

- `AllPersistenceIdsQuery`: This returns a live stream that emits all persistence IDs. This query can be used by calling `readJournal.persistenceIds()`.

- `CurrentPersistenceIdsQuery`: This returns a stream, the same as `AllPersistenceIds`, but does not keep a live subscriber for new incoming events. Therefore, this variant only emits the persistence IDs in the journal. This query can be used by calling `readJournal.currentPersistenceIds()`.

- `EventsByPersistenceIdQuery`: This returns a live stream that emits all events from a given persistence ID. This query can be used by calling `readJournal.eventsByPersistenceId("some-persistence-id")`.

- `CurrentEventsByPersistenceIdQuery`: This returns a stream, the same as `EventsByPersistenceId`, but only emitting the current events in the journal for a given persistence ID. This query can be used by calling `readJournal.currentEventsByPersistenceId("some-persistence-id")`.

- `EventsByTag`: This returns a stream that emits all events that contain a tag that matches the given tag. This stream can contain events from different persistent IDs since it only filters by tag. This query can be used by calling `readJournal.eventsByTag("some-tag")`.

- `CurrentEventsByTag`: This returns a stream the same as `EventByTag`, but only emitting the current events in the journal that contain a tag that matches the given tag. This query can be used by calling `readJournal.currentEventsByTag("some-tag")`.

How it works...

In this recipe, we have reviewed what are the different predefined queries by Akka persistence query. We have seen it is possible to query all events, query events by persistence ID, or query events by tag. Also, it is possible to have a live stream listening for new incoming events or just use the variant to read the events that are currently in the journal. In the next recipe, *Persistence query for LevelDB*, we are going to provide a real example of the usage of Akka persistence query.

Akka persistence query is marked as an experimental module in Akka 2.4.17. However, from Akka 2.5.0, Akka persistence query has been promoted to a fully supported module and is no longer experimental.

Persistence query for LevelDB

Akka persistence query provides the functionality to read the journal and also receive live events that are getting persisted thanks to an Akka Stream. Implementations of Akka persistence query differ depending on which underlying technology we select. In this recipe, we will be using the LevelDB plugin to query all current events in a journal, and we will also create a stream to subscribe to real-time events. To learn more about Akka Streams, refer to `Chapter 8`, *Akka Streams*.

Getting ready

To step through this recipe, we need to import the `hello-Akka` project in the IDE; other prerequisites are the same as earlier as we have downloaded the `akka-persistence` dependency. We will also need the persistence query dependency. We will also make use of the classes created in the *Recovering state of the actor* recipe for this recipe.

How to do it...

For this recipe, we need to perform the following steps:

1. First, we need to get the required dependencies. Open `build.sbt` and make sure these lines are present:

   ```
   libraryDependencies +=  "com.typesafe.akka" %% "akka-
   persistence-query-experimental" % "2.4.17"
   ```

2. Run `sbt compile` to ensure that `sbt` resolves the new dependency.

3. Make sure `reference.conf` inside `src/main/resources` contains the following values:

   ```
   akka.persistence.journal.plugin =
   "akka.persistence.journal.leveldb"
   akka.persistence.snapshot-store.plugin =
   "akka.persistence.snapshot-store.local"
   akka.persistence.journal.leveldb.dir = "target/friend/journal"
   akka.persistence.snapshot-store.local.dir =
   "target/friend/snapshots"
   ```

4. Create a file named `FriendJournalReader.scala` inside the `com.packt.chapter6` package. This file will create two persistent actors and use persistence query to listen to those events. The content should look like this:

   ```scala
   package com.packt.chapter6

   import akka.actor.ActorSystem
   import akka.persistence.Recovery
   import akka.persistence.query.PersistenceQuery
   import akka.persistence.query.journal.leveldb
   .scaladsl.LeveldbReadJournal
   import akka.stream.ActorMaterializer
   import akka.stream.scaladsl.Sink
   import scala.concurrent.duration._

   object FriendJournalReader extends App {
     implicit val system = ActorSystem()
     import system.dispatcher
     implicit val mat = ActorMaterializer()(system)
     val queries =
       PersistenceQuery(system).readJournalFor[LeveldbReadJournal]
       (LeveldbReadJournal.Identifier)

     val laura = system.actorOf(FriendActor.props("Laura",
   ```

```
Recovery()))
val maria = system.actorOf(FriendActor.props("Maria",
Recovery()))
laura ! AddFriend(Friend("Hector"))
laura ! AddFriend(Friend("Nancy"))
maria ! AddFriend(Friend("Oliver"))
maria ! AddFriend(Friend("Steve"))
system.scheduler.scheduleOnce(5 second, maria,
AddFriend(Friend("Steve")))
system.scheduler.scheduleOnce(10 second, maria,
RemoveFriend(Friend("Oliver")))
Thread.sleep(2000)

queries.allPersistenceIds().map(id => system.log.info(s"Id
received [$id]")).to(Sink.ignore).run()
queries.eventsByPersistenceId("Laura").map(e =>
log(e.persistenceId, e.event)).to(Sink.ignore).run()
queries.eventsByPersistenceId("Maria").map(e =>
log(e.persistenceId, e.event)).to(Sink.ignore).run()

def log(id: String, evt: Any) = system.log.info(s"Id [$id]
Event [$evt]")
}
```

5. Once we have all code ready, let's run the app either in IntelliJ or the command line:

```
hveiga$ sbt "runMain com.packt.chapter6.FriendJournalReader"
[info] Running com.packt.chapter6.FriendJournalReader
[INFO] [akka://default/user/$b] Recovery completed. Current
state:
[INFO] [akka://default/user/$a] Recovery completed. Current
state:
[INFO] [akka.actor.ActorSystemImpl(default)] Id received [Maria]
[INFO] [akka.actor.ActorSystemImpl(default)] Id received [Laura]
[INFO] [akka.actor.ActorSystemImpl(default)] Id [Maria] Event
[FriendAdded(Friend(Oliver))]
[INFO] [akka.actor.ActorSystemImpl(default)] Id [Laura] Event
[FriendAdded(Friend(Hector))]
[INFO] [akka.actor.ActorSystemImpl(default)] Id [Laura] Event
[FriendAdded(Friend(Nancy))]
[INFO] [akka.actor.ActorSystemImpl(default)] Id [Maria] Event
[FriendAdded(Friend(Steve))]
[INFO] [akka.actor.ActorSystemImpl(default)] Id [Maria] Event
[FriendAdded(Friend(Steve))]
[INFO] [akka.actor.ActorSystemImpl(default)] Id [Maria] Event
[FriendRemoved(Friend(Oliver))]
```

How it works...

In this recipe, we demonstrated how to use Akka persistent query with LevelDB. To do that, we are using the classes, actors, and events we were using in the *Handling failure in event sourcing* recipe. To begin, we create two `FriendActor` instances with different persistent IDs, `Laura` and `Maria`. With the actors created, we send some `AddFriend` messages to create some events and we schedule two others to happen in the future. Afterward, we define three different streams. To run the different queries, we need to get `readJournal` from actor system extension, `PersistenceQuery`. We call `readJournalFor`, providing `LeveldbReadJournal.Identifier` to specify the LevelDB journal reader we want. In case of using other plugins, the provided class should match to the plugin.

The first stream we create is created using `allPersistenceId()`. This streams emits all persistent IDs in the journal. We can see in the `Id received [Maria]` and `Id received [Laura]` logs. The second and third streams use `eventsByPersistenceId`, and we provide two different IDs: `Maria` and `Laura`. These streams log the different events being persisted. In the case of the `Laura` ID, we can see two events in the output. In the case of the `Maria` ID, we can see four events in the output. These numbers match the number of messages sent to the actors. These queries provide a read capability into Akka persistence, which might come handy when replaying events. This is helpful, for example, in understanding how a persistent actor got into a particular state.

7

Remoting and Akka Clustering

In this chapter, we will cover the following topics:

- Enabling Akka applications for remoting
- Creating remote actors on different machines
- Looking up remote actors from different machines
- Deploying remote actors programmatically on different nodes
- Scaling out your application using remote actors
- Creating a chat-based application using remote actors
- Enabling Akka clustering for your project
- Using Distributed Publish-Subscribe in the cluster
- Cluster Sharding
- Sharing data between nodes in an Akka cluster
- Creating a singleton actor across clusters

Introduction

As mentioned before, Akka actors are distributed by default. This concept allows you to expand your actor system beyond a single JVM. Akka provides mechanisms to connect actors running in different JVMs seamlessly. In a production system, you want to ensure high availability and resiliency; Akka remoting and Akka clustering help you achieve this.

Every actor has an address that is unique within an actor system. This address has the following format: `<actor system>/<actor path>`. Although this format is correct within a local actor system, when you are accessing remote actors, the fully qualified format is this: `<protocol>://<actor system>@<host>:<port>/<actor path>`. This concept is also known as **location transparency**.

We need to differentiate between two ways of accessing remote actors:

- **Akka remoting**: This means that an actor knows the location of the remote actor and uses its fully qualified address to communicate with it. The communication occurs in a peer-to-peer fashion.
- **Akka clustering**: This provides a decentralized peer-to-peer-based cluster membership service with automatic failure detection. Here, members use the Gossip protocol to share information. Akka clustering is built on top of Akka remoting.

> Learn more about the Gossip protocol at `https://en.wikipedia.org/wiki/Gossip_protocol`.

> When using Akka remoting or clustering, several new variables come into play; some of these variables are: DNS issues, connection, issues, buffer overflow issues and so on. Any of them might drop your messages. When programming in a distributed environment, build your code assuming that things will not work as expected eventually. Moreover, messages need to be serialized to be sent through the wire. So ensure your objects are serializable.

Enabling Akka applications for remoting

Before you enable your application to use remoting, review the different transport protocols that you can use to communicate:

- `akka.tcp`: This is a remoting protocol that uses TCP as the network protocol backed by the Netty framework.
- `akka`: This is an experimental UDP-based remoting protocol that uses Aeron as the network protocol.

> You can learn more about *Aeron* at `https://github.com/real-logic/Aeron`.

We will use `akka.tcp` as it is the more stable remoting protocol currently. However, Akka plans to deprecate it in favor of `akka` once this new remoting layer becomes more mature.

Getting ready

To step through this recipe, we need to import the `Hello-Akka` project; all other prerequisites are the same as before. We need to bring the required dependencies for remoting this time.

How to do it...

For this recipe, perform the following steps:

1. Let's start getting the required dependencies. Edit the `build.sbt` file and add Akka's remote dependency, as follows:

   ```
   libraryDependencies += "com.typesafe.akka" % "akka-remote_2.11"
   % "2.4.17"
   ```

2. Then, run `sbt update` to retrieve the dependencies from the central repository.

3. Create `application.conf` in the `src/main/resources` directory.

4. Add the following configuration parameters:

   ```
   akka {
     actor {
       provider = "akka.remote.RemoteActorRefProvider"
     }
     remote {
       enabled-transports = ["akka.remote.netty.tcp"]
       netty.tcp {
         hostname = "127.0.0.1"
         port = 2552
       }
     }
   }
   ```

How it works...

In this recipe, we defined the required dependencies and configured our application to enable remoting capabilities. First, we changed the actor provider to `akka.remote.RemoteActorRefProvider`, which allows us to create and look up remote actors. Second, we defined which transport protocol to use for remoting. In this case, we picked `netty.tcp`. Also, we configured the hostname and port where we want our application to listen for incoming messages.

Creating remote actors on different machines

In this recipe, we are going to see how to create remote actors on different machines. We will need to start two separate Akka applications running on different ports (mimicking as if they are running on different machines) to demonstrate how to do it.

Getting ready

Just import the Hello-Akka project; the prerequisites are the same as before. We will also need to have the Akka remoting dependency in our build.sbt file.

How to do it...

1. Create a new file named application-1.conf in the src/main/resources directory with the following contents:

```
akka {
  actor {
    provider = "akka.remote.RemoteActorRefProvider"
  }
  remote {
    enabled-transports = ["akka.remote.netty.tcp"]
    netty.tcp {
      hostname = "127.0.0.1"
      port = 2552
    }
  }
}
```

2. Create a second new file named application-2.conf in the src/main/resources directory with the following contents:

```
akka {
  actor {
    provider = "akka.remote.RemoteActorRefProvider"
    deployment {
      /simpleRemoteActor {
        remote =
          "akka.tcp://HelloAkkaRemoting1@127.0.0.1:2552"
      }
```

```
      }
    }
    remote {
      enabled-transports = ["akka.remote.netty.tcp"]
      netty.tcp {
        hostname = "127.0.0.1"
        port = 2553
      }
    }
  }
```

3. Create a file named `SimpleActor.scala` in the `com.packt.chapter7` package with the following contents:

```
package com.packt.chapter7
import akka.actor.Actor

class SimpleActor extends Actor {
  def receive = {
    case _ =>
      println(s"I have been created at
        ${self.path.address.hostPort}")
  }
}
```

4. Create a file named `RemotingApplication.scala`. It will have two applications, namely `HelloAkkaRemoting1` and `HelloAkkaRemoting2`:

```
package com.packt.chapter7
import akka.actor.{ActorSystem, Props}

object HelloAkkaRemoting1 extends App {
  val actorSystem = ActorSystem("HelloAkkaRemoting1")
}

object HelloAkkaRemoting2 extends App {
  val actorSystem = ActorSystem("HelloAkkaRemoting2")
  println("Creating actor from HelloAkkaRemoting2")
  val actor = actorSystem.actorOf(Props[SimpleActor],
    "simpleRemoteActor")
  actor ! "Checking"
}
```

5. Run `HelloAkkaRemoting1`. Use the `application-1.conf` configuration by providing the `-Dconfig.resource=application-1.conf` flag in either IntelliJ or the command line:

```
hveiga$ sbt -Dconfig.resource=application-1.conf "runMain
com.packt.chapter7.HelloAkkaRemoting1"
[info] Running com.packt.chapter7.HelloAkkaRemoting1
[INFO] [run-main-0] [akka.remote.Remoting] Starting remoting
[INFO] [run-main-0] [akka.remote.Remoting] Remoting started;
listening on
addresses :[akka.tcp://HelloAkkaRemoting1@127.0.0.1:2552]
[INFO] [run-main-0] [akka.remote.Remoting] Remoting now listens
on addresses:
[akka.tcp://HelloAkkaRemoting1@127.0.0.1:2552]
```

6. In a different command-line shell, run the second application, `HelloAkkaRemoting2`, to create the actor remotely. For this, you need to provide the second configuration, `application-2.conf`, using `-Dconfig.resource=application-2.conf`:

```
hveiga$ sbt -Dconfig.resource=application-2.conf "runMain
com.packt.chapter7.HelloAkkaRemoting2"
[info] Running com.packt.chapter7.HelloAkkaRemoting2
[INFO] [akka.remote.Remoting] Starting remoting
[INFO] [akka.remote.Remoting] Remoting started; listening on
addresses:
[akka.tcp://HelloAkkaRemoting2@127.0.0.1:2553]
[INFO] [akka.remote.Remoting] Remoting now listens on addresses:
[akka.tcp://HelloAkkaRemoting2@127.0.0.1:2553]
Creating actor from HelloAkkaRemoting2
```

7. You should see the following message in the first command-line shell:

```
I have been created at HelloAkkaRemoting1
```

How it works...

In this recipe, we demonstrated how it is possible to create an actor remotely. For this, we created two different remote-enabled actor systems. The first one uses `application-1.conf`, which configures the remote listener to listen in `127.0.0.1` and port `2552`. The second one uses `application-2.conf`, which configures the remote listener to listen in `127.0.0.1` as well, but port `2553`. It is not possible to configure both in the same port since there would be a collision. The configuration `application-2.conf` describes where `simpleRemoteActor` needs to be created by setting the value of the field remote `akka.tcp://HelloAkkaRemoting1@127.0.0.1:2552`. Based on this, the `HelloAkkaRemoting2` application creates the actor in the `HelloAkkaRemoting1` actor system and prints it in the standard output.

Looking up remote actors from different machines

It is useful to be able to check whether an actor is running on a remote machine. This can help make sure you don't create duplicate remote actors if they already exist. For this, we will use ActorSelection.

Getting ready

All the prerequisites are the same as before. We will reuse `SimpleActor.scala`, `application-1.conf`, and `application-2.conf` from the previous recipe.

How to do it...

1. Create a Scala file named `LookingUpRemoteApplication.scala` in the `com.packt.chapter7` package.

2. Add the following two apps. One app will create an actor remotely; the other will look for the remote actor:

   ```
   package com.packt.chapter7
   import akka.actor.{ActorRef, ActorSystem, Props}
   import scala.concurrent.duration._
   ```

```
object LookingUpActorSelection extends App {
  val actorSystem = ActorSystem("LookingUpActors")
  implicit val dispatcher = actorSystem.dispatcher
  val selection = actorSystem.actorSelection(
    "akka.tcp://LookingUpRemoteActors@127.0.0.1:2553
      /user/remoteActor")
  selection ! "test"
  selection.resolveOne(3 seconds).onSuccess {
    case actorRef : ActorRef =>
      println("We got an ActorRef")
      actorRef ! "test"
  }
}

object LookingUpRemoteActors extends App {
  val actorSystem = ActorSystem("LookingUpRemoteActors")
  actorSystem.actorOf(Props[SimpleActor], "remoteActor")
}
```

3. Run the `LookingUpRemoteActor` application using the `application-2.conf`
   configuration by passing the `-Dconfig.resource=application-2.conf` flag
   in either IntelliJ or the command line:

```
hveiga$ sbt -Dconfig.resource=application-2.conf "runMain
com.packt.chapter7.LookingUpRemoteActors"
[info] Running com.packt.chapter7.LookingUpRemoteActors
[INFO] [akka.remote.Remoting] Starting remoting
[INFO] [akka.remote.Remoting] Remoting started; listening on
addresses :
[akka.tcp://LookingUpRemoteActors@127.0.0.1:2553]
[INFO] [akka.remote.Remoting] Remoting now listens on addresses:
[akka.tcp://LookingUpRemoteActors@127.0.0.1:2553]
```

4. Then, run the `LookingUpActorSelection` application in a different command-
   line shell using the `application-1.conf` configuration by passing the
   `-Dconfig.resource=application-1.conf` flag in either IntelliJ or the
   command line:

```
hveiga$ sbt -Dconfig.resource=application-1.conf "runMain
com.packt.chapter7.LookingUpActorSelection" [info] Running
com.packt.chapter7.LookingUpActorSelection
[INFO] [akka.remote.Remoting] Starting remoting
[INFO] [akka.remote.Remoting] Remoting started; listening on
addresses:
[akka.tcp://LookingUpActors@127.0.0.1:2552]
[INFO] [akka.remote.Remoting] Remoting now listens on addresses:
[akka.tcp://LookingUpActors@127.0.0.1:2552]
```

```
We got an ActorRef
```

5. You should see the following statements in the first shell, where the remote actor is running:

```
I have been created at LookingUpRemoteActors
I have been created at LookingUpRemoteActors
```

How it works...

In this recipe, we used ActorSelection to look up a remote actor. To begin with, we started a remote application that created an actor named `remoteActor`. Then, we started an application that looked for it by passing `akka.tcp://LookingUpRemoteActors@127.0.0.1:2553/user/remoteActor` to ActorSelection.

ActorSelection traverses the hierarchy of the actors in the path to look for the desired actor. ActorSelection does not create any actors if the entered path is not inhabited by a previously created actor. To get `ActorRef` from an actor, we need to call `resolveOne()`, which returns the actual reference to the actor. This operation takes time and happens asynchronously; this is why the method returns a `Future[ActorRef]`.

Here, we used `onSuccess()`; however, we could have used `Await.result` for retrieving the result from the future and blocking the thread inside the actor, which is not recommended.

Deploying remote actors programmatically on different nodes

In this recipe, we will see how to create remote actors programmatically without explicitly defining them in the configuration.

Getting ready

All the prerequisites are the same as before. We will reuse `SimpleActor.scala`, `application-1.conf`, and `application-2.conf` from the previous recipe.

How to do it...

1. Create a file named `RemoteActorProgramatically.scala`. Inside this, define two small Scala applications--`RemoteActorsProgrammatically1` and `RemoteActorsProgrammatically`--with an `ActorSystem`. In the second file, create an actor of the type SampleActor, using the `withDeploy` method:

```scala
package com.packt.chapter7
import akka.actor.{ActorSystem, Address, Deploy, Props}
import akka.remote.RemoteScope

object RemoteActorsProgrammatically1 extends App {
  val actorSystem =
    ActorSystem("RemoteActorsProgramatically1")
}

object RemoteActorsProgrammatically2 extends App {
  val actorSystem =
    ActorSystem("RemoteActorsProgramatically2")
  println("Creating actor from RemoteActorsProgramatically2")
  val address = Address("akka.tcp",
    "RemoteActorsProgramatically1", "127.0.0.1", 2552)
  val actor = actorSystem.actorOf(
    Props[SampleActor].withDeploy(Deploy(scope =
      RemoteScope(address))), "remoteActor")
    actor ! "Checking"
}
```

2. Run `RemoteActorsProgrammatically1` using the `application-1.conf` configuration by passing the `-Dconfig.resource=application-1.conf` flag in either IntelliJ or the command line:

```
hveiga$ sbt -Dconfig.resource=application-1.conf "runMain
com.packt.chapter7.RemoteActorsProgrammatically1"
[info] Running com.packt.chapter7.RemoteActorsProgramatically1
[INFO] [akka.remote.Remoting] Starting remoting
[INFO] [akka.remote.Remoting] Remoting started; listening on
addresses:
[akka.tcp://RemoteActorsProgramatically1@127.0.0.1:2552]
[INFO] [akka.remote.Remoting] Remoting now listens on addresses:
[akka.tcp://RemoteActorsProgramatically1@127.0.0.1:2552]
```

3. In a different command-line shell, run the second application
   RemoteActorsProgrammatically2, which will create the actor remotely. For
   this, you need to provide the second configuration, application-2.conf, using
   -Dconfig.resource=application-2.conf:

```
hveiga$ sbt -Dconfig.resource=application-2.conf "runMain
com.packt.chapter7.RemoteActorsProgrammatically2"
[info] Running com.packt.chapter7.RemoteActorsProgramatically2
[INFO] [akka.remote.Remoting] Starting remoting
[INFO] [akka.remote.Remoting] Remoting started; listening on
addresses:
[akka.tcp://RemoteActorsProgramatically2@127.0.0.1:2553]
[INFO] [run-main-0] [akka.remote.Remoting] Remoting now listens
on addresses:
[akka.tcp://RemoteActorsProgramatically2@127.0.0.1:2553]
Creating actor from RemoteActorsProgramatically2
```

4. You should see the following message in the first command-line shell:

```
I have been created at RemoteActorsProgramatically1
```

How it works...

So, it is possible to deploy your remote actor programmatically. To accomplish this, you
need to use the withDeploy method, which allows you to specify where you want to
deploy your actor. As a reminder, Props defines the contract to create your actor. Every
time you want to instantiate a new actor, you provide a Props object to an actor system;
this creates the actors as per the Props configuration.

By default, deploy uses LocalScope to deploy your actors. Using remote and providing a
fully qualified address, the actor system knows where to create the actors.

Scaling out your application using remote actors

One of the key points of distributed programming is its ability to scale up the performance of your application horizontally. Let's assume a scenario where an actor receives messages to be processed, and this processing takes some time:

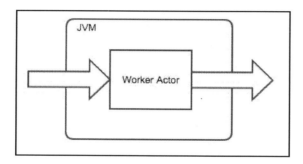

Everything works as expected until the rate of messages starts increasing. Then you realize that the bottleneck of your system is your actor, so you decide to create a pool of actors for processing the messages:

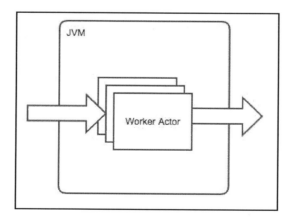

This solution works well; however, sooner or later you will notice an increase in CPU and memory usage, as the rate of messages keeps growing. To solve this, you decide to scale your system vertically and run your application in a larger machine with more CPU and memory.

However, at some point, your CPU and RAM would again reach the limit. Then you realize that throwing more hardware is not a long-term solution. Therefore, as an alternate solution, you decide to scale your system horizontally using Akka remoting. You redesign your solution to have a master node and a set of worker nodes to do the processing. Your master node will be responsible for forwarding the processing tasks to worker nodes. The worker nodes will send a notice to the master informing it that they are ready to work. Master nodes keep a list of the available worker nodes and watch for terminated messages. This approach allows you to elastically control the number of worker machines:

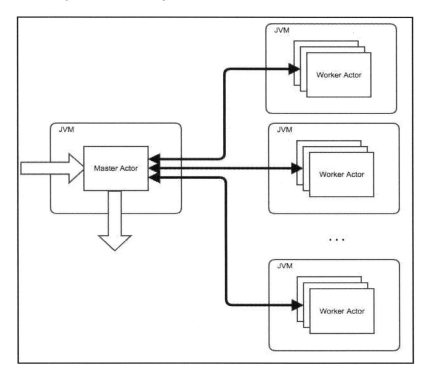

Getting ready

All the prerequisites are the same as before. We will reuse the `application.conf` discussed previously and also create new configurations, a `WorkerActor` class, a `MasterActor` class, and a few case classes that will define the messages exchanged by them. These classes will be similar to the ones we created previously.

How to do it...

1. Create a new file named `application-3.conf` in the `src/main/resources` directory with the following contents:

```
akka {
  actor {
    provider = "akka.remote.RemoteActorRefProvider"
  }
  remote {
    enabled-transports = ["akka.remote.netty.tcp"]
    netty.tcp {
      hostname = "127.0.0.1"
      port = 2554
    }
  }
}
```

2. Create a Scala Akka actor that will do the work and print the information once done. Let's name it `WorkerActor`. Use `Thread.sleep` to simulate the time spent doing the processing (this is only for testing purposes and should not be done in a production environment). In this file, define case classes as messages:

```
package com.packt.chapter7
import akka.actor.{Actor, ActorRef}

case class Work(workId: String)
case class WorkDone(workId: String)

class WorkerActor extends Actor {
  def receive = {
    case Work(workId) =>
      Thread.sleep(3000) //simulates time spent working
      sender ! WorkDone(workId)
      println(s"Work $workId was done by worker actor")
  }
}
```

3. Create a Scala Akka actor that will do the work and print the information once it's done. Let's name it `MasterActor`. This actor will keep a list of the available worker actors as well as have some logic to check whether a worker actor has stopped and then remove it from the list if it has:

```
package com.packt.chapter7
import akka.actor.{Actor, ActorRef, Terminated}
import scala.util.Random
```

```
case class RegisterWorker(workerActor: ActorRef)

class MasterActor extends Actor {
  var workers = List.empty[ActorRef]
  def receive = {
    case RegisterWorker(workerActor) =>
      context.watch(workerActor)
      workers =  workerActor :: workers
    case Terminated(actorRef) =>
      println(s"Actor ${actorRef.path.address} has been
      terminated. Removing from available workers.")
      workers = workers.filterNot(_ == actorRef)
    case work: Work if workers.isEmpty =>
      println("We cannot process your work since
        there is no workers.")
    case work: Work =>
      workers(Random.nextInt(workers.size)) ! work
    case WorkDone(workId) =>
      println(s"Work with id $workId is done.")
  }
}
```

4. Create two small Scala objects `ScalingOutWorker` and
   `ScalingOutMaster` with an `ActorSystem` inside each. Let's name the file
   `ScalingOutApplication.scala`. In the worker app, first look up the master
   actor `ActorRef` and then create a pool of 10 actors. In the master app, send work
   messages to `MasterActor` to simulate that work is coming from a third party:

```
package com.packt.chapter7
import akka.actor.{ActorRef, ActorSystem, Props}
import akka.routing.RoundRobinPool
import scala.concurrent.duration._

object ScalingOutWorker extends App {
  val actorSystem = ActorSystem("WorkerActorSystem")
  implicit val dispatcher = actorSystem.dispatcher
  val selection = actorSystem.actorSelection(
    "akka.tcp://MasterActorSystem@127.0.0.1:2552
    /user/masterActor")
  selection.resolveOne(3 seconds).onSuccess {
    case masterActor : ActorRef =>
      println("We got the ActorRef for the master actor")
      val pool = RoundRobinPool(10)
      val workerPool =
      actorSystem.actorOf(
        Props[WorkerActor].withRouter(pool), "workerActor")
        masterActor ! RegisterWorker(workerPool)
```

```
      }
    }

    object ScalingOutMaster extends App {
      val actorSystem = ActorSystem("MasterActorSystem")
      val masterActor = actorSystem.actorOf(Props[MasterActor],
        "masterActor")
      (1 to 100).foreach(i => {
        masterActor ! Work(s"$i")
        Thread.sleep(5000) //Simulates sending work to
          the master actor every 5 seconds
      })
    }
```

5. The first time, run the master application using the `application-1.conf` configuration by passing the `-Dconfig.resource=application-1.conf` flag in either IntelliJ or the command line:

```
hveiga$ sbt -Dconfig.resource=application-1.conf "runMain
com.packt.chapter7.ScalingOutMaster"
[info] Running com.packt.chapter7.ScalingOutMaster
[INFO] [akka.remote.Remoting] Starting remoting
[INFO] [akka.remote.Remoting] Remoting started; listening on
addresses:
[akka.tcp://MasterActorSystem@127.0.0.1:2552]
[INFO] [akka.remote.Remoting] Remoting now listens on addresses:
[akka.tcp://MasterActorSystem@127.0.0.1:2552]
We cannot process your work since there is no workers.
```

6. The second time, run the worker application using the `application-2.conf` configuration by passing the `-Dconfig.resource=application-2.conf` flag in either IntelliJ or the command line:

```
hveiga$ sbt -Dconfig.resource=application-2.conf "runMain
com.packt.chapter7.ScalingOutWorker"
[info] Running com.packt.chapter7.ScalingOutWorker
[INFO] [akka.remote.Remoting] Starting remoting
[INFO] [akka.remote.Remoting] Remoting started; listening on
addresses:
[akka.tcp://WorkerActorSystem@127.0.0.1:2553]
[INFO] [akka.remote.Remoting] Remoting now listens on addresses:
[akka.tcp://WorkerActorSystem@127.0.0.1:2553]
We got the ActorRef for the master actor
Work 5 was done by worker actor
```

7. The third time, run the worker application using the `application-3.conf` configuration by passing the `-Dconfig.resource=application-3.conf` flag in either IntelliJ or the command line:

```
hveiga$ sbt -Dconfig.resource=application-3.conf "runMain
com.packt.chapter7.ScalingOutWorker"
[info] Running com.packt.chapter7.ScalingOutWorker
[INFO] [akka.remote.Remoting] Starting remoting
[INFO] [akka.remote.Remoting] Remoting started; listening on
addresses:
[akka.tcp://WorkerActorSystem@127.0.0.1:2554]
[INFO] [run-main-0] [akka.remote.Remoting] Remoting now listens
on addresses:
[akka.tcp://WorkerActorSystem@127.0.0.1:2554]
We got the ActorRef for the master actor
Work 23 was done by worker actor
```

8. Then, kill the second application and look for the output in the master node:

```
Actor akka.tcp://WorkerActorSystem@127.0.0.1:2553 has been
terminated.
Removing from available workers.
```

9. Now the other worker will process all the messages:

```
Work with id 24 is done.
Work with id 25 is done.
Work with id 26 is done.
Work with id 27 is done.
```

How it works

In the preceding application, we created two actors:

1. `MasterActor`: This actor listens for new work messages and sends them to a random worker actor. If there are no worker actors available, it simply drops the message. Also, it registers workers and stores their `ActorRefs` in a list. Every time a worker actor tries to register itself, it calls `context.watch`; this allows you to have a terminated message to remove the stopped worker from the list.

2. `WorkerActor`: This actor waits for work messages and simulates some processing with `Thread.sleep`. Once done, it sends back a `WorkDone` message.

We also have two small Scala apps:

1. `ScalingOutMaster`: This app creates a master actor and it listens in port `2552` for messages to come since we used `application-1.conf` when executing the application. Also, we send a work message to the `MasterActor` every 5 seconds.

2. `ScalingOutWorker`: This app uses `ActorSelection` to find the remote master actor. After that, it resolves its `ActorRef`. Once this is ready, it creates a RoundRobinPool of 10 worker actors and sends a register message to `MasterActor`. Thanks to the register message, `MasterActor` knows the existence of these worker actors.

When we run our `ScalingOutMaster` application, it prints out `We cannot process your work since there is no workers.` until we start the `ScalingOutWorker` application. Then we see messages such as `Work with id X is done.` since the worker is processing our work messages.

As we have seen, we could run the `ScalingOutWorker` application multiple times in different nodes (or different ports within the same machine) to be able to scale out our application horizontally. In our example, we just run it twice using `application-2.conf` and `application-3.conf`.

Important note

It is not advisable to call `Thread.sleep` in production code. This call will block one of your threads, which will decrease the performance of your application. Moreover, `MasterActor` is a single point of failure in this architecture. Make sure you design your systems with no single point of failure to avoid unexpected issues.

Messages need to be serialized to be sent through the network when using remoting. By default, Akka uses Java serializers to serialize the classes; however, they are not performant. It is advisable to look for other serializer libraries, such as Protobuf or Kryo, which will serialize the classes into smaller messages in less time than the Java ones.

Creating a chat-based application using remote actors

A good example of using remote actors is a server-client system. In this recipe, we are going to develop a small chat application where clients will be connected to a remote server that will forward messages to the connected clients.

Getting ready

All the prerequisites are the same as before. We will reuse the previous `application.conf` and also create new actors, a server actor class, a client actor class, and a client interface actor class to handle the input from the command line.

How to do it...

1. To begin with, create a file named `ChatServer.scala` with the following contents:

```scala
package com.packt.chapter7
import akka.actor.{Actor, ActorRef, Props, Terminated}

object ChatServer {
  case object Connect
  case object Disconnect
  case object Disconnected
  case class Message(author: ActorRef, body: String,
    creationTimestamp : Long = System.currentTimeMillis())
  def props = Props(new ChatServer())
}

class ChatServer extends Actor {
  import ChatServer._
  var onlineClients = Set.empty[ActorRef]
  def receive = {
    case Connect =>
      onlineClients += sender
      context.watch(sender)
    case Disconnect =>
      onlineClients -= sender
      context.unwatch(sender)
      sender ! Disconnected
    case Terminated(ref) =>
      onlineClients -= ref
    case msg: Message =>
      onlineClients.filter(_ != sender).foreach(_ ! msg)
  }
}
```

2. Then, create a file named `ChatClient.scala` with the following contents:

```scala
package com.packt.chapter7
import akka.actor.{Actor, ActorRef, Props}
```

```
import com.packt.chapter7.ChatServer.{Connect, Disconnect,
  Disconnected, Message}
import akka.pattern.ask
import akka.pattern.pipe
import scala.concurrent.duration._
import akka.util.Timeout

object ChatClient {
  def props(chatServer: ActorRef) = Props(new
    ChatClient(chatServer))
}

class ChatClient(chatServer: ActorRef) extends Actor {
  import context.dispatcher
  implicit val timeout = Timeout(5 seconds)
  override def preStart = { chatServer ! Connect }

  def receive = {
    case Disconnect =>
      (chatServer ? Disconnect).pipeTo(self)
    case Disconnected =>
      context.stop(self)
    case body : String =>
      chatServer ! Message(self, body)
    case msg : Message =>
      println(s"Message from [${msg.author}] at
        [${msg.creationTimestamp}]: ${msg.body}")
  }
}
```

3. Now we need to create a helper to read the user input from the command line. Create a file named ChatClientInterface.scala with the following contents:

```
package com.packt.chapter7
import akka.actor.{Actor, ActorRef, Props}
import com.packt.chapter7.ChatServer.Disconnect
import scala.io.StdIn._

object ChatClientInterface {
  case object Check
  def props(chatClient: ActorRef) = Props(new
    ChatClientInterface(chatClient))
}

class ChatClientInterface(chatClient: ActorRef)
  extends Actor {
    import ChatClientInterface._
    override def preStart() = {
```

```
        println("You are logged in. Please type and press
          enter to send messages. Type 'DISCONNECT'
          to log out.")
        self ! Check
      }

    def receive = {
    case Check =>
      readLine() match {
        case "DISCONNECT" => chatClient ! Disconnect
        println("Disconnecting...")
        context.stop(self)
        case msg =>
        chatClient ! msg
        self ! Check
      }
    }
  }
```

4. Create a file named `ChatApplication.scala` with the following contents:

```scala
package com.packt.chapter7
import akka.actor.{ActorRef, ActorSystem, Props}
import scala.concurrent.duration._

object ChatClientApplication extends App {
  val actorSystem = ActorSystem("ChatServer")
  implicit val dispatcher = actorSystem.dispatcher
  val chatServerAddress =
    "akka.tcp://ChatServer@127.0.0.1:2552/user/chatServer"
  actorSystem.actorSelection(chatServerAddress).resolveOne(3
  seconds).onSuccess {
    case chatServer : ActorRef =>
      val client = actorSystem.actorOf(
        ChatClient.props(chatServer), "chatClient")
    actorSystem.actorOf(ChatClientInterface.props(client),
      "chatClientInterface")
  }
}

object ChatServerApplication extends App {
  val actorSystem = ActorSystem("ChatServer")
  actorSystem.actorOf(ChatServer.props, "chatServer")
}
```

5. Run the chat server. Execute the `ChatServerApplication` application using the `application-1.conf` configuration by passing the `-Dconfig.resource=application-1.conf` flag in either IntelliJ or the command line:

```
hveiga$ sbt -Dconfig.resource=application-1.conf "runMain
com.packt.chapter7.ChatServerApplication"
[info] Running com.packt.chapter7.ChatServerApplication
[INFO] [akka.remote.Remoting] Starting remoting
[INFO] [akka.remote.Remoting] Remoting started; listening on
addresses: [akka.tcp://ChatServer@127.0.0.1:2552]
[INFO] [akka.remote.Remoting] Remoting now listens on addresses:
[akka.tcp://ChatServer@127.0.0.1:2552]
```

6. Run the chat client. Execute the `ChatClientApplication` application using the `application-1.conf` configuration by passing the `-Dconfig.resource=application-2.conf` flag in either IntelliJ or the command line:

```
hveiga$ sbt -Dconfig.resource=application-2.conf "runMain
com.packt.chapter7.ChatClientApplication"
[info] Running com.packt.chapter7.ChatClientApplication
[INFO] [akka.remote.Remoting] Starting remoting
[INFO] [akka.remote.Remoting] Remoting started; listening on
addresses:
[akka.tcp://ChatServer@127.0.0.1:2553]
[INFO] [run-main-0] [akka.remote.Remoting] Remoting now listens
on addresses:
[akka.tcp://ChatServer@127.0.0.1:2553]
You are logged in. Please type and press enter to send messages.
Type 'DISCONNECT' to log out.
```

7. Do the same procedure to run a different client using `application-3.conf`:

```
hveiga$ sbt -Dconfig.resource=application-3.conf "runMain
com.packt.chapter7.ChatClientApplication"
[info] Running com.packt.chapter7.ChatClientApplication
[INFO] [akka.remote.Remoting] Starting remoting
[INFO] [akka.remote.Remoting] Remoting started; listening on
addresses:
[akka.tcp://ChatServer@127.0.0.1:2554]
[INFO] [run-main-0] [akka.remote.Remoting] Remoting now listens
on addresses:
[akka.tcp://ChatServer@127.0.0.1:2554]
You are logged in. Please type and press enter to send messages.
Type 'DISCONNECT' to log out.
```

8. Then type something in the command-line shell and you should see the message in the other client:

```
# Output client one
Message from [Actor[akka.tcp://ChatServer@127.0.0.1:2554
/user/chatClient#1617614523]] at [1485716003725]: Hello
Hey, how are you?
# Output client two
Hello
Message from
[Actor[akka.tcp://ChatServer@127.0.0.1:2553/user/chatClient#-
757506747]] at [1485716010867]: Hey, how are you?
```

How it works...

In this recipe, we demonstrated how to use Akka remoting to create a client-server system to send messages from one client to another. When clients get created, they use ActorSelection to look up the `ChatServer` actor. Then a `ClientInterface` actor gets created to deal with the command-line input from the user. In less than 200 lines, we have created a usable chat room.

Enabling Akka clustering for your project

We know how to interact with remote actors--create them, look them up, and send messages. However, Akka remoting requires you to know the actual addresses of actors in order to connect to them. Akka clustering is a layer on top of Akka remoting that helps you manage remote actors to provide a decentralized fault-tolerant service.

Akka clustering brings in a few new concepts:

- **Node**: This is a logical member of a cluster. It is defined by a `hostname:port:uid` tuple.
- **Cluster**: This is a set of nodes joined together through a membership service. Akka clustering utilizes the Gossip protocol to maintain a decentralized registry of nodes in a cluster.
- **Leader**: A single node in the cluster acts as a leader. The leader manages the convergence and membership state transitions.
- **Seed nodes**: These are a set of nodes that are used by other nodes to join the cluster.

- **Failure detector**: This is responsible for trying to detect whether a node is unreachable from the rest of the cluster. Akka cluster uses The Phi Accrual Failure Detector by Hayashibara and others.
- **Role**: This provides a mechanism to give different responsibilities to different members within the cluster. Each member can have from *0* to *n* roles assigned to it.

Every node in a cluster has a life cycle:

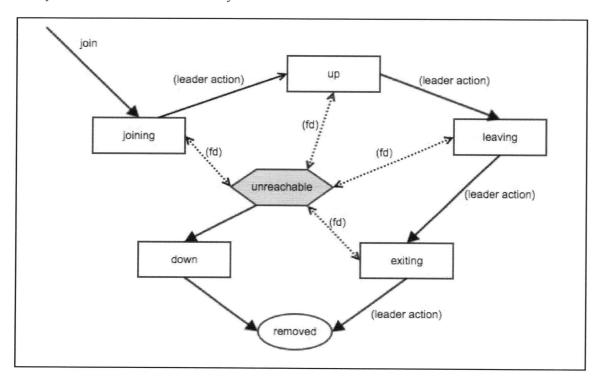

The possible states of a node in a cluster are as follows:

- **Joining**: This is the state when a node is trying to join a cluster
- **Up**: This is the regular operating state
- **Leaving/Existing**: This is the state that is used during the removal process
- **Down**: This is the state where the node is no longer part of the cluster decisions
- **Removed**: This is the state where the node is no longer a member of the cluster

The leader of a cluster is always responsible for acting on the member nodes and changing their states within the cluster. These decisions are taken based on the information shared among the nodes through the Gossip protocol. The leader can keep tabs on a member from **joining** to the **up** state when a node is joining the cluster, and it can mark a member from **exiting** to the **removed** state when a node is leaving the cluster.

In a distributed environment, we need to account for network failures as well. Akka clustering provides failure detection to detect **unreachable** nodes and a bit of configuration to be able to automatically mark them down or even remove them from the cluster. Note that the leader cannot take action while there is no convergence. This means all members need to agree on the state of each of the nodes in order to proceed and let other nodes join or be removed.

Akka clustering does not come as an isolated module, but it has a small ecosystem around it to help with most common tasks. These modules are Cluster Tools, Cluster Sharding, Cluster metrics, Cluster HTTP Management, Cluster Client, and more. We will revisit some of these in detail in the following recipes.

Getting ready

To step through this recipe, we need to import the `Hello-Akka` project; all other prerequisites are the same as before. We will need to bring the required dependencies for clustering this time.

How to do it...

For this recipe, perform the following steps:

1. Bring the required dependencies to begin with.
2. Edit the `build.sbt` file and add the Akka remote dependency as follows:

```
libraryDependencies += "com.typesafe.akka" %
  "akka-cluster_2.11" % "2.4.17"
```

   Then run `sbt update` to retrieve the dependencies from the central repository.

3. Create `application-cluster.conf` in the `src/main/resources` directory.
4. Add the following configuration parameters:

```
akka {
  actor {
```

```
      provider = "akka.cluster.ClusterActorRefProvider"
    }
    remote {
      enabled-transports = ["akka.remote.netty.tcp"]
      netty.tcp {
        hostname = "127.0.0.1"
        port = 2552
      }
    }
    cluster {
      seed-nodes = [
        "akka.tcp://ClusterSystem@127.0.0.1:2552",
        "akka.tcp://ClusterSystem@127.0.0.1:2553"]
    }
  }
```

How it works...

In this recipe, we included the required dependencies to use Akka clustering and created a configuration that enabled it. Now we are using `akka.cluster.ClusterActorRefProvider` as the actor provider. The configuration specifies the seed nodes to join the cluster. Since we have defined the remote hostname and port to be `127.0.0.1` and `2552`, respectively, the node running with this configuration will be a seed node, thanks to `akka.tcp://ClusterSystem@127.0.0.1:2552`.

Using Distributed Publish-Subscribe in the cluster

Akka clustering provides a fault-tolerant decentralized service to deploy actors. However, you need to know in advance in which node your actors are living to be able to interact with them. One module that can help us achieve this is Distributed Publish-Subscribe. This module brings the concept of a standard pub-sub pattern within our cluster.

This pattern provides a mediator actor that keeps an eventually consistent registry of actors across the cluster. This allows any actor on any node to send a message to a registered actor on any other node. Moreover, you can subscribe an actor to a topic. Once an actor publishes to that topic, all the subscribers get a copy of the message:

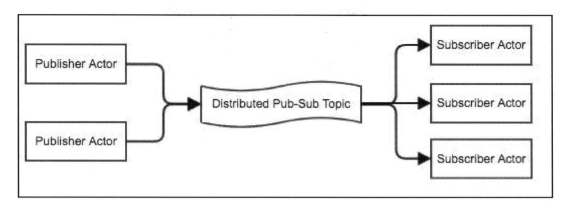

Getting ready

For this recipe, we will set up a cluster of nodes running on the same machine. For this, we will use two different ports specified in two different `application.conf` files. We will run an application that will have a notification publisher and notification subscriber in each node.

How to do it...

1. Bring the required dependencies to begin with.
2. Edit the `build.sbt` file and add the Akka remote dependency as follows:

```
libraryDependencies += "com.typesafe.akka" %
  "akka-cluster-tools_2.11" % "2.4.17"
```

Then, run `sbt update` to retrieve the dependencies from the central repository.

3. Create a new file named `application-cluster-1.conf` in the `src/main/resources` directory with the following contents:

```
akka {
  actor {
    provider = "akka.cluster.ClusterActorRefProvider"
  }
  remote {
    log-remote-lifecycle-events = off
    enabled-transports = ["akka.remote.netty.tcp"]
    netty.tcp {
```

```
          hostname = "127.0.0.1"
          port = 2552
        }
      }
      cluster {
        seed-nodes = [
          "akka.tcp://ClusterSystem@127.0.0.1:2552",
          "akka.tcp://ClusterSystem@127.0.0.1:2553"
        ]
      }
    }
```

4. Create a new file named `application-cluster-2.conf` in the `src/main/resources` directory with the following contents:

```
    akka {
      actor {
        provider = "akka.cluster.ClusterActorRefProvider"
      }
      remote {
        log-remote-lifecycle-events = off
        enabled-transports = ["akka.remote.netty.tcp"]
        netty.tcp {
          hostname = "127.0.0.1"
          port = 2553
        }
      }
      cluster {
        seed-nodes = [
          "akka.tcp://ClusterSystem@127.0.0.1:2552",
          "akka.tcp://ClusterSystem@127.0.0.1:2553"
        ]
      }
    }
```

5. Code the `NotificationPublisher`. Create a file named `NotificationPublisher.scala` in the `com.packt.chapter7` package with the following contents:

```
    package com.packt.chapter7
    import akka.actor.Actor
    import akka.cluster.pubsub.DistributedPubSub
    import akka.cluster.pubsub.DistributedPubSubMediator.Publish

    class NotificationPublisher extends Actor {
      val mediator =
        DistributedPubSub(context.system).mediator
```

```
    def receive = {
      case notification: Notification =>
        mediator ! Publish("notification", notification)
    }
  }
```

6. Now code the `NotificationSubscriber`. **Create a file named**
   `NotificationSubscriber.scala` in the `com.packt.chapter7` package with
   the following contents:

```
package com.packt.chapter7
import akka.actor.Actor
import akka.cluster.Cluster
import akka.cluster.pubsub.DistributedPubSub
import akka.cluster.pubsub.DistributedPubSubMediator.
  {Subscribe, SubscribeAck}

case class Notification(title: String, body: String)

class NotificationSubscriber extends Actor {
  val mediator = DistributedPubSub(context.system).mediator
  mediator ! Subscribe("notification", self)
  val cluster = Cluster(context.system)
  val clusterAddress = cluster.selfUniqueAddress

  def receive = {
    case notification: Notification =>
      println(s"Got notification in node $clusterAddress =>
        $notification")
    case SubscribeAck(Subscribe("notification",
      None, `self`)) ⇒ println("subscribing");
  }
}
```

7. Create a file named `DistributedPubSubApplication.scala` with the
   following contents:

```
package com.packt.chapter7
import akka.actor.{ActorSystem, Props}
import akka.cluster.Cluster
import scala.concurrent.duration._
import scala.util.Random

object DistributedPubSubApplication extends App {
  val actorSystem = ActorSystem("ClusterSystem")
  val cluster = Cluster(actorSystem)
  val notificationSubscriber =
```

```
      actorSystem.actorOf(Props[NotificationSubscriber])
    val notificationPublisher =
      actorSystem.actorOf(Props[NotificationPublisher])
    val clusterAddress = cluster.selfUniqueAddress
    val notification = Notification(s"Sent from
    $clusterAddress", "Test!")
    import actorSystem.dispatcher
    actorSystem.scheduler.schedule(Random.nextInt(5) seconds,
    5 seconds, notificationPublisher, notification)
  }
```

8. Once you have the entire code ready, run the application. First, run the
   `DistributedPubSubApplication` application using the `application-cluster-1.conf` configuration by passing the
   `-Dconfig.resource=application-cluster-1.conf` flag in either IntelliJ or
   the command line:

```
hveiga$ sbt -Dconfig.resource=application-cluster-1.conf "runMain
com.packt.chapter7.DistributedPubSubApplication"
[info] Running com.packt.chapter7.DistributedPubSubApplication
[INFO] [akka.remote.Remoting] Starting remoting
[INFO] [akka.remote.Remoting] Remoting started; listening on
addresses:
[akka.tcp://ClusterSystem@127.0.0.1:2552]
[INFO] [akka.cluster.Cluster(akka://ClusterSystem)] Cluster Node
[akka.tcp://ClusterSystem@127.0.0.1:2552] - Starting up...
[INFO] [akka.cluster.Cluster(akka://ClusterSystem)] Cluster Node
[akka.tcp://ClusterSystem@127.0.0.1:2552] - Registered cluster
JMX MBean
[akka:type=Cluster]
[INFO] [akka.cluster.Cluster(akka://ClusterSystem)] Cluster Node
[akka.tcp://ClusterSystem@127.0.0.1:2552] - Node
[akka.tcp://ClusterSystem@127.0.0.1:2552] is JOINING, roles []
[INFO] [akka.cluster.Cluster(akka://ClusterSystem)] Cluster Node
[akka.tcp://ClusterSystem@127.0.0.1:2552] - Leader is moving node
[akka.tcp://ClusterSystem@127.0.0.1:2552] to [Up]
Got notification in node UniqueAddress(
akka.tcp://ClusterSystem@127.0.0.1:2552,-1403384901) =>
Notification(Sent from UniqueAddress(
akka.tcp://ClusterSystem@127.0.0.1:2552,-1403384901),Test!)
Got notification in node UniqueAddress(
akka.tcp://ClusterSystem@127.0.0.1:2552,-1403384901) =>
Notification(Sent from UniqueAddress(
akka.tcp://ClusterSystem@127.0.0.1:2552,-1403384901),Test!)
```

9. Then, run the `DistributedPubSubApplication` application using the
   `application-cluster-2.conf` configuration by passing the
   `-Dconfig.resource=application-cluster-2.conf` flag in either IntelliJ or
   the command line:

```
hveiga$ sbt -Dconfig.resource=application-cluster-2.conf "runMain
com.packt.chapter7.DistributedPubSubApplication"
[info] Running com.packt.chapter7.DistributedPubSubApplication
[INFO] [akka.remote.Remoting] Starting remoting
[INFO] [akka.remote.Remoting] Remoting started; listening on
addresses:
[akka.tcp://ClusterSystem@127.0.0.1:2553]
[INFO] [akka.cluster.Cluster(akka://ClusterSystem)] Cluster Node
[akka.tcp://ClusterSystem@127.0.0.1:2553] - Starting up...
[INFO] [akka.cluster.Cluster(akka://ClusterSystem)] Cluster Node
[akka.tcp://ClusterSystem@127.0.0.1:2553] - Registered cluster
JMX MBean
[akka:type=Cluster]
[INFO] [akka.cluster.Cluster(akka://ClusterSystem)] Cluster Node
[akka.tcp://ClusterSystem@127.0.0.1:2553] - Started up
successfully
[INFO] [akka.cluster.Cluster(akka://ClusterSystem)] Cluster Node
[akka.tcp://ClusterSystem@127.0.0.1:2553] - Welcome from
[akka.tcp://ClusterSystem@127.0.0.1:2552]
Got notification in node UniqueAddress(
akka.tcp://ClusterSystem@127.0.0.1:2553,-1370252985) =>
Notification(Sent from UniqueAddress(
akka.tcp://ClusterSystem@127.0.0.1:2553,-1370252985),Test!)
```

10. Once you have both the applications running, you will be able to see the
    messages published and received by the nodes in both the command lines:

```
# Node running in port 2552
Got notification in node UniqueAddress(
akka.tcp://ClusterSystem@127.0.0.1:2552,-1403384901) =>
Notification(Sent from UniqueAddress(
akka.tcp://ClusterSystem@127.0.0.1:2553,-1370252985),Test!)
Got notification in node UniqueAddress(
akka.tcp://ClusterSystem@127.0.0.1:2552,-1403384901) =>
Notification(Sent from UniqueAddress(
akka.tcp://ClusterSystem@127.0.0.1:2552,-1403384901),Test!)
# Node running in port 2553
Got notification in node UniqueAddress(
akka.tcp://ClusterSystem@127.0.0.1:2553,-1370252985) =>
Notification(Sent from UniqueAddress(
akka.tcp://ClusterSystem@127.0.0.1:2552,-1403384901),Test!)
Got notification in node UniqueAddress(
```

```
akka.tcp://ClusterSystem@127.0.0.1:2553,-1370252985) =>
Notification(Sent from UniqueAddress(
akka.tcp://ClusterSystem@127.0.0.1:2553,-1370252985),Test!)
```

How it works...

In the preceding application, we created a simple cluster consisting of two members: one running in port 2552 (using `application-cluster-1.conf`) and another running in port 2553 (using `application-cluster-2.conf`).

The actor system consists of two actors:

- `NotificationSubscriber`: This actor subscribes itself to the topic called **notification** by sending a subscribe message to the mediator. The mediator actor is accessed through the `DistributedPubSub` extension. It sends a `SubscribeAck` message once the subscription is ready. From then on, any message published to the notification topic will be received by this actor.
- `NotificationPublisher`: This actor gets a reference of the mediator through the `DistributedPubSub` extension. Every time it receives a message of the type `Notification`, it publishes to the notification topic by sending a Publish message to the mediator.

The application also scheduled a notification message to be sent every 5 seconds with the title `Sent from [clusterAddress]` to be able to identify where the messages are coming from.

When we run the first application, we see our cluster starting up and moving our node from joining to the up state:

```
Cluster Node [akka.tcp://ClusterSystem@127.0.0.1:2552] - Node
[akka.tcp://ClusterSystem@127.0.0.1:2552] is JOINING, roles []
Cluster Node [akka.tcp://ClusterSystem@127.0.0.1:2552] - Leader is
moving node [akka.tcp://ClusterSystem@127.0.0.1:2552] to [Up]
```

Then, we start our second application:

```
Cluster Node [akka.tcp://ClusterSystem@127.0.0.1:2552] - Node
[akka.tcp://ClusterSystem@127.0.0.1:2553] is JOINING, roles []
Cluster Node [akka.tcp://ClusterSystem@127.0.0.1:2552] - Leader is moving
node [akka.tcp://ClusterSystem@127.0.0.1:2553] to [Up]
Cluster Node [akka.tcp://ClusterSystem@127.0.0.1:2553] - Welcome from
[akka.tcp://ClusterSystem@127.0.0.1:2552]
```

Distributed Publish-Subscribe also allows you to send messages to the mediator in a point-to-point fashion, using the Put, Send, and Remove messages.

Cluster Sharding

Akka Cluster Sharding is a helper module that automatically distributes actors across multiple cluster nodes. These actors have an identifier and they are commonly known as entities. Each actor entity runs only at one location, and you can interact with them through the `ClusterSharding` extension. A shard is a group of entities that is managed together through an EntityId.

Cluster Sharding takes care of routing the message to the expected destination, so you don't need to know where the actors are running. It needs a persistent store to store actor information. We will configure our app to use the distributed data store, which will be the default as of Akka 2.5.0. We will learn more about distributed data in the next recipe.

Cluster Sharding is used when you have stateful actors where the size of the state does not fit the memory of a single machine. We can easily scale an application beyond a single machine, thanks to Cluster Sharding.

In this recipe, we are going to test this feature in the following scenario: we are receiving current temperature data from a city. At some point, you decide to scale the app globally, but the data won't fit on a single machine. So we scale up using Cluster Sharding.

Getting ready

For this recipe, we will set up a cluster of two nodes running on the same machine. For this, we will use two different ports specified in two different `application.conf` files.

How to do it...

1. Bring the required dependencies to begin with.
2. Edit the `build.sbt` file and add Akka Sharding and distributed data dependencies as follows:

```
libraryDependencies += "com.typesafe.akka" %
  "akka-cluster-sharding_2.11" % "2.4.17"
libraryDependencies += "com.typesafe.akka" %
  "akka-distributed-data-experimental_2.11" % "2.4.17"
```

Then run `sbt update` to retrieve the dependencies from the central repository.

3. Create a new file named `application-cluster-sharding-1.conf` in the `src/main/resources` directory with the following contents:

```
akka {
  actor {
    provider = "akka.cluster.ClusterActorRefProvider"
  }
  remote {
    log-remote-lifecycle-events = off
    enabled-transports = ["akka.remote.netty.tcp"]
    netty.tcp {
      hostname = "127.0.0.1"
      port = 2552
    }
  }
  cluster {
    seed-nodes = [
      "akka.tcp://ClusterSystem@127.0.0.1:2552",
      "akka.tcp://ClusterSystem@127.0.0.1:2553"
    ]
    sharding.state-store-mode = ddata
  }
}
```

4. Create a new file named `application-cluster-sharding-2.conf` in the `src/main/resources` directory with the following contents:

```
akka {
  actor {
    provider = "akka.cluster.ClusterActorRefProvider"
  }
  remote {
    log-remote-lifecycle-events = off
    enabled-transports = ["akka.remote.netty.tcp"]
    netty.tcp {
      hostname = "127.0.0.1"
      port = 2553
    }
  }
  cluster {
    seed-nodes = [
      "akka.tcp://ClusterSystem@127.0.0.1:2552",
      "akka.tcp://ClusterSystem@127.0.0.1:2553"
    ]
    sharding.state-store-mode = ddata
```

```
    }
  }
```

5. Start coding `TemperatureActor`. Create a file named
   `TemperatureActor.scala` in the `com.packt.chapter7` package with the
   following contents:

```
package com.packt.chapter7
import akka.actor.{Actor, PoisonPill, ReceiveTimeout}
import akka.cluster.Cluster
import akka.cluster.sharding.ShardRegion
import akka.cluster.sharding.ShardRegion.Passivate
import scala.concurrent.duration._

object TemperatureActor {
  case class Location(
    country: String, city: String) {
      override def toString = s"$country-$city" }
  case class UpdateTemperature(location: Location,
    currentTemp: Double)
  case class GetCurrentTemperature(location: Location)

  val extractEntityId: ShardRegion.ExtractEntityId = {
    case msg@UpdateTemperature(location, _) ⇒
      (s"$location", msg)
    case msg@GetCurrentTemperature(location) ⇒
      (s"$location", msg)
  }
  val numberOfShards = 100
  val extractShardId: ShardRegion.ExtractShardId = {
    case UpdateTemperature(location, _) ⇒
      (s"$location".hashCode % numberOfShards).toString
    case GetCurrentTemperature(location) ⇒
      (s"$location".hashCode % numberOfShards).toString
  }
  val shardName = "Temperature"
}

class TemperatureActor extends Actor {
  import TemperatureActor._
  var temperatureMap = Map.empty[Location, Double]
  override def preStart() = {
    println(s"I have been created at
      ${Cluster(context.system).selfUniqueAddress}")
  }
  def receive = {
    case update @ UpdateTemperature(location, temp) =>
      temperatureMap += (location -> temp)
```

```
         println(s"Temp updated: $location")
      case GetCurrentTemperature(location) =>
         sender ! temperatureMap(location)
   }
}
```

6. Create a file named `ClusterShardingApplication.scala` with the following contents:

```scala
package com.packt.chapter7
import akka.actor.{ActorRef, ActorSystem, Props}
import akka.cluster.sharding.{ClusterSharding,
  ClusterShardingSettings}
import com.packt.chapter7.TemperatureActor.{
  GetCurrentTemperature, Location, UpdateTemperature}
import akka.pattern.ask
import akka.util.Timeout
import scala.concurrent.duration._

object ClusterShardingApplication extends App {
  val actorSystem = ActorSystem("ClusterSystem")
  import actorSystem.dispatcher
  val temperatureActor: ActorRef =
    ClusterSharding(actorSystem).start(
      typeName = TemperatureActor.shardName,
      entityProps = Props[TemperatureActor],
      settings = ClusterShardingSettings(actorSystem),
      extractEntityId = TemperatureActor.extractEntityId,
      extractShardId = TemperatureActor.extractShardId)
  //Let's simulate some time has passed. Never use
    Thread.sleep in production!
    Thread.sleep(30000)
  val locations = Vector(Location("USA","Chicago"),
    Location("ESP", "Madrid"),Location("FIN", "Helsinki"))
  temperatureActor ! UpdateTemperature(locations(0), 1.0)
  temperatureActor ! UpdateTemperature(locations(1), 20.0)
  temperatureActor ! UpdateTemperature(locations(2), -10.0)

  implicit val timeout = Timeout(5 seconds)
  locations.foreach {
    case location =>
      (temperatureActor ?
        GetCurrentTemperature(location)).onSuccess {
          case x: Double =>
            println(s"Current temperature in $location is $x")
        }
  }
}
```

7. Once you have the entire code ready, run the application. First, run the
   `ClusterShardingApplication` application using the `application-cluster-sharding-1.conf` configuration by passing the
   `-Dconfig.resource=application-cluster-sharding-1.conf` flag in either
   IntelliJ or the command line:

```
hveiga$ sbt -Dconfig.resource=application-cluster-sharding-1.conf
"runMain
com.packt.chapter7.ClusterShardingApplication"
[info] Running com.packt.chapter7.ClusterShardingApplication
[INFO] [akka.remote.Remoting] Starting remoting
[INFO] [akka.remote.Remoting] Remoting started; listening on
addresses:
[akka.tcp://ClusterSystem@127.0.0.1:2552]
[INFO] [akka.cluster.Cluster(akka://ClusterSystem)] Cluster Node
[akka.tcp://ClusterSystem@127.0.0.1:2552] - Starting up...
[INFO] [akka.cluster.Cluster(akka://ClusterSystem)] Cluster Node
[akka.tcp://ClusterSystem@127.0.0.1:2552] - Registered cluster
JMX MBean
[akka:type=Cluster]
[INFO] [akka.cluster.Cluster(akka://ClusterSystem)] Cluster Node
[akka.tcp://ClusterSystem@127.0.0.1:2552] - Started up
successfully
[INFO] [akka.cluster.Cluster(akka://ClusterSystem)] Cluster Node
[akka.tcp://ClusterSystem@127.0.0.1:2552] - Node
[akka.tcp://ClusterSystem@127.0.0.1:2552] is JOINING, roles []
[INFO] [akka.cluster.Cluster(akka://ClusterSystem)] Cluster Node
[akka.tcp://ClusterSystem@127.0.0.1:2552] - Leader is moving node
[akka.tcp://ClusterSystem@127.0.0.1:2552] to [Up]
[INFO] [akka.tcp://ClusterSystem@127.0.0.1:2552/system/sharding
/TemperatureCoordinator] Singleton manager starting singleton
actor
[akka://ClusterSystem/system/sharding/TemperatureCoordinator
/singleton]
[INFO] [akka.tcp://ClusterSystem@127.0.0.1:2552/system/sharding
/TemperatureCoordinator] ClusterSingletonManager state change
[Start -> Oldest]
```

8. Then, run the same application using the `application-cluster-sharding-2.conf` configuration by passing the
   `-Dconfig.resource=application-cluster-sharding-2.conf` flag in either
   IntelliJ or the command line:

```
hveiga$ sbt -Dconfig.resource=application-cluster-sharding-2.conf
"runMain
com.packt.chapter7.ClusterShardingApplication"
```

```
[info] Running com.packt.chapter7.ClusterShardingApplication
[INFO] [akka.remote.Remoting] Starting remoting
[INFO] [akka.remote.Remoting] Remoting started; listening on
addresses:
[akka.tcp://ClusterSystem@127.0.0.1:2553]
[INFO] [akka.cluster.Cluster(akka://ClusterSystem)] Cluster Node
[akka.tcp://ClusterSystem@127.0.0.1:2553] - Starting up...
[INFO] [akka.cluster.Cluster(akka://ClusterSystem)] Cluster Node
[akka.tcp://ClusterSystem@127.0.0.1:2553] - Registered cluster
JMX MBean
[akka:type=Cluster]
[INFO] [akka.cluster.Cluster(akka://ClusterSystem)] Cluster Node
[akka.tcp://ClusterSystem@127.0.0.1:2553] - Started up
successfully
[INFO] [akka.cluster.Cluster(akka://ClusterSystem)] Cluster Node
[akka.tcp://ClusterSystem@127.0.0.1:2553] - Welcome from
[akka.tcp://ClusterSystem@127.0.0.1:2552]
[INFO] [akka.tcp://ClusterSystem@127.0.0.1:2553/system/sharding
/TemperatureCoordinator] ClusterSingletonManager state change
[Start -> Younger]
```

9. After a few seconds (we set `Thread.sleep()` on purpose), you should see the following messages in either of the command-line shells:

```
I have been created at
UniqueAddress(akka.tcp://ClusterSystem@127.0.0.1:2552,917600962)
Temp updated: USA-Chicago
I have been created at
UniqueAddress(akka.tcp://ClusterSystem@127.0.0.1:2552,917600962)
Temp updated: FIN-Helsinki
I have been created at
UniqueAddress(akka.tcp://ClusterSystem@127.0.0.1:2553,1986921980)
Temp updated: ESP-Madrid
```

10. Finally, you should see the following messages asking for the current temperature in those cities. And, you should see these messages in both the command-line shells since we asked for this information in each of the applications we ran:

```
Current temperature in USA-Chicago is 1.0
Current temperature in ESP-Madrid is 20.0
Current temperature in FIN-Helsinki is -10.0
```

How it works...

In this recipe, we understood how Cluster Sharding can help us scale up our application. First, we defined a `TemperatureActor` class that simply holds temperature information for a given location. Then, we created these actors through the `ClusterSharding` extension. When defining sharding for actors, we need to provide the following:

- `Type name`: This defines the entity name
- `Props`: This refers to the prop object of the actor that we want to create
- `Settings`: This refers to Sharding settings. It allows you to further configure your sharding, for example, to run different shards on different cluster nodes depending on their roles.
- `ExtractEntityId`: This is an application-specific function that defines an entity, in our case, Country-City.
- `ExtractShardId`: This is an application-specific function that defines a shard. Normally, you might want multiple shards that will distribute your actors (and, therefore, the data going to those actors) across your cluster nodes uniformly.

As we can see, when we run our applications, the temperature actors get created in a node we did not define in advance. Also, we can see that we can access those actors seamlessly through the `ClusterSharding` extension from any cluster node. This makes scaling up a simple task.

Sharing data between nodes in an Akka cluster

Another interesting task you can accomplish through an Akka cluster is to have distributed data across all the nodes. The distributed data module allows you to use **Conflict-Free Replicated Data Types** (**CRDTs**) to have eventually consistent data structures. CRDTs permit you to execute updates from any node without coordination. In the case of update collision, the algorithm uses a monotonic merge function to resolve the issue.

This data is spread across cluster nodes via replication, and all the updates to these data structures are advertised by a Gossip protocol. The idea behind using Gossip is that all members should converge and decide the current state of a given data structure. By default, the Akka distributed data module provides the following data structures; however, it is possible to create your own custom `ReplicatedData` types:

- **Counters**: `GCounter` and `PNCounter`
- **Sets**: `GSet` and `ORSet`
- **Maps**: `ORMap`, `ORMultiMap`, `LWWMap`, and `PNCounterMap`
- **Registers**: `LWWRegister` and `Flag`

A good example would be to have a replicated set of subscriptions in all your nodes. This could be achieved using other tools, such as Hazelcast; however, we will use `ORSet` and distributed data for the task.

Important note

This is an experimental module as of Akka 2.4.X, so some APIs might change in newer releases. These data structures are eventually consistent, which means they might return an outdated value when you read them.

Getting ready

For this recipe, we will set up a cluster of two nodes running on the same machine. For this, we will use two different ports specified in two different `application.conf`. Specifically, we will reuse `application-cluster-1.conf` and `application-cluster-2.conf` from the previous recipes.

How to do it...

1. Bring the required dependencies to begin with.
2. Edit the `build.sbt` file and add the Akka distributed data dependencies as follows:

```
libraryDependencies += "com.typesafe.akka" %
  "akka-distributed-data-experimental_2.11" % "2.4.17"
```

Then run `sbt update` to retrieve the dependencies from the central repository.

3. Start coding `SubscriptionManager`. Create a file named
   `SubscriptionManager.scala` in the `com.packt.chapter7` package with the
   following contents:

```scala
package com.packt.chapter7
import akka.actor.{Actor, ActorRef, Props}
import akka.cluster.Cluster
import akka.cluster.ddata._
import akka.cluster.ddata.Replicator._

object SubscriptionManager {
  case class Subscription(id: Int, origin: String,
    creationTimestamp: Long)
  case class AddSubscription(subscription: Subscription)
  case class RemoveSubscription(subscription: Subscription)
  case class GetSubscriptions(consistency: ReadConsistency)

  trait GetSubscriptionsResult
  case class GetSubscriptionsSuccess(subscriptions:
    Set[Subscription]) extends GetSubscriptionsResult
  case object GetSubscriptionsFailure extends
    GetSubscriptionsResult
  def props = Props(new SubscriptionManager())
  val subscriptionKey = "subscription_key"
}

class SubscriptionManager extends Actor {
  import SubscriptionManager._
  val replicator = DistributedData(context.system).replicator
  implicit val node = Cluster(context.system)
  private val DataKey = ORSetKey[Subscription]
    (subscriptionKey)
  replicator ! Subscribe(DataKey, self)

  def receive = {
    case AddSubscription(subscription) =>
      println(s"Adding: $subscription")
      replicator ! Update(DataKey, ORSet.empty[Subscription],
        WriteLocal)(_ + subscription)
    case RemoveSubscription(subscription) =>
      println(s"Removing $subscription")
      replicator ! Update(DataKey, ORSet.empty[Subscription],
        WriteLocal)(_ - subscription)
    case GetSubscriptions(consistency) =>
      replicator ! Get(DataKey, consistency, request =
        Some(sender()))
    case g @ GetSuccess(DataKey, Some(replyTo: ActorRef)) =>
```

```
      val value = g.get(DataKey).elements
      replyTo ! GetSubscriptionsSuccess(value)
    case GetFailure(DataKey, Some(replyTo: ActorRef)) =>
      replyTo ! GetSubscriptionsFailure
    case _: UpdateResponse[_] => // ignore
    case c @ Changed(DataKey) =>
      val data = c.get(DataKey)
      println(s"Current elements: ${data.elements}")
  }
}
```

4. Create a file named `DistributedDataApplication.scala` with the following contents:

```
package com.packt.chapter7
import akka.actor.ActorSystem
import akka.cluster.Cluster
import akka.cluster.ddata.Replicator.{ReadFrom, ReadMajority}
import akka.pattern.ask
import akka.util.Timeout
import com.packt.chapter7.SubscriptionManager._
import scala.concurrent.Await
import scala.concurrent.duration._
import scala.util.Random

object DistributedDataApplication extends App {
  val actorSystem = ActorSystem("ClusterSystem")
  Cluster(actorSystem).registerOnMemberUp {
    val subscriptionManager =
      actorSystem.actorOf(SubscriptionManager.props)
    val subscription = Subscription(Random.nextInt(3),
  Cluster(actorSystem).selfUniqueAddress.toString,
    System.currentTimeMillis())
  subscriptionManager ! AddSubscription(subscription)
  //Let's simulate some time has passed.
  Never use Thread.sleep in production!
  Thread.sleep(10000)
  implicit val timeout = Timeout(5 seconds)
  val readMajority = ReadMajority(timeout = 5.seconds)
  val readFrom = ReadFrom(n = 2, timeout = 5.second)
  Await.result(subscriptionManager ?
    GetSubscriptions(readMajority),
    5 seconds) match {
      case GetSubscriptionsSuccess(subscriptions) =>
      println(s"The current set of subscriptions is
        $subscriptions")
      case GetSubscriptionsFailure =>
      println(s"Subscription manager was not able to get
```

```
      subscriptions successfully.")
  }
  subscriptionManager ! RemoveSubscription(subscription)
  Await.result(subscriptionManager ?
    GetSubscriptions(readFrom),
    5 seconds) match {
      case GetSubscriptionsSuccess(subscriptions) =>
        println(s"The current set of subscriptions is
          $subscriptions")
      case GetSubscriptionsFailure =>
        println(s"Subscription manager was not able to get
        subscriptions successfully.")
    }
  }
}
```

5. Once you have the entire code ready, run the application. First, run the
   `DistributedDataApplication` application using the `application-
   cluster-1.conf` configuration by passing the
   `-Dconfig.resource=application-cluster-1.conf` flag in either IntelliJ or
   the command line:

```
hveiga$ sbt -Dconfig.resource=application-cluster-1.conf "runMain
com.packt.chapter7.DistributedDataApplication"
[info] Running com.packt.chapter7.DistributedDataApplication
[INFO] [akka.remote.Remoting] Starting remoting
[INFO] [akka.remote.Remoting] Remoting started; listening on
addresses :
[akka.tcp://ClusterSystem@127.0.0.1:2552]
[INFO] [akka.cluster.Cluster(akka://ClusterSystem)] Cluster Node
[akka.tcp://ClusterSystem@127.0.0.1:2552] - Starting up...
[INFO] [akka.cluster.Cluster(akka://ClusterSystem)] Cluster Node
[akka.tcp://ClusterSystem@127.0.0.1:2552] - Registered cluster
 JMX MBean [akka:type=Cluster]
[INFO] [akka.cluster.Cluster(akka://ClusterSystem)] Cluster Node
[akka.tcp://ClusterSystem@127.0.0.1:2552] - Started up
successfully
[INFO] [akka.cluster.Cluster(akka://ClusterSystem)] Cluster Node
[akka.tcp://ClusterSystem@127.0.0.1:2552] - Node [
akka.tcp://ClusterSystem@127.0.0.1:2552] is JOINING, roles []
[INFO] [akka.cluster.Cluster(akka://ClusterSystem)] Cluster Node
[akka.tcp://ClusterSystem@127.0.0.1:2552] - Leader is moving node
[akka.tcp://ClusterSystem@127.0.0.1:2552] to [Up]
Adding: Subscription(0,UniqueAddress(
akka.tcp://ClusterSystem@127.0.0.1:2552,365975562),1485560015753)
Current elements: Set(Subscription(0,UniqueAddress(
akka.tcp://ClusterSystem@127.0.0.1:2552,365975562)
```

```
,1485560015753))
```

6. Within 10 seconds, run the same application using the `application-cluster-2.conf` configuration by passing the `-Dconfig.resource=application-cluster-2.conf` flag in either IntelliJ or the command line:

```
hveiga$ sbt -Dconfig.resource=application-cluster-2.conf "runMain
com.packt.chapter7.DistributedDataApplication"
[info] Running com.packt.chapter7.DistributedDataApplication
[INFO] [akka.remote.Remoting] Starting remoting
[INFO] [akka.remote.Remoting] Remoting started; listening on
addresses :
[akka.tcp://ClusterSystem@127.0.0.1:2553]
[INFO] [akka.cluster.Cluster(akka://ClusterSystem)] Cluster Node
[akka.tcp://ClusterSystem@127.0.0.1:2553] - Starting up...
[INFO] [akka.cluster.Cluster(akka://ClusterSystem)] Cluster Node
[akka.tcp://ClusterSystem@127.0.0.1:2553] - Registered cluster
JMX MBean [akka:type=Cluster]
[INFO] [akka.cluster.Cluster(akka://ClusterSystem)] Cluster Node
[akka.tcp://ClusterSystem@127.0.0.1:2553] - Started up
successfully
[INFO] [akka.cluster.Cluster(akka://ClusterSystem)] Cluster Node
[akka.tcp://ClusterSystem@127.0.0.1:2553] - Welcome from
[akka.tcp://ClusterSystem@127.0.0.1:2552]
Adding: Subscription(0,UniqueAddress(
akka.tcp://ClusterSystem@127.0.0.1:2553,789082718),1485560021259)
Current elements: Set(Subscription(0,UniqueAddress(
akka.tcp://ClusterSystem@127.0.0.1:2553,789082718)
,1485560021259))
```

7. After a few seconds (we set `Thread.sleep()` on purpose), you should see the following messages in either of command-line shells:

```
Current elements: Set(Subscription(0,UniqueAddress(
akka.tcp://ClusterSystem@127.0.0.1:2553,789082718)
,1485560021259), Subscription(0,UniqueAddress(
akka.tcp://ClusterSystem@127.0.0.1:2552,365975562),
1485560015753))
```

8. Finally, you should see the deletion subscription messages and an empty set once all the subscriptions have been deleted:

```
Current elements: Set()
```

How it works...

In this recipe, we set up a cluster with two nodes and created a `SubscriptionManager` actor in each one of them. This actor acts as the manager of your replicated data structure. In this case, we had an `ORSet` of subscriptions that get distributed, thanks to the replicator coming from the distributed data extension.

After you add two subscriptions, one from each node, you can access both the subscriptions from any node. When accessing a replicated dataset, you need to provide some level of consistency. In our example, we used `ReadMajority` and `ReadFrom`; however, you can use any of the following:

- `ReadLocal`: This means the value will come from the local replicate.
- `ReadFrom(n)`: This means the value will be read and merged from n replicas, including the local replica.
- `ReadMajority`: This means the value will be read and merged from at least $N/2 + 1$ replicas, where N is the number of nodes in the cluster.
- `ReadAll`: This means the value will be read and merged from all the nodes in the cluster.

Depending on your use case, you will need to use these consistently.

Creating a singleton actor across clusters

In some scenarios, it is required for you to have a singleton object within your whole cluster. The Akka Cluster Singleton module provides means to accomplish this task in an easy way.

This module picks the oldest node in the cluster to create your singleton actor. If this node gets removed from the cluster, then the module uses the same logic to decide where to deploy your singleton actor. First, it selects the oldest node in the cluster to recreate your singleton actor. Second, the module ensures that there is only one instance of your actor running within the whole cluster.

To demonstrate this behavior, we will make use of Auto Downing. This feature of Akka Cluster automatically marks a node Down and removes it from the cluster after a configurable amount of time. This feature is off by default.

Getting ready

For this recipe, we will set up a cluster of two nodes running on the same machine. For this, we will use two different ports specified in two different `application.conf` files.

How to do it...

1. Bring the required dependencies to begin with.
2. Edit the `build.sbt` file and add the Akka cluster tools dependency as follows:

```
libraryDependencies += "com.typesafe.akka" %
  "akka-cluster-tools_2.11" % "2.4.17"
```

Then run `sbt update` to retrieve the dependencies from the central repository.

3. Create a new file named `application-cluster-autodown-1.conf` in the `src/main/resources` directory with the following contents:

```
akka {
  actor {
    provider = "akka.cluster.ClusterActorRefProvider"
  }
  remote {
    log-remote-lifecycle-events = off
    enabled-transports = ["akka.remote.netty.tcp"]
    netty.tcp {
      hostname = "127.0.0.1"
      port = 2552
    }
  }
  cluster {
    seed-nodes = [
      "akka.tcp://ClusterSystem@127.0.0.1:2552",
      "akka.tcp://ClusterSystem@127.0.0.1:2553"
    ]
    auto-down-unreachable-after = 5s
  }
}
```

4. Create a new file named `application-cluster-autodown-2.conf` in the `src/main/resources` directory with the following contents:

```
akka {
  actor {
    provider = "akka.cluster.ClusterActorRefProvider"
  }
  remote {
    log-remote-lifecycle-events = off
    enabled-transports = ["akka.remote.netty.tcp"]
    netty.tcp {
      hostname = "127.0.0.1"
      port = 2553
    }
  }
  cluster {
    seed-nodes = [
      "akka.tcp://ClusterSystem@127.0.0.1:2552",
      "akka.tcp://ClusterSystem@127.0.0.1:2553"
    ]
    auto-down-unreachable-after = 5s
  }
}
```

5. Start coding `ClusterAwareSimpleActor`. Create a file named `ClusterAwareSimpleActor.scala` in the `com.packt.chapter7` package with the following contents:

```
package com.packt.chapter7
import akka.actor.Actor
import akka.cluster.Cluster

class ClusterAwareSimpleActor extends Actor {
  val cluster = Cluster(context.system)
  def receive = {
    case _ => println(s"I have been created at
      ${cluster.selfUniqueAddress}")
  }
}
```

6. Create a file named `ClusterSingletonApplication.scala` with the following contents:

```
package com.packt.chapter7
import akka.actor.{ActorSystem, PoisonPill, Props}
import akka.cluster.Cluster
import akka.cluster.singleton._
```

```
import scala.concurrent.duration._

object ClusterSingletonApplication extends App {
  val actorSystem = ActorSystem("ClusterSystem")
  val cluster = Cluster(actorSystem)
  val clusterSingletonSettings =
    ClusterSingletonManagerSettings(actorSystem)
  val clusterSingletonManager =

ClusterSingletonManager.props(Props[ClusterAwareSimpleActor],
      PoisonPill, clusterSingletonSettings)
    actorSystem.actorOf(clusterSingletonManager,
     "singletonClusteAwareSimpleActor")
  val singletonSimpleActor =
    actorSystem.actorOf(ClusterSingletonProxy.props(
      singletonManagerPath = "/user
        /singletonClusteAwareSimpleActor",
    settings = ClusterSingletonProxySettings(actorSystem)),
      name = "singletonSimpleActorProxy")
    import actorSystem.dispatcher
    actorSystem.scheduler.schedule(10 seconds, 5 seconds,
      singletonSimpleActor, "TEST")
}
```

7. Once you have the entire code ready, run the application. First, run the
   ClusterSingletonApplication application using the application-
   cluster-autodown-1.conf configuration by passing the
   -Dconfig.resource=application-cluster-autodown-1.conf flag in either
   IntelliJ or the command line:

```
hveiga$ sbt -Dconfig.resource=application-cluster-autodown-1.conf
"runMain
com.packt.chapter7.ClusterSingletonApplication"
[info] Running com.packt.chapter7.ClusterSingletonApplication
[INFO] [akka.remote.Remoting] Starting remoting
[INFO] [akka.remote.Remoting] Remoting started; listening on
addresses :
[akka.tcp://ClusterSystem@127.0.0.1:2552]
[INFO] [akka.cluster.Cluster(akka://ClusterSystem)] Cluster Node
[akka.tcp://ClusterSystem@127.0.0.1:2552] - Starting up...
[INFO] [akka.cluster.Cluster(akka://ClusterSystem)] Cluster Node
[akka.tcp://ClusterSystem@127.0.0.1:2552] - Registered cluster
JMX MBean [akka:type=Cluster]
[INFO] [akka.cluster.Cluster(akka://ClusterSystem)] Cluster Node
[akka.tcp://ClusterSystem@127.0.0.1:2552] - Started up
successfully
[INFO] [akka.cluster.Cluster(akka://ClusterSystem)] Cluster Node
```

```
[akka.tcp://ClusterSystem@127.0.0.1:2552] - Node
[akka.tcp://ClusterSystem@127.0.0.1:2552] is JOINING, roles []
[INFO] [akka.cluster.Cluster(akka://ClusterSystem)] Cluster Node
[akka.tcp://ClusterSystem@127.0.0.1:2552] - Leader is moving node
[akka.tcp://ClusterSystem@127.0.0.1:2552] to [Up]
[INFO] [akka.tcp://ClusterSystem@127.0.0.1:2552/user/
singletonClusteAwareSimpleActor] Singleton manager starting
singleton actor
[akka://ClusterSystem/user/singletonClusteAwareSimpleActor
/singleton]
[INFO] [akka.tcp://ClusterSystem@127.0.0.1:2552/user
/singletonClusteAwareSimpleActor]
ClusterSingletonManager state change [Start -> Oldest]
[INFO] [akka.tcp://ClusterSystem@127.0.0.1:2552/user
/singletonSimpleActorProxy]
Singleton identified at [akka://ClusterSystem/user/
singletonClusteAwareSimpleActor/singleton]
I have been created at
UniqueAddress(akka.tcp://ClusterSystem@127.0.0.1:2552,-979488016)
```

8. Second, run the same application using the `application-cluster-autodown-2.conf` configuration by passing the `-Dconfig.resource=application-cluster-autodown-2.conf` flag in either IntelliJ or the command line:

```
hveiga$ sbt -Dconfig.resource=application-cluster-autodown-2.conf
"runMain
com.packt.chapter7.ClusterSingletonApplication"
[info] Running com.packt.chapter7.ClusterSingletonApplication
[INFO] [akka.remote.Remoting] Starting remoting
[INFO] [akka.remote.Remoting] Remoting started; listening on
addresses :
[akka.tcp://ClusterSystem@127.0.0.1:2553]
[INFO] [akka.cluster.Cluster(akka://ClusterSystem)] Cluster Node
[akka.tcp://ClusterSystem@127.0.0.1:2553] - Starting up...
[INFO] [akka.cluster.Cluster(akka://ClusterSystem)] Cluster Node
[akka.tcp://ClusterSystem@127.0.0.1:2553] - Registered cluster
JMX MBean [akka:type=Cluster]
[INFO] [akka.cluster.Cluster(akka://ClusterSystem)] Cluster Node
[akka.tcp://ClusterSystem@127.0.0.1:2553] - Started up
successfully
[INFO] [akka.cluster.Cluster(akka://ClusterSystem)] Cluster Node
[akka.tcp://ClusterSystem@127.0.0.1:2553] - Welcome from
[akka.tcp://ClusterSystem@127.0.0.1:2552]
[INFO] [akka.tcp://ClusterSystem@127.0.0.1:2553/user/
singletonSimpleActorProxy] Singleton identified at
[akka.tcp://ClusterSystem@127.0.0.1:2552/user
```

```
/singletonClusteAwareSimpleActor/singleton]
[INFO] [akka.tcp://ClusterSystem@127.0.0.1:2553/user
/singletonClusteAwareSimpleActor]
ClusterSingletonManager state change [Start -> Younger]
```

9. You should see messages only in the first command-line shell since the singleton actor is running there. Now stop the first application and look at how the module moves the singleton to the second node in the cluster and starts printing out:

```
[WARN] [akka.tcp://ClusterSystem@127.0.0.1:2553/system
/cluster/core/daemon]
Cluster Node [akka.tcp://ClusterSystem@127.0.0.1:2553] -
Marking node(s) as UNREACHABLE [Member(address =
akka.tcp://ClusterSystem@127.0.0.1:2552, status = Up)]
[INFO] [akka.cluster.Cluster(akka://ClusterSystem)] Cluster Node
[akka.tcp://ClusterSystem@127.0.0.1:2553] - Leader is auto-
downing unreachable node
[akka.tcp://ClusterSystem@127.0.0.1:2552]
[INFO] [akka.cluster.Cluster(akka://ClusterSystem)] Cluster Node
[akka.tcp://ClusterSystem@127.0.0.1:2553] - Marking unreachable
node
[akka.tcp://ClusterSystem@127.0.0.1:2552] as [Down]
[INFO] [akka.cluster.Cluster(akka://ClusterSystem)] Cluster Node
[akka.tcp://ClusterSystem@127.0.0.1:2553] - Leader is removing
unreachable node
[akka.tcp://ClusterSystem@127.0.0.1:2552]
[INFO] [akka.tcp://ClusterSystem@127.0.0.1:2553/user
/singletonClusteAwareSimpleActor]
Previous oldest removed [akka.tcp://ClusterSystem@127.0.0.1:2552]
[INFO] [akka.tcp://ClusterSystem@127.0.0.1:2553/user
/singletonClusteAwareSimpleActor]
Younger observed OldestChanged: [None -> myself]
[INFO] [akka.tcp://ClusterSystem@127.0.0.1:2553/user
/singletonClusteAwareSimpleActor]
Singleton manager starting singleton actor
[akka://ClusterSystem/user/singletonClusteAwareSimpleActor
/singleton]
[INFO] [akka.tcp://ClusterSystem@127.0.0.1:2553/user
/singletonClusteAwareSimpleActor]
ClusterSingletonManager state change [Younger -> Oldest]
[INFO] [akka.tcp://ClusterSystem@127.0.0.1:2553/user
/singletonSimpleActorProxy]
Singleton identified at [akka://ClusterSystem/user/
singletonClusteAwareSimpleActor/singleton]
I have been created at
UniqueAddress(akka.tcp://ClusterSystem@127.0.0.1:2553,-96051361)
```

How it works...

In this recipe, we learned how to have a singleton actor across a cluster. For this, we had made use of `ClusterSingletonManager` and `ClusterSingletonProxy`:

- `ClusterSingletonManager`: This is a manager that needs to be instantiated in every node of the cluster. It takes care of ensuring that there is only one instance of your actor. This class must **not** be used to interact with the singleton actor.
- `ClusterSingletonProxy`: This is a proxy that routes your messages to the singleton instance wherever it lives within the cluster.

Once we configured `ClusterAwareSimpleActor` using `ClusterSingletonManager`, we got the corresponding actor reference from `ClusterSingletonProxy`. Note that we need to know the actor path in advance to be able to access the actor correctly. Then, we scheduled a message to be sent every 5 seconds to the singleton actor.

When we are running both the applications, we can see in the logs that the actor is only living in the first node (because it was created before); therefore, we only see the output statements in the first command-line shell. When we stop the first application, we see how the cluster reacts, marking the node Down and removing it from the cluster. After this, the Akka Cluster singleton realizes that there is no instance of the actor running, as the node where it was running dies and new instance in the second node is created. Then this new instance starts printing out the statements to the second command-line shell. The Akka Cluster Singleton allows you to configure the hand-over retry interval and minimum retries through the `akka.cluster.singleton.hand-over-retry-interval` configuration parameters and `akka.cluster.singleton.min-number-of-hand-over-retries`.

Note that while this might seem appealing to use, you need to consider that having a single actor performing a task within a whole cluster might become a bottleneck. Dealing with a stateful actor is another aspect you need to account for. If the node where the actor is living dies and this actor gets recreated in some other node, you might need to use Akka Persistence to ensure the state remains.

See also

- Learn more about the *Gossip protocol* at `https://en.wikipedia.org/wiki/Gossip_protocol`
- Learn more about *Aeron* at `https://github.com/real-logic/Aeron`
- Learn more about *The Phi Accrual Failure Detector* at `http://fubica.lsd.ufcg.edu.br/hp/cursos/cfsc/papers/hayashibara04theaccrual.pdf`

8

Akka Streams

In this chapter, we will cover the following topics:

- Creating simple Akka streams
- Transforming and consuming streams
- Creating stream sources, flows, and sinks
- Custom stream processing
- Error handling in Akka Streams
- Pipelining and parallelizing streams
- Working with streaming I/O
- Integrating streams with Akka actors
- Working with graphs
- Processing RabbitMQ messages with Akka Streams
- Integrating Akka Streams with Kafka using Reactive Kafka

Introduction

Nowadays, we live in a world where more and more things are getting connected to the Internet. These things generate helpful information that is usually delivered in real time. Streaming helps you ingest, process, analyze, and store data in a quick and responsive manner. Unlike batching, streaming happens in a real-time (or near real-time) fashion, which brings a new set of challenges--race conditions, network failures, buffers, and so on.

Akka Streams is a module built on top of Akka to make the ingestion and processing of streams easier, using the actor model under the hood. It provides easy-to-use APIs to create streams that leverage the power of the Akka toolkit without explicitly defining actor behaviors and messages. This allows you to focus on logic and forget about all of the boilerplate code required to manage the actor. Akka Streams follows the Reactive Streams manifesto, which defines a standard for asynchronous stream processing.

Akka Streams has backpressure mechanisms enabled by default. This feature allows components to signal other components in the stream that they are ready to process new elements. If some part of the processing takes longer (for example, an insertion into a database), we can throttle the consumer until things go back to normal.

 Learn more about Reactive Streams at `http://www.reactive-streams.org/`.

Creating simple Akka Streams

A stream is a set of components with different responsibilities. Some components consume data, some transform data, and others deliver data. Akka Streams uses these components as modular pieces that you put together to create a runnable stream. These pieces help you not only understand the overall design of your topology, but they also aid in maintainability. In addition, they are reusable, which allows us to use the **don't repeat yourself** (**DRY**) principle.

Each stream topology basically consists of the following:

- **Source**: This is the entry point to your stream. There must be at least one in every stream.
- **Sink**: This is the exit point of your stream. There must be at least one in every stream.
- **Flow**: This is the component responsible for manipulating the elements of the stream. You can have none or any number of them.

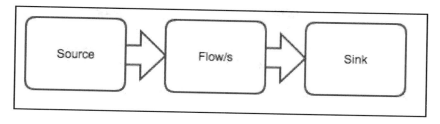

These components are also known as stages. There are multiple built-in stages that allow you to do the most common operations. These operations range from mapping, filtering, and merging to more complicated functions, such as `statefulMapConcat`. We will review most of these out-of-the-box stages in the *Working with Graphs* recipe. To get started with Akka Streams, we are going to create a simple application that will check some files.

Getting ready

To step through this recipe, import the `Hello-Akka` project; all the other prerequisites are the same as before. We need to get the required dependencies for stream this time.

How to do it...

For this recipe, perform the following steps:

1. Get the required dependencies. This time, use Akka version 2.4.17.
2. Edit the `build.sbt` file and add the Akka Streams dependency, as follows:

```
libraryDependencies += "com.typesafe.akka" %
  "akka-stream_2.11" % "2.4.17"
```

3. Now create a file named `SimpleStreamsApplication.scala`. Once you do this, define your stream and run it:

```
package com.packt.chapter8

import akka.actor.ActorSystem
import akka.stream.ActorMaterializer
import akka.stream.scaladsl.{Sink, Source}

object SimpleStreamsApplication extends App {
  implicit val actorSystem = ActorSystem("SimpleStream")
  implicit val actorMaterializer = ActorMaterializer()
```

```
val fileList = List("src/main/resources/testfile1.text",
  "src/main/resources/testfile2.txt",
  "src/main/resources/testfile3.txt")

val stream = Source(fileList)
  .map(new java.io.File(_))
  .filter(_.exists())
  .filter(_.length() != 0)
  .to(Sink.foreach(f => println(s"Absolute path:
    ${f.getAbsolutePath}")))
    stream.run()
}
```

4. Create two files inside `src/main/resources`. Create a file named `testfile2.txt` and leave it empty. Create a file named `testfile3.txt` and add some text to it, such as `Hello World Akka Streams!`.

5. Run the `SimpleStreamsApplication` application in either IntelliJ or CommandLine:

```
hveiga$ sbt "runMain com.packt.chapter8.SimpleStreamsApplication"
[info] Running com.packt.chapter8.SimpleStreamsApplication
Absolute path: /code/chapter8/testfile3.txt
```

How it works...

In this recipe, we created a small stream that could read a list of filenames and emit each element through the stream. It maps these filenames to the files, filters out non-existent or empty files, and finally prints out the absolute path of non-empty files. Since the only non-empty file is `testfile3.txt`, we saw `Absolute path: /code/chapter8/testfile3.txt` in the output.

In order to be able to run a stream, an `ActorMaterializer` is required. `ActorMaterializer` is responsible for creating the underlying actors with the specific functionality you define in your stream. Since `ActorMaterializer` creates actors, it also needs an `ActorSystem`. This is the reason why we implicitly defined one in our sample code.

It's also good to mention the type of `stream` in the code. The `stream` has a type of `RunnableGraph[NotUsed]`. It is also possible to understand any stream as a graph. Such graphs would have nodes and connections. In Akka Streams, these nodes would be represented by the stages of the stream (sources, flows, and sinks). Connections, on the other hand, is about how you would link each stage with the others. We will see more about this in the following recipes.

How to transform streams and consume them

As mentioned before, a Source is responsible for consuming elements and emitting them through the stream. A Flow is responsible for transforming elements as they go. In this recipe, we will revisit the out-of-the-box transforming functions a Flow provides. In a later recipe, we will see how we can create more complicated Flows using the Graph DSL.

Getting ready

We will use the same prerequisites as that of the previous recipe. This time, we will implement a stream to do a word count. We will consume a GZIP compressed file and count the occurrences of each word.

How to do it...

For this recipe, perform the following steps:

1. Create a test file named `gzipped-file` inside `src/main/resources` with the following contents:

   ```
   hello world from akka streams! No seriously,
   HELLO WORLD FROM AKKA STREAMS!!!
   ```

2. Then compress the file. This can be easily achieved using the `gzip gzipped-file` command. You should end up with a compressed file named `gzipped-file.gz`.

3. Now create a file named `TransformingStreamsApplication.scala`. Define your stream as follows:

```scala
package com.packt.chapter8

import java.nio.file.Paths

import akka.actor.ActorSystem
import akka.stream.ActorMaterializer
import akka.stream.scaladsl._

object TransformingStreamsApplication extends App {

  implicit val actorSystem = ActorSystem("TransformingStream")
  implicit val actorMaterializer = ActorMaterializer()
  val MaxGroups = 100

  val path = Paths.get("src/main/resources/gzipped-file.gz")

  val stream = FileIO.fromPath(path)
    .via(Compression.gunzip())
    .map(_.utf8String.toUpperCase)
    .mapConcat(_.split(" ").toList)
    .collect { case w if w.nonEmpty =>
      w.replaceAll("""[p{Punct}&&[^.]]""",
      "").replaceAll(System.lineSeparator(), "") }
    .groupBy(MaxGroups, identity)
    .map(_ -> 1)
    .reduce((l, r) => (l._1, l._2 + r._2))
    .mergeSubstreams
    .to(Sink.foreach(println))

  stream.run()
}
```

4. Run the `TransformingStreamsApplication` application in either IntelliJ or CommandLine:

```
hveiga$ sbt "runMain
com.packt.chapter8.TransformingStreamsApplication"
[info] Running com.packt.chapter8.TransformingStreamsApplication
(NO,1)
(STREAMS,2)
(SERIOUSLY,1)
(HELLO,2)
(FROM,2)
```

```
(WORLD,2)
(AKKA,2)
```

How it works...

This word count scenario brings with it a few new concepts and stages. To begin with, we used a different Source for our stream. FileIO is a Source stage provided in the Akka Streams library, where you can provide a path to consume a file and emit it through the stream in the `ByteString` format.

After that, we uncompressed the file to read the contents. To do so, we used the helper Flow, namely `Compression.gunzip()`. This Flow object is provided as an intermediate processing stage using the method `Via`. `Via` expects a Flow and allows you to modularize your streams. You can instantiate the Flow somewhere else and just reference it there. Next, we mapped ByteStrings to UTF8 uppercase strings. We did this using the `map` method. This method takes one element of a given type and returns another. This new element does not necessarily need to be of the same type.

Afterward, we turned our string to multiple elements. `MapConcat` takes one element and outputs from 0 to n elements. In this case, we split our line by spaces and returned each word as a different element. `MapConcat` is semantically similar to `flatMap` in the Scala Collections API. Then, we collected each non-empty element and replaced all the new lines and punctuation signs. We used the filter function to achieve this. Filter takes one element and lets it through, depending on the given predicate.

Subsequently, we grouped our elements using the `groupBy` method. The `groupBy` method demultiplexes the incoming stream into separate output streams, one for each element key. We used `identity` as our key, so each word would generate a different output stream. One important aspect to mention is that `groupBy` does not permit unlimited output substreams; this is why you need to provide a max substream value (in our case, set to `100`). Thereafter, we mapped each word to a tuple (word, 1) and used `reduce` to sum all the elements in each substream.

Finally, we used `mergeSubstreams` to flatten the substream into by performing a merge operation. Then, we used a simple `Sink.foreach` to print each of the values to the standard output.

Creating stream sources, flows, and sinks

Now that we are more familiar with the different stages, let's see how we can modularize and reuse them. Akka Streams provides a large number of stages out of the box. We could group them into the following categories:

- Source stages
- Sink stages
- Processing stages
- Timer-driven stages
- Back pressure aware stages
- Nesting and flattening stages
- Time aware stages
- Fan-in stages
- Fan-out stages

In this recipe, we will reuse the code from the previous recipe to demonstrate how to make it modular. We will create two different streams that will use the same immutable stages but will run independently.

Getting ready

We will use the same prerequisites as the previous recipe. This time, we will implement a stream to do a word count. We will consume a GZIP compressed file and count the occurrences of each word.

How to do it...

For this recipe, perform the following steps:

1. Creating a test file named `gzipped-file` inside `src/main/resources` with the following contents:

   ```
   hello world from akka streams! No seriously,
   HELLO WORLD FROM AKKA STREAMS!!!
   ```

2. Then compress the file. This can be easily achieved using the `gzip gzipped-file` command.

3. Now create a file named `ModularizingStreamsApplication.scala`. Define your stream as follows:

```
package com.packt.chapter8

import java.nio.file.Paths

import akka.actor.ActorSystem
import akka.stream.ActorMaterializer
import akka.stream.scaladsl._
import akka.util.ByteString

object ModularizingStreamsApplication extends App {
  implicit val actorSystem =
    ActorSystem("TransformingStream")
  implicit val actorMaterializer = ActorMaterializer()

  val MaxGroups = 1000

  val path = Paths.get("src/main/resources/gzipped-file.gz")
  val source = FileIO.fromPath(path)

  val gunzip = Flow[ByteString].via(Compression.gunzip())
  val utf8UppercaseMapper =
    Flow[ByteString].map(_.utf8String.toUpperCase)
  val utf8LowercaseMapper =
    Flow[ByteString].map(_.utf8String.toLowerCase)
  val splitter = Flow[String].mapConcat(_.split(" ").toList)
  val punctuationMapper = Flow[String].map(_.replaceAll("""
    [p{Punct}&&[^.]]""", "").replaceAll(
    System.lineSeparator(), ""))
  val filterEmptyElements = Flow[String].filter(_.nonEmpty)
  val wordCountFlow = Flow[String]
    .groupBy(MaxGroups, identity)
    .map(_ -> 1)
    .reduce(((l, r) => (l._1, l._2 + r._2)))
    .mergeSubstreams

  val printlnSink = Sink.foreach(println)

  val streamUppercase = source
    .via(gunzip)
    .via(utf8UppercaseMapper)
    .via(splitter)
    .via(punctuationMapper)
```

```
      .via(filterEmptyElements)
      .via(wordCountFlow)
      .to(printlnSink)
    val streamLowercase = source
      .via(gunzip)
      .via(utf8LowercaseMapper)
      .via(splitter)
      .via(punctuationMapper)
      .via(filterEmptyElements)
      .via(wordCountFlow)
      .to(printlnSink)

  streamUppercase.run()
  streamLowercase.run()
  }
```

4. Run the `TransformingStreamsApplication` application in either IntelliJ or CommandLine:

```
hveiga$ sbt "runMain
com.packt.chapter8.ModularizingStreamsApplication"
[info] Running com.packt.chapter8.ModularizingStreamsApplication
(no,1)
(NO,1)
(world,2)
(STREAMS,2)
(streams,2)
(SERIOUSLY,1)
(from,2)
(HELLO,2)
(hello,2)
(FROM,2)
(seriously,1)
(WORLD,2)
(akka,2)
(AKKA,2)
```

How it works...

In this recipe, we created two different streams to count words. We took a different approach here, as compared to the previous recipes. First, we instantiated our Source. Second, we instantiated our Flow stages. As we can see in the code, it is possible to have more than one stage in a Flow, as we saw in `wordCountFlow`. This Flow is actually a composition of `groupBy`, `map`, `reduce`, and `mergeSubstream`; however, we can use it now as one stage instead of many. This composing capability allows you to have difficult Flow stages defined as a single unit, and therefore, easy to manage. Last, we instantiated `Sink.foreach` to print out every element in the stream.

Afterward, we created our two different streams by reusing the stages and only having the uppercase or lowercase stage different. Keep in mind that we could have simplified the code even more to something like this:

```
val sourceGunzip = source.via(gunzip)
val reusableProcessingFlow = Flow[String].via(splitter)
  .via(punctuationMapper)
  .via(filterEmptyElements)
  .via(wordCountFlow)

val streamLowercase = sourceGunzip
  .via(utf8LowercaseMapper)
  .via(reusableProcessingFlow)
  .to(printlnSink)
```

Since any combination is possible, the decision about how granular it could be with the stages is up to the developer. Also, it is good to mention that since these streams do not depend on each other, the order in which they would be started is not important.

Custom stream processing

Sometimes, all the out-of-the-box Akka Streams stages do not cover a specific scenario you need. Akka Streams provides a set of APIs to create your own custom stage. Since Streams are essentially processing graphs, to create a custom stage, you need to extend the `GraphStage` abstraction. Let's not confuse `GraphDSL` with `GraphStage`. The main difference between `GraphDSL`, which is used to compose multiple stages into a single stage, and `GraphStage` is that the latter cannot be decomposed into smaller pieces.

At this point, we need to learn a bit about how Akka Streams works internally. To begin with, there is the concept of shape. A shape defines the number of input and output ports in your stage (known as inlets and outlets). For example, SourceShape has only one outlet. A SinkShape has one inlet. A FlowShape has one inlet and one outlet. It is also possible to have an AmorphousShape, which has an arbitrary number of inlets and outlets. Every GraphStage also encompasses stage logic. This logic defines a set of handlers (InHandler or OutHandler) that implement the behavior of the different ports. All of the logic should extend GraphStageLogic and can be stateful or stateless, depending on your use case.

These handlers are also part of the backpressure mechanism. We will demonstrate how to use them in this recipe.

Getting ready

We will use the same prerequisites as that of the previous recipe. This time, we will implement a custom source and a custom sink using GraphStage.

How to do it...

For this recipe, perform the following steps:

1. Create a file named HelloAkkaStreamsSource.scala inside the com.packt.chapter8 package. This class will extend GraphStage. Define a SourceShape emitting String elements. The content should look like this:

```scala
package com.packt.chapter8

import akka.stream.{Attributes, Outlet, SourceShape}
import akka.stream.stage._

class HelloAkkaStreamsSource extends
  GraphStage[SourceShape[String]] {

  val out: Outlet[String] = Outlet("SystemInputSource")
  override val shape: SourceShape[String] = SourceShape(out)

  override def createLogic(inheritedAttributes: Attributes):
  GraphStageLogic =
    new GraphStageLogic(shape) {

      setHandler(out, new OutHandler {
        override def onPull() = {
```

```
          val line = "Hello World Akka Streams!"
          push(out, line)
        }
      })
    }
  }
```

2. Then, create a file named `WordCounterSink.scala` inside the `com.packt.chapter8` package. This class will extend `GraphStage`. Define a `SinkShape` pulling string elements. The content should look like this:

```scala
package com.packt.chapter8

import akka.stream.{Attributes, Inlet, SinkShape}
import akka.stream.stage._

import scala.concurrent.duration._

class WordCounterSink extends GraphStage[SinkShape[String]] {
  val in: Inlet[String] = Inlet("WordCounterSink")
  override val shape: SinkShape[String] = SinkShape(in)

  override def createLogic(inheritedAttributes: Attributes):
    GraphStageLogic = new TimerGraphStageLogic(shape) {
      var counts = Map.empty[String, Int].withDefaultValue(0)

      override def preStart(): Unit = {
        schedulePeriodically(None, 5 seconds)
        pull(in)
      }

      setHandler(in, new InHandler {
        override def onPush(): Unit = {
          val word = grab(in)
          counts += word -> (counts(word) + 1)
          pull(in)
        }
      })

      override def onTimer(timerKey: Any) =
        println(s"At ${System.currentTimeMillis()}
        count map is $counts")
    }
}
```

3. Lastly, create a file named `CustomStagesApplication.scala` with the following content:

```scala
package com.packt.chapter8

import akka.actor.ActorSystem
import akka.stream.ActorMaterializer
import akka.stream.scaladsl.{Flow, Sink, Source}

object CustomStagesApplication extends App {

  implicit val actorSystem = ActorSystem("CustomStages")
  implicit val actorMaterializer = ActorMaterializer()

  val source = Source.fromGraph(new HelloAkkaStreamsSource())
  val upperCaseMapper = Flow[String].map(_.toUpperCase())
  val splitter = Flow[String].mapConcat(_.split(" ").toList)
  val punctuationMapper = Flow[String].map(_.replaceAll("""
  [p{Punct}&&[^.]]""", "").replaceAll(
    System.lineSeparator(), ""))
  val filterEmptyElements = Flow[String].filter(_.nonEmpty)
  val wordCounterSink = Sink.fromGraph(new WordCounterSink())

  val stream = source
    .via(upperCaseMapper)
    .via(splitter)
    .via(punctuationMapper)
    .via(filterEmptyElements)
    .to(wordCounterSink)

  stream.run()
}
```

4. Run the `CustomStagesApplication` application in either IntelliJ or CommandLine:

```
hveiga$ sbt "runMain com.packt.chapter8.CustomStagesApplication"
[info] Running com.packt.chapter8.CustomStagesApplication
At 1486357674134 count map is Map(HELLO -> 104733,
WORLD -> 104733, AKKA -> 104733, STREAMS -> 104733)
At 1486357679121 count map is Map(
HELLO -> 420147, WORLD -> 420147, AKKA -> 420147, STREAMS ->
420146)
```

How it works...

In this recipe, we implemented two custom stages. First, we created a custom Source stage. Since a Source emits elements into a stream, we implemented GraphStageLogic with an OutHandler. This handler provides the onPull method that will be called by the downstream stages when there is demand for new elements. In this example, we pushed a string.

Secondly, we created a custom Sink stage. This time, we implemented TimerGraphStageLogic with an InHandler since a Sink receives elements from a stream. TimerGraphStageLogic provides APIs to schedule messages within the stage. To request for more elements from the upstream, we used the pull and grab methods. These methods help consume elements from the stream and manage back pressure. Pull requests an element from the stream. Calling this method twice before an element has arrived will make it throw an exception. The grab method actually returns the element that comes from the stream. Therefore, it is required to call pull, and then grab to receive an element. In addition, we scheduled a None timer key to be periodically sent to the stage every 5 seconds. Every time the scheduler is triggered, the onTimer method is called with the timer key.

Finally, we used Source.fromGraph and Sink.fromGraph to instantiate our Source and Sink objects.

Error handling in Akka streams

It is a common mistake to develop applications assuming that there will be no unexpected issues. Akka provides a set of supervision strategies to deal with errors that happen in actors. Akka Streams is no different and provides a similar approach to deal with unexpected exceptions. For instance, these exceptions might occur when an element in the stream is not the expected type. In this recipe, we will see how to handle such errors.

Getting ready

We will use the same prerequisites as before. We will define a supervision strategy to handle certain types of error.

How to do it...

For this recipe, perform the following steps:

1. Create a file named `HandlingErrorsApplication.scala` inside the `com.packt.chapter8` package. This object will create a stream with two custom supervision strategies: one for a particular flow and one for the whole stream. The content should look like this:

```scala
package com.packt.chapter8

import akka.actor.ActorSystem
import akka.stream.{ActorAttributes, ActorMaterializer,
ActorMaterializerSettings, Supervision}
import akka.stream.scaladsl._

object HandlingErrorsApplication extends App {
  implicit val actorSystem = ActorSystem("HandlingErrors")
  val streamDecider: Supervision.Decider = {
    case e: IndexOutOfBoundsException =>
      println("Dropping element because of
      IndexOufOfBoundException. Resuming.")
      Supervision.Resume
    case _ => Supervision.Stop
  }

  val flowDecider: Supervision.Decider = {
    case e: IllegalArgumentException =>
      println("Dropping element because of
        IllegalArgumentException. Restarting.")
      Supervision.Restart
    case _ => Supervision.Stop
  }

  val actorMaterializerSettings =
    ActorMaterializerSettings(actorSystem)
      .withSupervisionStrategy(streamDecider)
  implicit val actorMaterializer =
    ActorMaterializer(actorMaterializerSettings)
  val words = List("Handling", "Errors", "In",
    "Akka", "Streams", "")

  val flow = Flow[String].map(word => {
    if(word.length == 0) throw new
      IllegalArgumentException("
        Empty words are not allowed") word
  }).withAttributes(
```

```
    ActorAttributes.supervisionStrategy(flowDecider))

  //We map and get the third character with array(2)
    Source(words).via(flow).map(array =>
    array(2)).to(Sink.foreach(println)).run()
}
```

2. Run the `HandlingErrorsApplication` application in either IntelliJ or the command line:

```
hveiga$ sbt "runMain
com.packt.chapter8.HandlingErrorsApplication"
[info] Running com.packt.chapter8.HandlingErrorsApplication
n
r
Dropping element because of IndexOufOfBoundException. Resuming.
k
r
Dropping element because of IllegalArgumentException. Restarting.
```

How it works...

In this recipe, we demonstrated how we can handle errors using supervision strategies. It is possible to set supervision strategies in two different levels: stream or stage. First, we have a supervision strategy called `streamDecider` that will be resumed if there is any `IndexOutOfBoundsException` and will stop in any other case. Second, we have a supervision strategy named `flowDecider` that will resume if there is any `IllegalArgumentException` and will stop in any other case. There are three possibilities when handling an error:

- `Stop`: The stream is completed with a failure.
- `Resume`: The element gets dropped and the stream keeps running and processing subsequent elements.
- `Restart`: The element gets dropped and the stream keeps running; however, it restarts the stage beforehand. For stateful stages, the state will be lost since the restart happens by creating a new instance of the stage.

To set the supervision strategy for all the stages in the stream, we need to pass the decider instance as part of `ActorMaterializerSettings` by calling `withSupervisionStrategy`. On the contrary, if we want our strategy to only apply to specific stages, we need to use `withAttributes` and pass `ActorAttributes.supervisionStrategy` to these specific stages. `Attributes` provide a way of controlling and tweaking your stages. The supervision strategy is just one aspect of what you can control through `Attributes`.

Pipelining and parallelizing streams

As seen in the previous recipes, Akka Streams provides a set of high-level APIs to process streams using actors as the underlying technology. `ActorMaterializer` is responsible for making this happen. `ActorMaterializer` allocates the resources and instantiates the classes required to have to turn your defined stream into a `RunnableGraph`. By default, all the processing stages are combined and executed sequentially. Therefore, a stage is limited to run at most once at any given time.

Having a sequential execution might be desired in some scenarios; however, other use cases could benefit from parallelizing some processing tasks. Akka Streams provides a method called `async` to indicate when a stage should run asynchronously and have its own internal actor. By default, all the stages not marked `async` will run in a single actor. Asynchronous stages have internal buffers to make the passing of messages more efficient. This is to reduce the overhead introduced by content switching.

In this recipe, we will demonstrate the different approaches for pipelining and parallelizing. We will use a washer/dryer example and use `GraphDSL` to create parallel stages. In a later recipe, we will explain `GraphDSL` in detail.

Getting ready

In this recipe, we will create three small applications: one to demonstrate synchronous pipelining, one to demonstrate asynchronous pipelining, and one to demonstrate parallelizing.

How to do it...

For this recipe, perform the following steps:

1. Create a file named `PipeliningParallelizing.scala` inside the `com.packt.chapter8` package. This trait contains all the stages necessary to form our different applications. The content should look like this:

```scala
package com.packt.chapter8

import akka.NotUsed
import akka.actor.ActorSystem
import akka.stream.{ActorMaterializer, FlowShape}
import akka.stream.scaladsl.{Balance, Flow,
GraphDSL, Merge, Sink, Source}
import scala.util.Random

trait PipeliningParallelizing extends App {
  implicit val actorSystem =
    ActorSystem("PipeliningParallelizing")
  implicit val actorMaterializer = ActorMaterializer()

  case class Wash(id: Int)
  case class Dry(id: Int)
  case class Done(id: Int)

  val tasks = (1 to 5).map(Wash)

  def washStage = Flow[Wash].map(wash => {
    val sleepTime = Random.nextInt(3) * 1000
    println(s"Washing ${wash.id}. It will take
      $sleepTime milliseconds.")
    Thread.sleep(sleepTime)
    Dry(wash.id)
  })

  def dryStage = Flow[Dry].map(dry => {
    val sleepTime = Random.nextInt(3) * 1000
    println(s"Drying ${dry.id}. It will take
      $sleepTime milliseconds.")
    Thread.sleep(sleepTime)
    Done(dry.id)
  })

  val parallelStage = Flow.fromGraph(
    GraphDSL.create() { implicit builder =>
    import GraphDSL.Implicits._
```

```
    val dispatchLaundry = builder.add(Balance[Wash](3))
    val mergeLaundry = builder.add(Merge[Done](3))

    dispatchLaundry.out(0) ~> washStage.async ~>
      dryStage.async ~> mergeLaundry.in(0)
    dispatchLaundry.out(1) ~> washStage.async ~>
      dryStage.async ~> mergeLaundry.in(1)
    dispatchLaundry.out(2) ~> washStage.async ~>
      dryStage.async ~> mergeLaundry.in(2)

    FlowShape(dispatchLaundry.in, mergeLaundry.out)
  })

  def runGraph(testingFlow: Flow[Wash,
    Done, NotUsed]) = Source(tasks).via(testingFlow).to(
    Sink.foreach(println)).run()
}
```

2. Create a file named `PipeliningParallelizingApplications.scala` in the `com.packt.chapter8.` package. This file will have three application objects with our stages set up a bit differently. The content should look like this:

```
package com.packt.chapter8

import akka.stream.scaladsl._

object SynchronousPipeliningApplication extends
  PipeliningParallelizing {
    runGraph(Flow[Wash].via(washStage).via(dryStage))
}

object AsynchronousPipeliningApplication extends
  PipeliningParallelizing {
    runGraph(Flow[Wash].via(
      washStage.async).via(dryStage.async))
}

object ParallelizingApplication extends
  PipeliningParallelizing {
    runGraph(Flow[Wash].via(parallelStage))
}
```

3. First, run the `SynchronousPipeliningApplication` application in either IntelliJ or the command line:

```
hveiga$ sbt "runMain
com.packt.chapter8.SynchronousPipeliningApplication"
[info] Running
com.packt.chapter8.SynchronousPipeliningApplication
Washing 1. It will take 1000 milliseconds.
Drying 1. It will take 2000 milliseconds.
Done(1)
Washing 2. It will take 2000 milliseconds.
Drying 2. It will take 2000 milliseconds.
Done(2)
Washing 3. It will take 2000 milliseconds.
Drying 3. It will take 1000 milliseconds.
Done(3)
Washing 4. It will take 1000 milliseconds.
Drying 4. It will take 1000 milliseconds.
Done(4)
Washing 5. It will take 0 milliseconds.
Drying 5. It will take 2000 milliseconds.
Done(5)
```

4. Second, run the `AsynchronousPipeliningApplication` application in either IntelliJ or CommandLine:

```
hveiga$ sbt "runMain
com.packt.chapter8.AsynchronousPipeliningApplication"
[info] Running
com.packt.chapter8.AsynchronousPipeliningApplication
Washing 1. It will take 2000 milliseconds.
Washing 2. It will take 0 milliseconds.
Drying 1. It will take 0 milliseconds.
Washing 3. It will take 1000 milliseconds.
Drying 2. It will take 0 milliseconds.
Done(1)
Done(2)
Washing 4. It will take 0 milliseconds.
Drying 3. It will take 2000 milliseconds.
Washing 5. It will take 0 milliseconds.
Drying 4. It will take 2000 milliseconds.
Done(3)
Drying 5. It will take 0 milliseconds.
Done(4)
Done(5)
```

5. Last, run the `ParallelizingApplication` application in either IntelliJ or CommandLine:

```
hveiga$ sbt "runMain com.packt.chapter8.ParallelizingApplication"
[info] Running com.packt.chapter8.ParallelizingApplication
Washing 1. It will take 0 milliseconds.
Washing 2. It will take 2000 milliseconds.
Drying 1. It will take 1000 milliseconds.
Done(1)
Washing 3. It will take 2000 milliseconds.
Drying 2. It will take 0 milliseconds.
Done(2)
Washing 4. It will take 1000 milliseconds.
Drying 3. It will take 1000 milliseconds.
Washing 5. It will take 0 milliseconds.
Drying 4. It will take 0 milliseconds.
Done(3)
Done(4)
Drying 5. It will take 1000 milliseconds.
Done(5)
```

How it works...

In this recipe, we demonstrated how streams behave within different execution boundaries. For this, we used a simple example of laundry with washing and drying tasks. First, we used the default behavior that encapsulates the execution within a single actor. When we execute this example, we see how the execution occurs sequentially: the **Sink** pulls an element; this element gets executed by `washStage`, then by `dryStage`, and finally, it reaches the **Sink**. Only when the element is successfully processed by the **Sink**, another element is pulled from the **Source**:

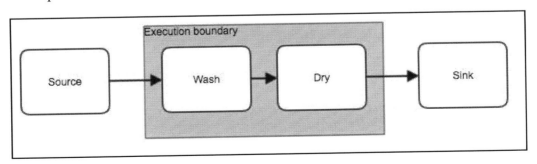

Second, we modified the asynchronous boundaries and provided the `async` modifier to both `washStage` and `dryStage`. This allows elements to be executed by `washStage` and `dryStage` asynchronously. Elements do no longer need to wait for both the stages to finish to be processed by the following stage, as we can see in the command-line output of the application:

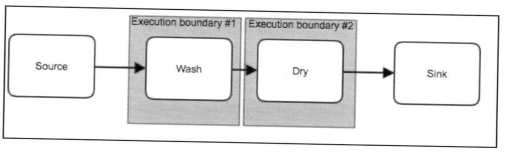

Finally, we used `GraphDSL` to parallelize the process into three different branches. A Balance is a stage with one input port and *n* output ports that distributes elements in the output ports as soon as there is demand. In our example, we had three output ports. A Merge is a stage with *n* input ports and one output port. This stage is responsible for merging different branches into a unique channel. After defining our graph, we return `FlowShape` to indicate this stage behaves as a flow with one input port and one output port. In this case, we can also see that the processing of messages happen asynchronously and in parallel by analyzing the command-line output:

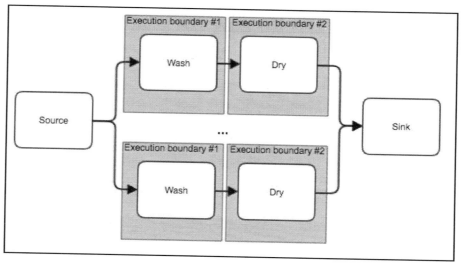

Working with streaming I/O

One of the most common scenarios of streaming is input-output applications. Nowadays, almost any modern application uses I/O to communicate with external entities or services. This is usually achieved by either listening on a port or pushing data to a remote system. For example, this concept is what the Internet of Things relies on when machines use I/O to contact with each other.

Akka Streams provide a set of Sources and Sinks to use files, InputStreams, and OutputStreams in your streams. In this recipe, we will create a stream to listen for words and count them as they come.

Getting ready

In this recipe, we will create a stream that will listen for TCP connections on port 1234. Once it receives an incoming message from the stream, it will count its words and return the counts in ByteString.

How to do it...

For this recipe, perform the following steps:

1. Create a file named WorkingIOStreamsApplication.scala inside the com.packt.chapter8 package. This object instantiates a stream to listen at 127.0.0.1 and port 1234. The content looks like this:

```
package com.packt.chapter8

import akka.actor.ActorSystem
import akka.stream.ActorMaterializer
import akka.stream.scaladsl.Tcp.{IncomingConnection,
ServerBinding}
import akka.stream.scaladsl._
import akka.util.ByteString

import scala.concurrent.Future

object WorkingIOStreamsApplication extends App {

  implicit val actorSystem = ActorSystem("WorkingIOStreams")
  implicit val actorMaterializer = ActorMaterializer()
```

```
val MaxGroups = 1000

val connections = Tcp().bind("127.0.0.1", 1234)
connections.runForeach(connection =>
  connection.handleWith(wordCount))

val wordCount =
  Flow[ByteString].map(_.utf8String.toUpperCase)
  .mapConcat(_.split(" ").toList)
  .collect { case w if w.nonEmpty =>
    w.replaceAll("""[p{Punct}&&[^.]]""",
    "").replaceAll(System.lineSeparator(), "") }
  .groupBy(MaxGroups, identity)
  .map(_ -> 1)
  .reduce((l, r) => (l._1, l._2 + r._2))
  .mergeSubstreams
  .map(x => ByteString(s"[${x._1} => ${x._2}]n"))
}
```

2. Then, run the `WorkingIOStreamsApplication` application in either IntelliJ or CommandLine:

```
hveiga$ sbt "runMain
com.packt.chapter8.WorkingIOStreamsApplication"
[info] Running com.packt.chapter8.WorkingIOStreamsApplication
```

3. After that, use a tool to push a stream to the TCP server. In our case, we will use `netcat` (nc in Mac OS):

```
echo -n "A very very repetitive message to
count words" | netcat 127.0.0.1 1234
```

4. You should see the following message coming back from your stream:

```
hveiga$ echo -n "A very very repetitive message to count words" |
netcat 127.0.0.1 1234
[A => 1]
[MESSAGE => 1]
[REPETITIVE => 1]
[WORDS => 1]
[COUNT => 1]
[TO => 1]
[VERY => 2]
```

How it works...

In this recipe, we demonstrated how to create a streaming application that listens for TCP connections. `Tcp.bind()` is responsible for creating the listener in the given hostname and port. In this case, the stream does not have a Sink explicitly defined. This is because we are using the helper method `runForeach`, which is an alias of `Sink.foreach`.

It is good to mention that each `connection` is a Flow that represents a real incoming connection, and it can be materialized only once. That's why this Flow cannot be reused as other Flows can. We used the `handleWith` method to provide a word count. This `wordCount` flow ingests the incoming messages from the TCP connection and returns the element emitted by the last transformation. In this case, it needs to be of the type `ByteString`:

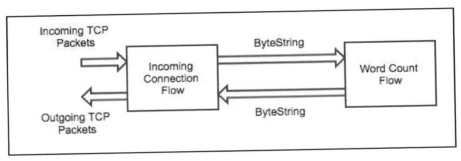

Integrating streams with Akka actors

The stages of a stream are ultimately lines of code that are **fused** and run on actors. This is why it is natural that Akka Stream has full integration with Akka actors. At the time of writing, there are multiple ways of interacting with Actors. One possibility is to use the traits named `ActorPublisher` and `ActorSubscriber`. These traits create an actor source or sink; however, they do not honor the back-pressure mechanism, and there are plans to decommission them in Akka 2.5+. Therefore, it is not recommended that you use them.

Instead of using `ActorPublisher` and `ActorSubscriber`, we will see `Source.queue` for our Source actor, `Sink.actorRefWithAck` for our Sink actor, and `mapAsync` plus `ask` for our Flow.

Getting ready

In this recipe, we will see how to create a Source that can emit elements into a stream, how to create a flow that can ask an actor, and how to create a Sink that pulls elements from a stream.

How to do it...

For this recipe, perform the following steps:

1. Create a file named `StringCleanerActor.scala` inside the `com.packt.chapter8` package. This class will be an actor responsible for removing punctuation characters from strings. The content should look like this:

```
package com.packt.chapter8

import akka.actor.Actor

class StringCleanerActor extends Actor {
  def receive = {
    case s : String =>
      println(s"Cleaning [$s] in StringCleaner")
      sender ! s.replaceAll("""[p{Punct}&&[^.]]""",
        "").replaceAll(System.lineSeparator(), "")
  }
}
```

2. Create a file named `SinkActor.scala` inside the `com.packt.chapter8` package. This class will be the Sink actor that will consume elements from the stream:

```
package com.packt.chapter8

import akka.actor.Actor
import com.packt.chapter8.SinkActor.{AckSinkActor,
  InitSinkActor}

object SinkActor {
  case object CompletedSinkActor
  case object AckSinkActor
  case object InitSinkActor
}
```

```
class SinkActor extends Actor {
  def receive = {
    case InitSinkActor =>
      println("SinkActor initialized")
      sender ! AckSinkActor
    case something =>
      println(s"Received [$something] in SinkActor")
      sender ! AckSinkActor
  }
}
```

3. Create a file named `SourceActor.scala` inside
   the `com.packt.chapter8` package. This class will be a Source actor that will
   emit elements into the stream. To achieve this, it needs the reference to the queue
   that we will pass as a class parameter:

```
package com.packt.chapter8

import akka.actor.{Actor, Props}
import akka.stream.scaladsl.SourceQueueWithComplete

import scala.concurrent.duration._

object SourceActor {
  case object Tick
  def props(sourceQueue: SourceQueueWithComplete[String]) =
    Props(new SourceActor(sourceQueue))
}

class SourceActor(sourceQueue:
  SourceQueueWithComplete[String]) extends Actor {
    import SourceActor._
    import context.dispatcher

  override def preStart() = {
    context.system.scheduler.schedule(0 seconds,
      5 seconds, self, Tick)
  }

  def receive = {
    case Tick =>
      println(s"Offering element from SourceActor")
      sourceQueue.offer("Integrating!!###
        Akka$$$ Actors? with}{ Akka** Streams")
  }
}
```

4. Once you create your actor classes, create the stream. Create a file named `IntegratingWithActorsApplication.scala` inside the `com.packt.chapter8` package with the following contents:

```
package com.packt.chapter8

import akka.actor.{ActorSystem, Props}
import akka.stream.{ActorMaterializer, OverflowStrategy}
import akka.stream.scaladsl._
import akka.pattern.ask
import akka.util.Timeout
import com.packt.chapter8.SinkActor.{AckSinkActor,
  CompletedSinkActor, InitSinkActor}

import scala.concurrent.duration._

object IntegratingWithActorsApplication extends App {

  implicit val actorSystem =
    ActorSystem("IntegratingWithActors")
  implicit val actorMaterializer = ActorMaterializer()

  implicit val askTimeout = Timeout(5 seconds)
  val stringCleaner =
    actorSystem.actorOf(Props[StringCleanerActor])
  val sinkActor = actorSystem.actorOf(Props[SinkActor])

  val source = Source.queue[String](100,
    OverflowStrategy.backpressure)
  val sink = Sink.actorRefWithAck[String](sinkActor,
    InitSinkActor, AckSinkActor, CompletedSinkActor)
  val queue = source
    .mapAsync(parallelism = 2)(elem => (stringCleaner ?
      elem).mapTo[String])
    .to(sink)
    .run()

  actorSystem.actorOf(SourceActor.props(queue))
}
```

5. Then, run the `WorkingIOStreamsApplication` application in either IntelliJ or CommandLine:

```
hveiga$ sbt "runMain
com.packt.chapter8.IntegratingWithActorsApplication"
[info] Running
com.packt.chapter8.IntegratingWithActorsApplication
```

```
Offering element from SourceActor
SinkActor initialized
Cleaning [Integrating!!### Akka$$$ Actors? with}{ Akka**
Streams] in StringCleaner
Received [Integrating Akka Actors with Akka Streams] in
SinkActor
```

How it works...

In this recipe, we demonstrated how to make Akka actors interact with streams. To begin with, we created a SourceActor responsible for pushing data into the stream. Akka Streams provides a `Source.queue` approach, where a queue is used to buffer elements while the stream is working on processing other elements. When instantiating the queue, you provide a buffer size and `OverflowStrategy`. This overflow strategy defines how the queue should behave when the buffer is full and you try to insert new elements. We used `backpressure` to slow down the producer of data and avoid the dropping of elements. However, other strategies allow you to drop elements from the buffer or even the whole buffer. You use `queue.offer` to push an element into the queue. Note that Akka Streams also provides a `Source.actorRef` approach, where there is no backpressure mechanism.

Second, we used a combination of `mapAsync` plus `ask` to have an asynchronous stage, where you send an element to an actor and wait for the actor to send a message back. In our example, this actor is `StringCleanerActor`. When using `ask`, it is necessary to set `Timeout` so the stream does not wait for your element to come back forever.

Finally, we had a Sink actor. Akka Streams provides a `Sink.actorRefWithAck` method where you need to pass the reference to your actor, a message to signal the stream has been initialized, a message to signal acks, and a message to signal the completion of the stream. In our case, we created three simple case objects: `InitSinkActor`, `AckSinkActor`, and `CompleteSinkActor`. When the actor receives `InitSinkActor`, it needs to send back an `AckSinkActor` message to signal it is ready to consume elements. The same happens when any other element comes to the actor. This is how you can implement back pressure, so no new message will be sent to your actor if your actor is not ready to continue with the processing of new elements. It is the same as Source; Akka Streams provides a variant, namely `Sink.actorRef`, where there is no back-pressure mechanism and messages pile up in the mailbox of your actor. This might lead to memory leaks if your actor is not able to process these messages at the same rate the stream is pushing them.

Working with graphs

Streams are ultimately graphs. Stages can be seen as graph nodes with a certain number of input and output ports, and streams define how these nodes are connected. Akka Streams brings a `GraphDSL` to design your streams in a more intuitive way. This `GraphDSL` can be used for multiple purposes:

- Design and compose complicated stages that would act as unique stages. These stages will also be reusable.
- Design runnable graphs.

A runnable graph is a type of stream where there is at least one Source and one Sink and all the ports of all the stages are connected. There are built-in stages available to combine different streams. The most common junction stages are as follows:

- `Merge`: This is a stage with *n* input ports and one output port. It merges all the incoming elements from the input with the output.
- `Balance`: This is a stage with one input port and *n* output port. It distributes incoming elements to output ports based on demand.
- `Broadcast`: This is a stage with one input port and *n* output ports. It pushes incoming elements to all the output ports.

There are other built-in stages, but we need to remember that if we need something that is not covered by the built-in stage, we can always create our custom stage, as explained in the previous section, *Custom Stream Processing*. Unlike other frameworks, Akka Streams allows you to have cyclic graphs; however, you need to pay special attention to avoid loops and possible thread deadlocks.

Getting ready

In this recipe, we will create a graph using `GraphDSL`, as follows:

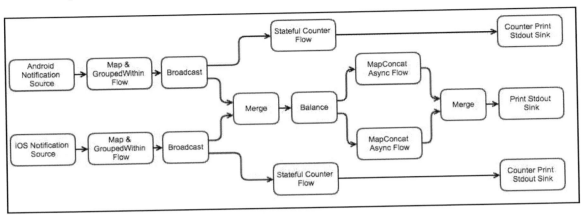

We will simulate an environment in which we would get notifications from Android and iOS phones. We will map each notification to a `GenericMsg` class and use it to count them separately with our stateful counter flows. Also, we will merge them, map them, and print them to the standard output.

How to do it...

For this recipe, perform the following steps:

1. Create a file named `StatefulCounterFlow.scala` inside the `com.packt.chapter8` package. This class will be `GraphStage` of `FlowShape` with a counter. The content should look like this:

```
package com.packt.chapter8

import akka.stream.{Attributes, FlowShape, Inlet, Outlet}
import akka.stream.stage.{GraphStage, GraphStageLogic,
   InHandler, OutHandler}
import com.packt.chapter8.
   WorkingWithGraphsApplication.GenericMsg

class StatefulCounterFlow extends
   GraphStage[FlowShape[Seq[GenericMsg], Int]] {

   val in: Inlet[Seq[GenericMsg]] =
```

```
        Inlet("IncomingGenericMsg")
  val out: Outlet[Int] = Outlet("OutgoingCount")
  override val shape: FlowShape[Seq[GenericMsg], Int] =
    FlowShape(in, out)

  override def createLogic(inheritedAttributes: Attributes):
    GraphStageLogic =
      new GraphStageLogic(shape) {
        var count = 0

        setHandler(in, new InHandler {
          override def onPush() = {
            val elem = grab(in)
            count += elem.size
            push(out, count)
          }
        })

        setHandler(out, new OutHandler {
          override def onPull() = {
            pull(in)
          }
        })
      }
  }
}
```

2. Create a file named `WorkingWithGraphs.scala` inside the `com.packt.chapter8` package. This class defines the whole stream using GraphDSL:

```
package com.packt.chapter8

import akka.actor.ActorSystem
import akka.stream._
import akka.stream.scaladsl.{Balance, Broadcast,
  Flow, GraphDSL, Merge, RunnableGraph, Sink, Source}
import scala.concurrent.duration._
import scala.util.Random


object WorkingWithGraphsApplication extends App {

  implicit val actorSystem = ActorSystem("WorkingWithGraphs")
  implicit val actorMaterializer = ActorMaterializer()

  trait MobileMsg {
    def id = Random.nextInt(1000)
```

```scala
    def toGenMsg(origin: String) = GenericMsg(id, origin)
}
class AndroidMsg extends MobileMsg
class IosMsg extends MobileMsg
case class GenericMsg(id: Int, origin: String)

val graph = RunnableGraph.fromGraph(
  GraphDSL.create() { implicit builder =>
    import GraphDSL.Implicits._

    //Sources
    val androidNotification = Source.tick(
      2 seconds, 500 millis, new AndroidMsg)
    val iOSNotification = Source.tick(700 millis,
      600 millis, new IosMsg)

    //Flow
    val groupAndroid = Flow[AndroidMsg].map(
    _.toGenMsg("ANDROID")).groupedWithin(5, 5
      seconds).async
    val groupIos = Flow[IosMsg].map(
    _.toGenMsg("IOS")).groupedWithin(5, 5 seconds).async
    def counter = Flow[Seq[GenericMsg]].via(new
      StatefulCounterFlow())
    val mapper = Flow[Seq[GenericMsg]].mapConcat(_.toList)

    //Junctions
    val aBroadcast =
      builder.add(Broadcast[Seq[GenericMsg]](2))
    val iBroadcast =
      builder.add(Broadcast[Seq[GenericMsg]](2))
    val balancer = builder.add(Balance[Seq[GenericMsg]](2))
    val notitificationMerge =
      builder.add(Merge[Seq[GenericMsg]](2))
    val genericNotitificationMerge =
      builder.add(Merge[GenericMsg](2))

    //Sink
    def counterSink(s: String) = Sink.foreach[Int](x =>
      println(s"$s: [$x]"))

    //Graph
    androidNotification ~> groupAndroid ~> aBroadcast ~>
    counter ~> counterSink("Android") aBroadcast ~>
    notitificationMerge
    iBroadcast ~> notitificationMerge
    iOSNotification ~> groupIos ~> iBroadcast ~> counter ~>
    counterSink("Ios")
```

```
notitificationMerge ~> balancer ~> mapper.async ~>
genericNotitificationMerge
balancer ~> mapper.async ~> genericNotitificationMerge

genericNotitificationMerge ~> Sink.foreach(println)

ClosedShape
})
graph.run()
}
```

3. Then, run the `WorkingWithGraphsApplication` application in either IntelliJ or CommandLine:

```
hveiga$ sbt "runMain
com.packt.chapter8.WorkingWithGraphsApplication"
[info] Running com.packt.chapter8.WorkingWithGraphsApplication
Ios: [5]
GenericMsg(904,IOS)
GenericMsg(410,IOS)
GenericMsg(584,IOS)
GenericMsg(350,IOS)
GenericMsg(143,IOS)
Android: [5]
GenericMsg(270,ANDROID)
GenericMsg(301,ANDROID)
GenericMsg(413,ANDROID)
GenericMsg(50,ANDROID)
GenericMsg(585,ANDROID)
```

How it works...

In this recipe, we demonstrated how to use the `GraphDSL`. To begin with, we defined our sources. To simulate our notifications coming from Android and iOS, we created two classes: `AndroidMsg` and `IosMsg`. We can emit elements periodically using `Source.tick`, as we did. Secondly, we defined our Flows to map, group, and count our elements.

Afterward, we instantiated our junctions: `Merge`, `Broadcast`, and `Balance`. It is worth mentioning that to be able to use junctions properly in the graph, we need to add them through `builder`. The `builder` is a helper to provide another graph. It returns the appropriate shape with the ports that you will need to connect. When creating any of the junctions, we need to provide the number of ports. For instance, `Merge(2)` means that this stage has two input ports and one output port. Finally, we defined a special Sink to print out the count of elements after `StatefulCounterFlow`.

Once we have all the stages ready, we just need to connect them. We connect each stage using the ~> method. This method is available by importing the Implicits from `GraphDSL`. As we said before, we need to connect all the ports in order to end up with `RunnableGraph`. For example, all the flows need to have one ~> before and one ~> after. However, our `Broadcast(2)` needs to have one ~> before and two ~> after to have all its ports connected. At last, we return `ClosedShape`. This tells `GraphDSL` that you want to have a runnable closed graph. Not connecting all the ports will throw an exception when instantiating the graph.

Processing RabbitMQ messages with Akka streams

Messaging brokers have become the central piece of many distributed and real-time systems. RabbitMQ is one of most commonly used brokers nowadays. It is an open source Advanced Message Queuing Protocol (AMQP) and Message Queue Telemetry Transport (MQTT) broker that provides a clustered high-availability solution to decouple applications using the publisher-subscriber pattern.

In this recipe, we will see how to consume AMQP messages from a RabbitMQ queue into your stream. Once consumed, we will transform the message and publish it back to RabbitMQ. To achieve this, we are going to use the AMQP module from Alpakka. Alpakka is a community-driven repository that provides useful Akka Streams stages for the most common protocols and formats. For example, there are connectors for Amazon S3, Amazon SQS, JMS, Cassandra, and many others.

 To check all the available Alpakka modules, visit their GitHub repository at `https://github.com/akka/alpakka`.

Getting ready

In order to test this recipe, we need to have a RabbitMQ broker installed and running. Follow this link to download and install RabbitMQ locally: `http://www.rabbitmq.com/download.html`. From this point, we will assume there is a local broker running on port `5672` with `username/password guest/guest`. Remember that these credentials are only valid if you access RabbitMQ locally. Remote connection will be rejected if the provided credentials are `guest/guest`:

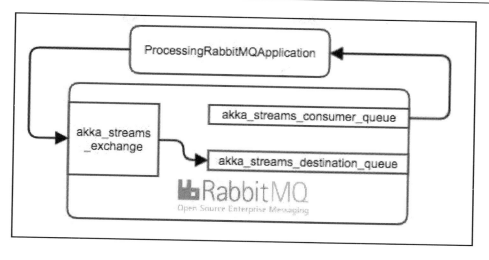

How to do it...

For this recipe, perform the following steps:

1. Get the required dependency. For this, add the following line to your `build.sbt` file:

```
libraryDependencies += "com.lightbend.akka" %
"akka-stream-alpakka-amqp_2.11" % "0.5"
```

2. Run `sbt update` to retrieve the dependencies from the central repository.

3. Create a file named `ProcessingRabbitMQApplication.scala` inside the `com.packt.chapter8` package. Here, define your AMQP Source and Sink and a mapping stage to apply uppercase to the String value. The content should look like this:

```
package com.packt.chapter8

import akka.actor.ActorSystem
import akka.stream.ActorMaterializer
import akka.stream.alpakka.amqp._
import akka.stream.alpakka.amqp.scaladsl.{AmqpSink,
  AmqpSource}
import akka.util.ByteString

object ProcessingRabbitMQApplication extends App {
```

```
implicit val actorSystem = ActorSystem("SimpleStream")
implicit val actorMaterializer = ActorMaterializer()

val consumerQueueName = "akka_streams_consumer_queue"
val consumerQueueDeclaration =
QueueDeclaration(consumerQueueName)
val sourceDeclarations = Seq(consumerQueueDeclaration)

val exchangeName = "akka_streams_exchange"
val exchangeDeclaration = ExchangeDeclaration(
exchangeName, "direct")
val destinationQueueName = "akka_streams_destination_queue"
val destinationQueueDeclaration =
QueueDeclaration(destinationQueueName)
val bindingDeclaration = BindingDeclaration(
destinationQueueName, exchangeName)
val sinkDeclarations = Seq(exchangeDeclaration,
destinationQueueDeclaration, bindingDeclaration)

val credentials = AmqpCredentials("guest", "guest")
val connectionSetting = AmqpConnectionDetails(
"127.0.0.1", 5672, Some(credentials))
val amqpSourceConfig = NamedQueueSourceSettings(
connectionSetting, consumerQueueName, sourceDeclarations)
val rabbitMQSource = AmqpSource(amqpSourceConfig, 1000)
val amqpSinkConfig = AmqpSinkSettings(connectionSetting,
Some(exchangeName), None, sinkDeclarations)
val rabbitMQSink = AmqpSink(amqpSinkConfig)

val stream = rabbitMQSource
.map(incomingMessage => {
  val upperCased =
    incomingMessage.bytes.utf8String.toUpperCase
  OutgoingMessage(bytes = ByteString(upperCased),
  immediate = false,
  mandatory = false,
  props = None)
})
.to(rabbitMQSink)

stream.run()
}
```

4. Run the application `ProcessingRabbitMQApplication` either in IntelliJ or CommandLine:

```
hveiga$ sbt "runMain
com.packt.chapter8.ProcessingRabbitMQApplication"
[info] Running com.packt.chapter8.ProcessingRabbitMQApplication
```

5. Open the web interface that the RabbitMQ server provides by accessing `http://localhost:15672/`. When it asks for the credentials, give the username `guest` and the password `guest`. If you go to the **Queues** tab now, you should see the two queues we created:

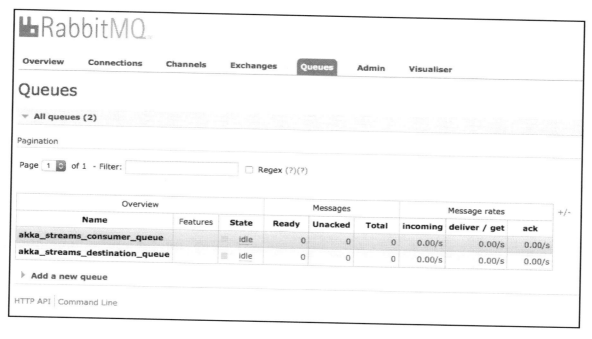

6. Click on **akka_streams_consumer_queue** and use the **Publish message** section to publish a message:

7. Finally, go back to the **Queues** tab and click on
   akka_streams_destination_queue. You should see there is a new message in the
   queue:

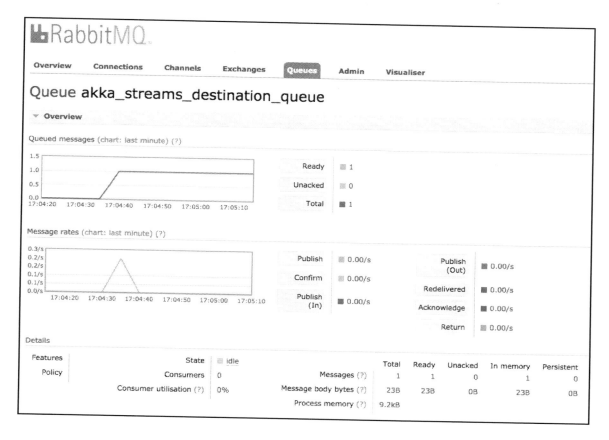

7. Then use the **Get messages** section to get a message and see the uppercase version of the message you published initially:

How it works...

In this recipe, we demonstrated how to use the AMQP connector that the Alpakka project provides. In our scenario, we consumed messages from an AMQP queue called **akka_streams_consumer_queue**. The `amqpSource` is a Source object responsible for taking these messages and pushing them into the stream using the `IncomingMessage` type. After that, we mapped them to `OutgoingMessage` so the `amqpSink` Sink object understands them and is able to push them to an AMQP exchange.

While configuring our source and sink, we also define our queues, exchange, and binding declarations. This is required because these elements need to exist in the RabbitMQ server before you use them. If you try to use them before declaring them, an exception will be thrown.

Integrating Akka Streams with Kafka using Reactive Kafka

Apache Kafka is a distributed messaging system that is becoming an industry favorite. A messaging system is commonly used to decouple application components and help scale out system architectures. Apache Kafka has the peculiarity of writing messages directly into the disk instead of memory. Initially, this might seem like a showstopper. However, this technique allows Apache Kafka to achieve extremely high message rates thanks to both sequential writes and the partitioning system. Kafka has demonstrated that it is capable of consuming and delivering millions of messages per second.

In this recipe, we will use Kafka 0.10.1. We will create two streams. The first one will publish to a Kafka topic. The second one will consume from it. Both the streams use the same topic, namely akka_streams_topic.

Getting ready

For this recipe, we will assume we have an Apache Kafka broker running locally on port 9092. In order to install it, follow the instructions in the official documentation at `https://kafka.apache.org/`. Note that we will be using Apache Kafka 0.10.1. This recipe might not be compatible with other Kafka versions.

How to do it...

For this recipe, perform the following steps:

1. Bring the required dependency. For this, add the following line to your `build.sbt` file:

   ```
   libraryDependencies += "com.typesafe.akka" %
       "akka-stream-kafka_2.11" % "0.13"
   ```

2. Run `sbt update` to retrieve the dependencies from the central repository.

3. Create a file named `ProcessingKafkaApplication.scala` inside the `com.packt.chapter8` package. Here, define a graph that will produce some messages to our Kafka topic and consume them. The content should look like this:

   ```scala
   package com.packt.chapter8

   import akka.actor.ActorSystem
   import akka.kafka.scaladsl.{Consumer, Producer}
   import akka.kafka.{ConsumerSettings,
       ProducerSettings, Subscriptions}
   import akka.stream.{ActorMaterializer, ClosedShape}
   import akka.stream.scaladsl.{Flow, GraphDSL,
       RunnableGraph, Sink, Source}
   import org.apache.kafka.clients.consumer.{ConsumerConfig,
       ConsumerRecord}
   import org.apache.kafka.clients.producer.ProducerRecord
   import org.apache.kafka.common.TopicPartition
   import org.apache.kafka.common.serialization.{
       ByteArrayDeserializer, ByteArraySerializer,
           StringDeserializer, StringSerializer}

   import scala.concurrent.duration._

   object ProcessingKafkaApplication extends App {
       implicit val actorSystem = ActorSystem("SimpleStream")
       implicit val actorMaterializer = ActorMaterializer()

       val bootstrapServers = "localhost:9092"
       val kafkaTopic = "akka_streams_topic"
       val partition = 0
       val subscription = Subscriptions.assignment(new
           TopicPartition(kafkaTopic, partition))

       val consumerSettings = ConsumerSettings(actorSystem,
   ```

```
    new ByteArrayDeserializer, new StringDeserializer)
    .withBootstrapServers(bootstrapServers)
    .withGroupId("akka_streams_group")
    .withProperty(ConsumerConfig.AUTO_OFFSET_RESET_CONFIG,
    "earliest")

val producerSettings = ProducerSettings(actorSystem,
    new ByteArraySerializer, new StringSerializer)
    .withBootstrapServers(bootstrapServers)

val runnableGraph = RunnableGraph.fromGraph(
    GraphDSL.create() { implicit builder =>
    import GraphDSL.Implicits._

    val tickSource = Source.tick(0 seconds, 5 seconds,
    "Hello from akka streams through ")
    val kafkaSource = Consumer.plainSource(
        consumerSettings, subscription)
    val kafkaSink = Producer.plainSink(producerSettings)
    val printlnSink = Sink.foreach(println)

    val mapToProducerRecord = Flow[String].map(elem =>
        new ProducerRecord[Array[Byte], String](
        kafkaTopic, elem))
    val mapFromConsumerRecord =
        Flow[ConsumerRecord[Array[Byte], String]].map(
        record => record.value())

    tickSource   ~> mapToProducerRecord   ~> kafkaSink
    kafkaSource ~> mapFromConsumerRecord ~> printlnSink

    ClosedShape
    })

    runnableGraph.run()
}
```

4. Run the `ProcessingKafkaApplication` application in either IntelliJ or CommandLine:

```
hveiga$ sbt "runMain
com.packt.chapter8.ProcessingKafkaApplication"
[info] Running com.packt.chapter8.ProcessingKafkaApplication
Hello from Akka Streams using Kafka!
Hello from Akka Streams using Kafka!
```

How it works...

In this recipe, we demonstrated how to produce and consume records from an Apache Kafka topic. Apache Kafka uses a Key-Value approach to deal with data. This Key-Value pair helps you distribute your records among all the available partitions in the Kafka cluster. Keys and Values need to be serialized and deserialized. For this purpose, Apache Kafka provides a set of predefined serializers and deserializers. In our case, we used `Array[Byte]` for Key and `String` for Value.

First, we produced data to the topic. For this purpose, we used `Source.tick` that emits a string element periodically. These string elements were then mapped to `ProducerRecord` objects. `ProducerRecord` is the type a producer understands to push data to the Apache Kafka cluster. Note that when instantiating a new `ProducerRecord`, it is required to set the Key and Value types, as well as which topic this record should be directed to. At last, we created our `Producer.plainSink` to publish the data. This producer is configured through the `ProducerSettings`. The `ProducerSettings` class and defined through parameters such as server connection details (`bootstrapServers`) or Key/Value serializers.

Once we have the producing part ready to fire new elements to our Kafka topic, we need to set up a second stream to consume these records. To start consuming them, we need to instantiate a Kafka source through `Consumer.plainSource`. To create it, we need to provide the `ConsumerSettings` and `Subscription` arguments. `ConsumerSettings` is similar to `ProducerSettings`; it defines the bootstrap servers, deserializers, group identifier, and special properties. In our example, we used `AUTO_OFFSET_RESET_CONFIG` to reset the offset config automatically in case the offset does not exist in the server. `Subscription` creates a subscription in the Apache Kafka broker that defines what topic and partition this consumer needs to read from. After fetching the elements, we map them from `ConsumerRecord` to `String`. `ConsumerRecord` is the object type a consumer emits when an event comes from Kafka. `ConsumerRecord` also needs to define the Key and Value types. After this, we simply used `println` to print our string elements; we can see it in our output: `Hello from Akka Streams using Kafka!`.

It is also possible to configure your consumer to use a different offset than 0. In some scenarios, you might want to resume your processing from an specific offset. This can be achieved by storing the offset in an external storage location and using the `Subscription.assignmentWithOffset` class when creating your consumer. In addition, our example commits offsets automatically. This means when we receive a message, we acknowledge it so the broker understands we don't need to consume it again. Some use cases require you to do the processing of messages; once done, let the Kafka broker know it needs to increment the offset. In this case, you need to use a combination of `Consumer.committableSource` and `Producer.commitableSink` to achieve this.

9
Akka HTTP

In this chapter, we will cover the following recipes:

- Creating a minimal HTTP server using Akka HTTP
- Consuming Akka HTTP services using a client-side API
- Writing routing DSL for HTTP servers
- Understanding the configuration of Akka HTTP
- Marshaling and unmarshaling data
- Encoding and decoding data
- Understanding directives
- Exception handling
- Uploading a file using Akka HTTP
- Building JSON support with Akka HTTP
- XML support with Akka HTTP

Introduction

Akka HTTP is a streaming-first library that focuses on leveraging Akka Streams and Akka actors. Akka HTTP is another module under the Lightbend umbrella that provides comprehensive and easy APIs to create both HTTP servers and clients.

Akka HTTP defines different layers to do so and lets the developer decide how abstracted he or she wants to be compared to the low-level implementation protocol, depending on the use case. From the low-level point of view, it allows you to have actors deal with the incoming HTTP messages as messages. From the high-level point of view, it provides a directive-based routing DSL that helps you define what to do with the incoming requests, depending on their headers or content. The library also provides great flexibility regarding marshaling, encoding, customization, and extensibility to cover all the possible scenarios.

Akka HTTP was initially developed as a different project named Spray. Currently, it is maintained by the Akka team, but it is also heavily driven by the community. Akka HTTP is also moving ahead with an asynchronous implementation of HTTP2, the newer version of the HTTP protocol created to speed up the communication of systems on the Internet.

Creating a minimal HTTP server using Akka HTTP

In this recipe, we will see how to create a minimal HTTP server using routing DSL. We will also make use of the HttpApp trait, which provides a precooked server ready to be run.

Getting ready

To step through this recipe, we need to import the Hello-Akka project; all the other prerequisites are the same as before. We need to get the required dependencies for http this time.

How to do it...

For this recipe, perform the following steps:

1. Get the required dependencies.
2. Edit the build.sbt file and add the Akka HTTP dependency as follows:

```
libraryDependencies += "com.typesafe.akka" %
   "akka-http_2.11" % "10.0.5"
```

3. Now create a file named `MinimalHttpServer.scala`. Define your server and a small object to run it:

```
package com.packt.chapter9

import akka.http.scaladsl.model.{ContentTypes, HttpEntity}
import akka.http.scaladsl.server.HttpApp
import akka.http.scaladsl.server.Directives._
import akka.http.scaladsl.settings.ServerSettings
import com.typesafe.config.ConfigFactory

object MinimalHttpServer extends HttpApp {
def route =
    pathPrefix("v1") {
      path("id" / Segment) { id =>
        get {
         complete(HttpEntity(ContentTypes.`text/html(UTF-8)`,
         s"<h1>Hello $id from Akka Http!</h1>"))
        } ~
        post {
          entity(as[String]) { entity =>
            complete(HttpEntity(ContentTypes.`text/html(
            UTF-8)`, s"<b>Thanks $id for posting
            your message <i>$entity</i></b>"))
          }
        }
      }
    }
}

object MinimalHttpServerApplication extends App {
    MinimalHttpServer.startServer("0.0.0.0", 8088,
    ServerSettings(ConfigFactory.load))
}
```

4. Run the `MinimalHttpServerApplication` application in either IntelliJ or the command-line shell:

```
hveiga$ sbt "runMain
com.packt.chapter9.MinimalHttpServerApplication"
[info] Running com.packt.chapter9.MinimalHttpServerApplication
Press RETURN to stop...
[INFO] [akka.actor.ActorSystemImpl(MinimalHttpServer)] Server
online at http://0:0:0:0:0:0:0:0:8088/
```

5. Now run a curl command to receive a GET response from your running server. To do so, run the `curl http://localhost:8088/v1/id/ALICE` command and you should see the server response printed out:

```
hveiga$ curl http://localhost:8088/v1/id/ALICE
<h1>Hello ALICE from Akka Http!</h1>
```

6. In the same command-line shell, run the following curl command to push the received response: `curl -X POST --data 'Akka Http is Cool' http://localhost:8088/v1/id/ALICE`. You should see the server response printed out:

```
hveiga$ curl -X POST --data 'Akka Http is Cool'
http://localhost:8088/v1/id/ALICE
<b>Thanks ALICE for posting your message
<i>Akka Http is Cool</i></b>
```

How it works...

In this recipe, we created a small HTTP server using `HttpApp`. This trait provides all of the code required to run a minimal HTTP server. When we extend the trait in our object, we need to implement routes, which define how to handle your incoming HTTP requests and respond to them. It is in routes that we can add different HTTP endpoints using directives. Directives are small code blocks and can be composed to form routes. In our example, we used the directives `pathPrefix`, `path`, `get`, `post`, and `entity`. As you can see, routing DSL is powerful and straightforward. Just by looking at the route definition, you understand how a request is going to be handled. We will see routing DSL in more depth in the *Writing routing DSL for http servers* recipe.

Once we define our routes, we need to run our server. For this, `HttpApp` provides the `startServer` method. The `startServer` method expects a hostname and port where the server will be listening as well as a `ServerSettings` object. This object is used to provide more advanced configurations for your servers, such as request or bind timeouts. When we run our application, we can see that there is a log that announces the server is ready to receive requests. In our case, we used curl to test a GET request as well as a POST request; however, it should be possible to use any other HTTP client, for example, a browser:

Once we are done with our server, we can just press **RETURN** and our App will terminate. This functionality is provided by the `HttpApp` trait as well.

Consuming Akka HTTP services using a client-side API

Akka HTTP provides capabilities to consume remote HTTP services. Other frameworks, such as Apache HttpComponents, also provide the same functionality; however, Akka HTTP is asynchronous and streaming-first by default. The Akka HTTP client API uses the same abstractions as the HTTP server API, but it adds the concept of connection pooling. This concept allows developers to reuse connections and improve performance.

It is important to mention that, since Akka HTTP is streaming-first and built on top of Akka streams, there is built-in back pressure. This means that it is required to consume the HTTP entities to signal the stream that you are good to receive new ones. This is required even if you want to discard them. Not doing so might impact your application negatively without apparent reason. The HTTP client API is divided into three levels of abstraction:

- **Connection level**: This represents the lowest level. It provides full control of HTTP connections. It is probably too low level for most use cases.
- **Host level**: This is similar to the connection level, but here you don't have to manage the HTTP connections yourself.
- **Request level**: This represents the highest level. The developer only deals with HTTP requests; the rest is handled by Akka HTTP internally. This is recommended for most use cases.

In this recipe, we will demonstrate how to use the Akka HTTP client API by making a `GET` request to their GitHub repository using the different API levels and checking how many open issues the Akka HTTP project has.

Getting ready

To step through this recipe, we need to import the `Hello-Akka` project and the required Akka HTTP dependency we added in the previous recipe.

How to do it...

For this recipe, perform the following steps:

1. First, use the connection-level API. Create a file named
   `ConnectionLevelClientAPIApplication.scala` in the
   `com.packt.chapter9` package. The content should be as follows:

```scala
package com.packt.chapter9

import akka.actor.ActorSystem
import akka.http.scaladsl.Http
import akka.http.scaladsl.model.HttpRequest
import akka.stream.ActorMaterializer
import akka.stream.scaladsl.{Sink, Source}

import scala.util.{Failure, Success}
import scala.concurrent.duration._

object ConnectionLevelClientAPIApplication extends App {

  implicit val system = ActorSystem()
  implicit val materializer = ActorMaterializer()
  implicit val executionContext = system.dispatcher

  val connectionFlow =
    Http().outgoingConnectionHttps("api.github.com")
  val akkaToolkitRequest = HttpRequest(uri = "/repos
  /akka/akka-http")

  val responseFuture =
    Source.single(akkaToolkitRequest).via(
    connectionFlow).runWith(Sink.head)

  responseFuture.andThen {
    case Success(response) =>
      response.entity.toStrict(5 seconds).map(
        _.data.decodeString("UTF-8")).andThen {
        case Success(json) =>
          val pattern = """.*"open_issues":(.*?),.*""".r
          pattern.findAllIn(json).matchData foreach { m =>
            println(s"There are ${m.group(1)} open issues
            in Akka Http.")
            materializer.shutdown()
            system.terminate()
          }
        case _ =>
```

```
        }
            case _ => println("request failed")
    }
}
```

2. After this, create a file named `HostLevelClientAPIApplication.scala` in the `com.packt.chapter9` package. This time we will use the host-level API. The content should look like this:

```scala
package com.packt.chapter9

import akka.actor.ActorSystem
import akka.http.scaladsl.Http
import akka.http.scaladsl.model.HttpRequest
import akka.stream.ActorMaterializer
import akka.stream.scaladsl.{Sink, Source}

import scala.concurrent.duration._
import scala.util.{Failure, Success}

object HostLevelClientAPIApplication extends App {

  implicit val system = ActorSystem()
  implicit val materializer = ActorMaterializer()
  implicit val executionContext = system.dispatcher

  val poolClientFlow =
    Http().cachedHostConnectionPoolHttps[String]
      ("api.github.com")
  val akkaToolkitRequest = HttpRequest(uri = "/repos
    /akka/akka-http") -> """.*"open_issues":(.*?),.*"""
  val responseFuture = Source.single(akkaToolkitRequest)
    .via(poolClientFlow).runWith(Sink.head)

  responseFuture.andThen {
    case Success(result) =>
      val (tryResponse, regex) = result
      tryResponse match {
        case Success(response) =>
          response.entity.toStrict(5
            seconds).map(_.data.decodeString(
              "UTF-8")).andThen {
              case Success(json) =>
              val pattern = regex.r
              pattern.findAllIn(json).matchData foreach {
                m => println(s"There are ${m.group(1)}
                open issues in Akka Http.")
                materializer.shutdown()
```

```
                    system.terminate()
              }
              case _ =>
              }
           case _ => println("request failed")
        }
      case _ => println("request failed")
    }
  }
}
```

3. Finally, **create a file named** `RequestLevelClientAPIApplication.scala` **in the** `com.packt.chapter9` **package with the following content:**

```scala
package com.packt.chapter9

import akka.actor.ActorSystem
import akka.http.scaladsl.Http
import akka.http.scaladsl.model.HttpRequest
import akka.stream.ActorMaterializer

import scala.concurrent.duration._
import scala.util.{Failure, Success}

object RequestLevelClientAPIApplication extends App {

  implicit val system = ActorSystem()
  implicit val materializer = ActorMaterializer()
  implicit val executionContext = system.dispatcher

  val akkaToolkitRequest = HttpRequest(uri =
    "https://api.github.com/repos/akka/akka-http")
  val responseFuture =
    Http().singleRequest(akkaToolkitRequest)

  responseFuture.andThen {
    case Success(response) =>
      response.entity.toStrict(5 seconds).map(
      case Success(json) =>
        val pattern = """.*"open_issues":(.*?),.*""".r
      pattern.findAllIn(json).matchData foreach { m =>
        println(s"There are ${m.group(1)} open issues
          in Akka Http.")
        materializer.shutdown()
        system.terminate()
      }
      case _ =>
    }
    case _ => println(s"request failed")
```

```
    }
  }
```

4. Once you have the code, run the three applications. First, run
   `ConnectionLevelClientAPIApplication` in either IntelliJ or the command
   line:

   ```
   hveiga$ sbt "runMain
   com.packt.chapter9.ConnectionLevelClientAPIApplication"
   [info] Running
   com.packt.chapter9.ConnectionLevelClientAPIApplication
   There are 352 open issues in Akka Http.
   ```

5. Then, run `HostLevelClientAPIApplication`:

   ```
   hveiga$ sbt "runMain
   com.packt.chapter9.HostLevelClientAPIApplication
   [info] Running com.packt.chapter9.HostLevelClientAPIApplication
   There are 352 open issues in Akka Http.
   ```

6. Lastly, run `RequestLevelClientAPIApplication`:

   ```
   hveiga$ sbt "runMain
   com.packt.chapter9.RequestLevelClientAPIApplication"
   [info] Running
   com.packt.chapter9.RequestLevelClientAPIApplication
   There are 352 open issues in Akka Http.
   ```

How it works...

In this recipe, we revisited how to use different Akka HTTP Client API levels to perform a GET request. To begin with, we used the Connection-Level Client API. This API relies heavily on Akka Streams. Akka HTTP treats connections as Akka Streams flows. This means a connection will receive a request as input and send a response as output. We used `Sink.head` to receive `Future[HttpResponse]`, which eventually holds the value of the response. To retrieve the actual content of the response, we need to get `entity` and decode it to UTF8. After all that, we simply extract the desired value, thanks to a regular expression, and print out the number of open issues.

Second, we used the Host-Level Client API. This is similar to the previous one; the main difference is that, with this API, we get our connection flow by calling `Http().cachedHostConnectionPoolHttps`. This flow holds a connection pool to a specific hostname and port and consumes a tuple of the type (`HttpRequest` and `T`). In our case, the type `T` was the string. This level is meant to be used when you access the same HTTP server multiple times using different requests that have a companion object of the type `T` to identify the request. Since some requests might fail, the output type is another tuple with (`Try[HttpResponse]` and `T`). `Http().cachedHostConnectionPoolHttps` does not preserve order, so the flow will push elements to the streams as soon as they are ready. Therefore, it is not rare to see responses in a different order of how you send requests.

At last, we used the request-level Client API. This is the recommended level for most use cases and the most straightforward level. Just by calling `Http().singleRequest`, Akka HTTP triggers the request in the execution context and gives a `Futute[HttpResponse]` back to consume the result when it becomes available.

In this example, we used HTTPs as our remote HTTP server; however, this recipe works exactly the same if you use HTTP.

Writing routing DSL for HTTP servers

Akka HTTP provides an elegant DSL for defining the layout of your REST API. This DSL allows you to compose different directives to route and handle your incoming requests. Directives are functions that either let the HTTP request through or reject it depending on its nature. There are over 150 distinct directives to handle the different aspects of the HTTP protocol and parameters of an HTTP request or response. For instance, there are method directives (`post`, `get`, `put`, `delete`, and so on) or path directives to match a certain path in the URI of the request.

Check all the predefined directives ordered alphabetically in `http://doc.akka.io/docs/akka-http/current/scala/http/routing-dsl/directives/alphabetically.html`.

In this recipe, we see how to easily write a **CRUD (Create, Read, Update, Delete)** REST API using memory as our storage solution. We will do it using an agnostic approach, where any type of data could be used. Also, we will see how these routes are modular and can be composed into more complex routes. In this particular example, we will use our REST API to store the current temperatures of locations.

Getting ready

To step through this recipe, import the `Hello-Akka` project and the required Akka HTTP dependency we added in the previous recipe.

How to do it...

For this recipe, perform the following steps:

1. First, start writing a trait that will handle all the requests for a given path and leave the methods for handling `get`, `post`, `put`, and `delete` requests unimplemented. Create a file named `InMemoryStorageRestApi.scala` inside the `com.packt.chapter9` package with the following content:

```scala
package com.packt.chapter9

import akka.http.scaladsl.server.Directives._
import akka.http.scaladsl.server._

import scala.collection.mutable

trait InMemoryStorageRestApi[K, V] {
  implicit val fixedPath: String

  def composedRoute(cache: mutable.Map[K, V]) =
    versionOneRoute {
      temperaturePathRoute {
        handleAllMethods(cache)
      }
    }

  private def versionOneRoute(route: Route) =
    pathPrefix("v1") {
      route
    }

  private def temperaturePathRoute(route: Route) =
```

```
      pathPrefix(fixedPath) {
        route
      }
    }

  private def handleAllMethods(cache: mutable.Map[K, V]) = {
    get { handleGet(cache) } ~
    post { handlePost(cache) } ~
    put { handlePut(cache) } ~
    delete { handleDelete(cache) }
  }

  def handleGet(cache: mutable.Map[K, V]): Route
  def handlePut(cache: mutable.Map[K, V]): Route
  def handlePost(cache: mutable.Map[K, V]): Route
  def handleDelete(cache: mutable.Map[K, V]): Route
}
```

2. Second, create the objects you are going to store in your cache. Create a file named TemperatureMeasurement.scala inside the com.packt.chapter9 package. Inside this, define your case class:

```
package com.packt.chapter9

case class TemperatureMeasurement(location: String,
  measurement: Double)
```

3. Now it's time to define the actual handlers for your REST API. Create a file named CRUDHandlers.scala inside the com.packt.chapter9 package. Inside the file, define four different traits. Each one will handle a different HTTP method: GET, PUT, POST, and delete. The content should be as follows:

```
package com.packt.chapter9

import akka.http.scaladsl.model.StatusCodes
import akka.http.scaladsl.server.Directives._
import akka.http.scaladsl.server.PathMatchers.Segment

trait GetRequestsHandler {
  def handleGet(cache: scala.collection.mutable.Map[String,
  TemperatureMeasurement]) =
    pathEndOrSingleSlash {
      complete {
        cache.map(keyValue => s"${keyValue._2.location},
          ${keyValue._2.measurement}")
          .mkString("n")
      }
    } ~
```

```
        path(Segment) { id =>
          complete {
            cache.get(id) match {
              case Some(TemperatureMeasurement(location,
                measurement)) => s"Temperature for
                $location is $measurement"
              case None => StatusCodes.NotFound -> s"Not
                temperature measurement for $id"
            }
          }
        }
    }

  trait PostRequestsHandler {
    def handlePost(cache: scala.collection.mutable.Map[String,
      TemperatureMeasurement]) =
        entity(as[String]) { content =>
        complete {
          content.split(",") match {
            case Array(location, _)
            if cache.contains(location) =>
              StatusCodes.Conflict -> s"$location has a
              value already. To update it please
                use PUT method."
            case Array(location, measurement) =>
              cache.put(location, TemperatureMeasurement(
                location, measurement.toDouble))
              s"Measurement inserted for $location"
          }
        }
      }
  }

  trait PutRequestsHandler {
    def handlePut(cache: scala.collection.mutable.Map[String,
      TemperatureMeasurement]) =
        path(Segment) { id =>
          entity(as[String]) { updatedMeasurement =>
            complete {
              cache.get(id) match {
              case Some(TemperatureMeasurement(location,
                measurement)) =>
                cache.put(id, TemperatureMeasurement(location,
                  updatedMeasurement.toDouble))
                s"New temperature for $location is
                  $updatedMeasurement"
              case None =>
                StatusCodes.NotFound -> s"Not temperature
```

```
                        measurement for $id"
                    }
                  }
                }
              }
          }

      trait DeleteRequestsHandler {
        def handleDelete(cache: scala.collection.mutable.Map[
          String, TemperatureMeasurement]) =
          path(Segment) { id =>
          complete {
            cache.get(id) match {
              case Some(TemperatureMeasurement(location,
                measurement)) =>
                cache.remove(id)
                s"Removed temperature for $location"
              case None =>
                StatusCodes.NotFound -> s"Not temperature
                  measurement for $id"
            }
          }
        }
      }
```

4. Finally, create a class that will mix all the traits and extend `HttpApp` to make it a runnable application. For this, create a file named `WritingRoutingDSL.scala` inside the `com.packt.chapter9` package. The content should be as follows:

```
package com.packt.chapter9

import akka.http.scaladsl.server.HttpApp
import akka.http.scaladsl.settings.ServerSettings
import com.typesafe.config.ConfigFactory

import scala.collection.mutable

class TemperatureInMemoryStorageRestApi(
cache: mutable.Map[String,
 TemperatureMeasurement]) extends HttpApp
  with InMemoryStorageRestApi[String, TemperatureMeasurement]
  with GetRequestsHandler
  with PostRequestsHandler
  with PutRequestsHandler
  with DeleteRequestsHandler {

  implicit val fixedPath = "temperature"
```

```
    val route = composedRoute(cache)
}

object TemperatureInMemoryStorageRestApiApplication
  extends App {
  val cache = mutable.Map.empty[String,
    TemperatureMeasurement]
  new TemperatureInMemoryStorageRestApi(
    cache).startServer("0.0.0.0", 8088,
      ServerSettings(ConfigFactory.load))
}
```

5. Once you have the code, run the three applications. First, run
   ConnectionLevelClientAPIApplication in either IntelliJ or the command
   line:

```
hveiga$ sbt "runMain
com.packt.chapter9.TemperatureInMemoryStorageRestApiApplication"
[info] Running
com.packt.chapter9.TemperatureInMemoryStorageRestApiApplication
Press RETURN to stop...
[INFO] [TemperatureInMemoryStorageRestApi-akka.actor.default-
dispatcher-4]
[akka.actor.ActorSystemImpl(TemperatureInMemoryStorageRestApi)]
Server online at http://0:0:0:0:0:0:0:0:8088/
```

6. To test it, open a different command-line shell and use CURL (or any other
   similar tool) to run a couple of requests:

```
hveiga$ curl -X POST --data "Chicago,20.0"
http://localhost:8088/v1/temperature/
Measurement inserted for Chicago
hveiga$ curl -X POST --data "Madrid,15.0"
http://localhost:8088/v1/temperature/
Measurement inserted for Madrid
hveiga$ curl -X GET http://localhost:8088/v1/temperature/
Madrid,15.0
Chicago,20.0
```

How it works...

In this recipe, we learned how to use the Akka HTTP routing DSL. We created a REST API to store the temperature values of various locations. To achieve this, we created a generalized trait: `InMemoryStorageRestApi`. This trait composes a route by matching all the incoming requests with two `pathPrefix` directives. The first one is the version prefix v1 that is used primarily to provide some versioning mechanism to our API (there is currently no universally accepted way of versioning your API, and this is just one of the common approaches). The second one is just a string we use to identify the resources in the URI path. After this, we had four unimplemented methods to handle the different HTTP methods. They matched, thanks to the HTTP method directives `get`, `post`, `put`, and `delete`. It is in the `CRUDHandlers.scala` file where we created four different handlers to handle these directives. This was to demonstrate how easy it is to modularize different parts of your API. This can be especially useful for testing and maintainability.

These handlers use other valuable directives. The `pathEndOrSingleSlash` method matches when the remaining portion of the URI is just a single slash or nothing. `path(Segment)` matches and extracts the remaining portion of the URI, `entity(as[String])` extracts the content of the HTTP request in String format, and, `complete` allows you to set the HTTP response for the given request. `complete` can take multiple values, but in this case, we were returning a tuple of (`StatusCode` and `ToResponseMarshallable`). `StatusCode` sets the HTTP status code of the response. `ToResponseMarshallable` represents an object that can be marshaled into an HTTP response, for example, a string.

Finally, we composed our complete API by defining the `TemperatureInMemoryStorageRestApi` class. This class extends our `InMemoryStorageRestApi` trait as well as the four traits that define the different HTTP method handles. In addition, it mixes in `HttpApp` to make a runnable server. After this, we ran our application and tested it using an HTTP client.

 It is not advisable to use a simple mutable map in memory storage. We used it in our recipe just for demonstration purposes.

Understanding the configuration of Akka HTTP

Akka HTTP comes with a handful of configuration parameters to fine-tune your application. As usual, with Akka-related projects, the configuration gets defined in the Typesafe configuration file `application.conf`. In this recipe, we will learn how to set and override the most common configuration parameters. Specifically, we will override a configuration parameter for the Akka HTTP server, another configuration parameter for the Akka HTTP client and finally we will see how to modify the default values when parsing HTTP Requests. This is valuable if you need to reject requests of specific characteristics.

Getting ready

To begin with, we need to differentiate between different sets of configuration parameters. Akka HTTP projects contain multiple modules:

- `Akka-http-core`: This contains configuration parameters for a low-level implementation, for both client and server APIs
- `Akka-http`: This contains configuration parameters for a high-level implementation. Currently, it is the Routing DSL configuration.

We will modify the following things:

Parameter	Module	Default	Why you might need to override it
`server.request-timeout`	akka-http-core	20 seconds	Your backend might take a long time to produce a response. Therefore, 20 seconds might not be enough.
`client.connecting-timeout`	akka-http-core	10 seconds	The remote server might be slow. Therefore, 10 seconds might not be enough.

max-content-length	akka-http-core	8 minutes	Your rest API runs in an embedded device. Large requests might not be acceptable.

How to do it...

For this recipe, perform the following steps:

1. To begin with, create a file named `application.conf` inside `src/main/resources`.

2. Inside this file, set the following configuration parameters:

```
akka.http {
  server.request-timeout = 60s
  client.connecting-timeout = 60s
  parsing.max-content-length = 1m
}
```

How it works...

In this recipe, we saw how to modify the configuration of Akka HTTP to fit our needs. In our case, we set only three configuration parameters to demonstrate how to do it. It is good to mention that overriding `akka.http.parsing` sets that configuration for both the server and client. However, it is possible to just set different parameters for each server and client. To do so, we need to set either `akka.http.server.parsing` or `akka.http.client.parsing`.

 Akka HTTP has many other configuration parameters to tweak and tune different aspects from both client and server APIs. You can find all the configuration parameters at `http://doc.akka.io/docs/akka-http/curr ent/scala/http/configuration.html`.

Marshaling and unmarshaling data

The HTTP protocol is primarily used to transfer information between remote systems. Data needs to be serialized into bytes to be able to be transferred from one point to another; however, manipulating bytes in your application is probably challenging and error-prone. The regular approach to this problem is to create classes in your code that represent the data you are sending or receiving. In addition, you could develop complementary code that would contain the logic to marshall your classes into a byte stream, and of course, unmarshal the incoming byte stream into your classes.

Akka HTTP gets APIs to do the marshaling and unmarshaling automatically as long as you provide the logic to do it. Depending on your use case, you might just want to marshal a part of your HTTP request or response. This is why Akka HTTP provides different levels for marshalers. If you just need to customize the serialization of the HTTP entity (basically the content and content type), you can extend `ToEntityMarshaller[T]` or `FromEntityUnmarshaller[T]`. If you need to provide more details, such as special headers, you will need to extend either `ToResponseMarshaller[T]`, `FromResponseUnmarshaller[T]`, `ToRequestMarshaller[T]`, or `FromRequestUnmarshaller[T]`. There are also XML and JSON marshalers; we will see them in later recipes.

In this recipe, we will see how to create our own entity marshaler and unmarshaler to serialize your case class using tab-separated values. After this, we will see how to integrate them into the Routing DSL.

Getting ready

To step through this recipe, we need to import the `Hello-Akka` project and the required Akka HTTP dependency we added in the previous recipe.

How to do it...

For this recipe, perform the following steps:

1. Create a file named `SpeedMeasurement.scala` inside the `com.packt.chapter9` package. This file will contain three definitions:

- A case class that will define `SpeedMeasurement`
- An object to turn a space-separated string into SpeedMeasurement
- A helper trait with the marshaler and unmarshaler

2. First, define the case class `SpeedMeasurement` in the `SpeedMeasurement.scala` file:

```
package com.packt.chapter9

case class SpeedMeasurement(timestamp: Long, latitude:
 Double, longitude: Double, value: Double) {
   val marshall = s"$timestamp $latitude $longitude
 $value" }
```

3. Second, define the object in the same file. The content should be as follows:

```
package com.packt.chapter9

object SpeedMeasurement {
  def unmarshall(str: String) = {
    str.split("s") match {
      case Array(timestamp, latitude, longitude, value) =>
        SpeedMeasurement(timestamp.toLong, latitude.toDouble,
          longitude.toDouble, value.toDouble)
    }
  }
}
```

4. Finally, define the `SpeedMeasurementMarshallingHelper` trait in the same file:

```
package com.packt.chapter9

import akka.http.scaladsl.marshalling.{Marshaller, _}
import akka.http.scaladsl.model._
import akka.http.scaladsl.unmarshalling.{Unmarshaller, _}

trait SpeedMeasurementMarshallingHelper {
  val contentType = ContentType(MediaTypes.`text/tab-
    separated-values`, HttpCharsets.`UTF-8`)
  implicit val utf8TextSpaceMarshaller:
    ToEntityMarshaller[SpeedMeasurement] =
      Marshaller.withFixedContentType(contentType) {
        speedMeasurement ⇒ HttpEntity(contentType,
        speedMeasurement.marshall) }
  implicit val utf8TextSpaceUnmarshaller:
```

```
        FromEntityUnmarshaller[SpeedMeasurement] =
            Unmarshaller.stringUnmarshaller.map(
                SpeedMeasurement.unmarshall)
    }
```

5. Now create a file to define our route and an object to run our application. Create a file named `MarshallingApplication.scala` inside the `com.packt.chapter9` package with the following content:

```scala
package com.packt.chapter9

import akka.http.scaladsl.model._
import akka.http.scaladsl.server.Directives._
import akka.http.scaladsl.server.HttpApp
import akka.http.scaladsl.settings.ServerSettings
import com.typesafe.config.ConfigFactory

object MarshallingServer extends HttpApp with
    SpeedMeasurementMarshallingHelper {
        var measurement: Option[SpeedMeasurement] = None

    val route =
    get {
        complete {
            measurement match {
                case None => StatusCodes.NotFound ->
                    "Speed Measurement is empty"
                case Some(value) => StatusCodes.OK -> value
            }
        }
    } ~
    post {
        entity(as[SpeedMeasurement]) { speedMeasurement =>
        complete {
            measurement = Some(speedMeasurement)
            StatusCodes.OK -> s"Speed Measurement now is
            $speedMeasurement"
        }
        }
    }
}

object MarshallingApplication extends App {
    MarshallingServer.startServer("0.0.0.0", 8088,
        ServerSettings(ConfigFactory.load))
}
```

6. Run the application in either Intellij or the command line:

```
hveiga$ sbt "runMain com.packt.chapter9.MarshallingApplication"
[info] Running com.packt.chapter9.MarshallingApplication
Press RETURN to stop...
[INFO] [02/21/2017 19:53:41.973] [MarshallingServer-
akka.actor.default-dispatcher-4]
[akka.actor.ActorSystemImpl(MarshallingServer)] Server
online at http://0:0:0:0:0:0:0:0:8088/
```

7. Run the following command with Curl or a similar HTTP client to test it out:

```
hveiga$ curl -X POST --data "140000000 40.42015 -3.70578 56.0"
http://localhost:8088/
Speed Measurement now is
SpeedMeasurement(140000000,40.42015,-3.70578,56.0)
hveiga$ curl -X GET http://localhost:8088/
140000000 40.42015 -3.70578 56.0
```

How it works...

In this recipe, you learned how to use the marshaling and unmarshaling capabilities of Akka HTTP to automatically receive and send requests and responses using your code classes. To achieve this, we had SpeedMeasurementMarshallingHelper. This trait contains both a marshaler and unmarshaler for the SpeedMeasurement type.

The utf8TextSpaceMarshaller class uses the help method Marshaller.withFixedContentType to turn a SpeedMeasurement into an HttpEntity. The same way utf8TextSpaceUnmarshaller uses the help of Unmarshaller.stringUnmarshaller to read the bytes from the wire and finally turn it into a SpeedMeasurement instance.

Note that both marshaler and unmarshaler are defined as implicit. This will be required for Akka HTTP to understand which marshaler to use in case we want to send or receive a SpeedMeasurement type. This happens either when we complete a request with the type SpeedMeasurement (as we did in the get part of our route) or when we want to unmarshal an entity into the SpeedMeasurement type using entity(as[SpeedMeasurement]) (as we are doing in the post part of our route).

Akka HTTP also has a set of built-in marshalers and unmarshalers to cover the most usual cases, such as `Array[Byte]`, String, or CSV.

You can follow the official documentation to find a list of all the out-of-the-box supported types, for marshalers, refer to `http://doc.akka.io/do cs/akka-http/current/scala/http/common/marshalling.html#predef ined-marshallers`, and for unmarshalers, refer to `http://doc.akka.io/d ocs/akka-http/current/scala/http/common/unmarshalling.html#pre defined-unmarshallers`.

Encoding and decoding data

Unlike marshaling/unmarshaling, encoding/decoding in HTTP is the process of transforming your HTTP entity into a different format. This formatting can be undone by the remote endpoint to understand the HTTP entity, and it usually happens using a formatting codec. HTTP primarily uses a compression codec to compress/uncompress your HTTP entity and save some bandwidth in transmission. The cost of this additional process is usually irrelevant compared to the benefits of less bandwidth and faster overall response times. Some of the popular codecs are gzip, compress, and deflate.

Akka HTTP provides a functionality to both server and client APIs to deal with codecs. In this recipe, we will create a server that will receive a compressed HTTP entity and decode it and prepare an HTTP response, encode it, and send it back to the client. To test this, we will also create some client code to send a compressed request and read the compressed response.

Getting ready

To step through this recipe, we need to import the `Hello-Akka` project and the required Akka HTTP dependency we added in the previous recipe.

How to do it...

For this recipe, perform the following steps:

1. Create a file named `EncodingDecodingServerApplication.scala` inside the `com.packt.chapter9` package. This file will contain the route to decode the gzip request and encode the result. The content should look like this:

    ```scala
    package com.packt.chapter9

    import akka.http.scaladsl.coding._
    import akka.http.scaladsl.model.StatusCodes
    import akka.http.scaladsl.server.Directives._
    import akka.http.scaladsl.server.HttpApp
    import akka.http.scaladsl.settings.ServerSettings
    import com.typesafe.config.ConfigFactory

    object EncodingDecodingServer extends HttpApp {
      val route =
        post {
          decodeRequestWith(Gzip, NoCoding) {
            entity(as[String]) { stringEntity =>
              encodeResponse {
                complete {
                  println(s"Received $stringEntity")
                  StatusCodes.OK -> s"Thank you for
                    your encoded request [$stringEntity]."
                }
              }
            }
          }
        }
    }

    object EncodingDecodingServerApplication extends App {
      EncodingDecodingServer.startServer("0.0.0.0", 8088,
        ServerSettings(ConfigFactory.load))
    }
    ```

2. Second, create client code. Create a file named `EncodingDecodingClientApplication.scala` inside the `com.packt.chapter9` package. Use the Request-Level Client API from Akka HTTP to perform two requests: one gzip compressed and the other uncompressed. The content should look like this:

    ```scala
    package com.packt.chapter9
    ```

```scala
import akka.actor.ActorSystem
import akka.http.scaladsl.Http
import akka.http.scaladsl.coding.{Encoder, Gzip, NoCoding}
import akka.http.scaladsl.model._
import akka.http.scaladsl.model.headers._
import akka.http.scaladsl.model.headers.HttpEncodings._
import akka.http.scaladsl.model.HttpMethods._
import headers.HttpEncodings
import akka.stream.ActorMaterializer
import akka.util.ByteString

import scala.concurrent.duration._
import scala.concurrent.Future
import scala.util.{Failure, Success}

object EncodingDecodingClientApplication extends App {
  implicit val system = ActorSystem()
  implicit val materializer = ActorMaterializer()

  import system.dispatcher

  val http = Http()
  val uriServer = "http://localhost:8088/"

  val requests = Seq (
    HttpRequest(POST, uriServer, List(`Accept-
      Encoding`(gzip)), HttpEntity("Hello!")),
    HttpRequest(POST, uriServer, List(`Content-
      Encoding`(gzip), `Accept-Encoding`(gzip)),
    HttpEntity(compress("Hello compressed!", Gzip))
    )
  )

  Future.traverse(requests)
    (http.singleRequest(_).map(decodeResponse)) andThen {
    case Success(responses) => responses.foreach(response =>
      response.entity.toStrict(5 seconds).map(
        _.data.decodeString("UTF-8")).andThen {
          case Success(content) => println(s"Response:
            $content")
          case _ =>
      })
    case Failure(e) => println(s"request failed $e")
  }

  private def decodeResponse(response: HttpResponse) = {
    val decoder = response.encoding match {
      case HttpEncodings.gzip => Gzip
```

```
    case HttpEncodings.identity => NoCoding
  }

  decoder.decode(response)
}

private def compress(input: String,
  encoder: Encoder): ByteString =
    encoder.encode(ByteString(input))
}
```

3. Now that you have the code ready, run the server code in either IntelliJ or the command line:

```
hveiga$ sbt "runMain
com.packt.chapter9.EncodingDecodingServerApplication"
[info] Running
com.packt.chapter9.EncodingDecodingServerApplication
Press RETURN to stop...
[INFO] [EncodingDecodingServer-akka.actor.default-dispatcher-3]
[akka.actor.ActorSystemImpl(EncodingDecodingServer)] Server
online at http://0:0:0:0:0:0:0:0:8088/
```

4. Afterward, run the client code in either IntelliJ or the command line. You should see the response back in the console:

```
hveiga$ sbt "runMain
com.packt.chapter9.EncodingDecodingClientApplication"
[info] Running
com.packt.chapter9.EncodingDecodingClientApplication
Response: Thank you for your encoded request [Hello!].
Response: Thank you for your encoded request [Hello compressed!].
```

5. Finally, check the server output. You should have received the following:

```
Received Hello!
Received Hello compressed!
```

How it works...

In this recipe, you learned how to use encoding and decoding with both server and client APIs from Akka HTTP. On the server side, we used the directives `decodeRequestWith` and `encodeRequest`. `decodeRequestWith` tries to decode the HTTP entity of the request based on the HTTP header `Content-Encoding` with the provided decoders, in our case, Gzip or NoCoding. `encodeRequest` tries to encode the HTTP entity of the response based on the HTTP header `Accept-Encoding`. If this header is not provided, Akka HTTP won't encode your response.

On the client side, we prepared two requests: one with no coding and one compressed with gzip. For the one with the gzip content, we had to provide the Content-Encoding header to inform the server that the content was encoded. We fired our requests using the Request-level client API and mapping the responses to receive the expected values. Finally, we just printed these values out, and we see the following in the console:

```
Response: Thank you for your encoded request [Hello!].
Response: Thank you for your encoded request [Hello compressed!].
```

Understanding directives

As mentioned before, Routing DSL is basically a set of directives that you can compose to route and handle your incoming HTTP requests. Directives are small code blocks that can do things such as transform, filter, extract, or complete an incoming request.

In this recipe, we will see how to create a custom directive to measure the number of times a particular path of a route is called and also how long it took to process it. We will make use of basic directives to compose more complex ones. For this task, we will make use of Dropwizard metrics. Dropwizard metrics is a popular, stable, and simple metrics library that has an easy API to gather and report information about an application.

Getting ready

To step through this recipe, we need to import the `Hello-Akka` project and the required Akka HTTP dependency we added in the previous recipe. Also, we will add the Dropwizard metrics dependency to complete this recipe.

How to do it...

For this recipe, perform the following steps:

1. Get the required dependencies.

2. Edit the `build.sbt` file and add the Dropwizard dependency as follows:

```
libraryDependencies += "io.dropwizard" %
  "dropwizard-core" % "1.0.6"
```

3. Now create a file named `MetricDirectives.scala` in the `com.packt.chapter9` package. This file will contain the trait that will bring the new directives to our routes. We will implement two directives--meter and timer. The content of this file should look like this:

```
package com.packt.chapter9

import akka.http.scaladsl.server.Directive0
import akka.http.scaladsl.server.Directives._
import com.codahale.metrics.MetricRegistry

trait MetricDirectives {
def meter(metricRegistry: MetricRegistry) : Directive0 = {
    extractMethod.flatMap[Unit] { httpMethod =>
      extractUri.flatMap { uri =>
        metricRegistry.meter(s"meter-
          Method[${httpMethod.value}]-
            Uri[${uri.path.toString}]").mark
            pass
      }
    }
  }

def timer(metricRegistry: MetricRegistry) : Directive0 = {
    extractMethod.flatMap[Unit] { httpMethod =>
      extractUri.flatMap { uri =>
val timer = metricRegistry.timer(s"timer-
          Method[${httpMethod.value}]-
            Uri[${uri.path.toString}]")
val timerContext = timer.time()
        mapRouteResult { x =>
          timerContext.stop()
          x
      }
    }
  }
```

```
        }
      }
```

4. Then, create a file named `CustomDirectivesApplication.scala` inside the `com.packt.chapter9` package. This file will have your route and an app to run your server. The contents of the file should look as follows:

```scala
package com.packt.chapter9

import java.util.concurrent.TimeUnit

import akka.http.scaladsl.server.Directives._
import akka.http.scaladsl.server.HttpApp
import akka.http.scaladsl.settings.ServerSettings
import com.codahale.metrics.{ConsoleReporter, MetricRegistry}
import com.typesafe.config.ConfigFactory

object CustomDirectivesServer extends HttpApp with
  MetricDirectives {
    private val metricRegistry = new MetricRegistry()
    ConsoleReporter.forRegistry(
      metricRegistry).build().start(10, TimeUnit.SECONDS)

    val route =
      timer(metricRegistry) {
        get {
          complete { Thread.sleep(200); "Hello from GET!" }
        } ~
        post {
          complete { Thread.sleep(500); "Hello from POST!" }
        } ~
        put {
          meter(metricRegistry) {
            complete { "Hello from PUT!" }
          }
        }
      }
  }

object CustomDirectivesApplication extends App {
  CustomDirectivesServer.startServer("0.0.0.0", 8088,
    ServerSettings(ConfigFactory.load))
}
```

5. Once the code is ready, run it in either IntelliJ or the command line. You should see your `ConsoleReporter` reporting metrics every 10 seconds. Initially, there are no metrics to report so you should see new empty lines:

```
hveiga$ sbt "runMain
com.packt.chapter9.CustomDirectivesApplication"
[info] Running com.packt.chapter9.CustomDirectivesApplication
Press RETURN to stop...
[INFO] [02/23/2017 17:02:24.814] [CustomDirectivesServer-
akka.actor.default-dispatcher-2]
[akka.actor.ActorSystemImpl(CustomDirectivesServer)] Server
online at http://0:0:0:0:0:0:0:0:8088/
===========================================================
```

6. Then use CURL or your preferred HTTP client to send some requests:

```
hveiga$ curl -X POST http://localhost:8088
Hello from POST!
hveiga$ curl -X POST http://localhost:8088
Hello from POST!
hveiga$ curl -X POST http://localhost:8088
Hello from POST!
hveiga$ curl -X GET http://localhost:8088
Hello from GET!
hveiga$ curl -X GET http://localhost:8088
Hello from GET!
hveiga$ curl -X PUT http://localhost:8088
Hello from PUT!
```

How it works...

In this recipe, you learned how routing DSL is not only elegant and useful but also extensible. We saw how to create new directives that we can integrate seamlessly into our routes. In this particular case, we defined two new directives--`meter` and `timer`. `meter` is responsible for measuring the rate of events. `timer` is responsible for measuring how long a computation takes. As we can see in the code, we reused other basic directives provided by Akka HTTP, such as `extractMethod`, `extractUri`, or `mapRouteResult`. This is advisable since the basic directives cover most of the common use cases; however, it is possible to create a directive from scratch by extending the `Directive[L] (implicit val ev: Tuple[L]).` abstract class.

Both our new directives returned `Directive0`. `Directive0` is just an alias for `Directive[Unit]` and it means this directive does not extract any values. In case your directive needs to extract one or more values, you will need to return `Directive1[T]` for one or `Directive[TupleN[T]]` for multiple values (where *N* is the total number of extracted values). Extractions are represented by tuples, which bring great flexibility.

Then, we saw how our `CustomDirectivesServer` object mixed with the `MetricDirectives` trait. This is the only step required to start using your shiny new directives. For testing purposes, we had `Thread.sleep` in GET and POST routes. This was only to demonstrate how the timer directive behaves; it should not be used in production code. Finally, to make both the directives work, we needed to provide a `MetricRegistry` function. This is a Dropwizard class that holds a registry of all the metrics you create. Moreover, we created a console reporter to report the values of these created metrics. Dropwizard provides many other reporters, such as JMX, HTTP, or Graphite.

Once we run our application, we execute three POST requests, two GET requests, and one PUT request. Therefore, we see that three timers were created (one for POST, one for GET, and one for PUT) in the output and one meter was created for PUT:

```
-- Meters ----------------------------
meter-Method[PUT]-Uri[/]
count = 1
mean rate = 0.01 events/second
1-minute rate = 0.04 events/second
5-minute rate = 0.14 events/second
15-minute rate = 0.18 events/second
-- Timers ----------------------------
timer-Method[GET]-Uri[/]
count = 2
mean rate = 0.02 calls/second
1-minute rate = 0.06 calls/second
...
99.9% <= 204.99 milliseconds
timer-Method[POST]-Uri[/]
count = 3
mean rate = 0.02 calls/second
1-minute rate = 0.08 calls/second
...
99.9% <= 532.52 milliseconds
timer-Method[PUT]-Uri[/]
count = 1
mean rate = 0.01 calls/second
1-minute rate = 0.04 calls/second
...
```

```
99.9% <= 1.45 milliseconds
```

Thanks to `Thread.sleep`, we can see how the timer works--GET has a time of ~200ms, POST of ~500ms , and PUT of ~1ms.

Exception handling

Like all the other Akka modules, Akka HTTP has great exception handling mechanisms. By default, if anything in your route throws an exception, the server returns a 500 response, which means there is an internal server error. This is a useful default behavior; however, you might need to do something more specific and respond in a different way depending on the exception thrown.

In this recipe, we will revisit how to add an exception handler to your routes. This allows you to customize the behavior of your route when exceptions are thrown.

Getting ready

To step through this recipe, we need to import the `Hello-Akka` project and the required Akka HTTP dependency we added in the previous recipe.

How to do it...

For this recipe, perform the following steps:

1. First, create a trait where you will define your exception handler. Create a file named `RouteExceptionHandler.scala` inside the `com.packt.chapter9` package. The content should be as follows:

    ```
    package com.packt.chapter9

    import akka.http.scaladsl.model.StatusCodes
    import akka.http.scaladsl.server.Directives._
    import akka.http.scaladsl.server.ExceptionHandler
    import akka.pattern.AskTimeoutException

    trait RouteExceptionHandler {

      val routeExceptionHandler = ExceptionHandler {
        case _: ArithmeticException =>
    ```

```
        complete {
          StatusCodes.BadRequest -> "You values are incorrect.
          Probably b needs to be different from 0"
        }
        case _: AskTimeoutException =>
          complete {
            StatusCodes.ServiceUnavailable -> "Internal
            actor is not responding within 500 millis"
          }
      }
    }
  }
```

2. To illustrate a different error, time out a `Future`. For this, create an actor that ignores all the messages. Create a file named `UnresponsiveActor.scala` inside the `com.packt.chapter9` package. The actor should look like this:

```
package com.packt.chapter9

import akka.actor.Actor

class UnresponsiveActor extends Actor {
  def receive = Actor.ignoringBehavior
}
```

3. Then, create a file named `HandlingExceptionsApplication.scala` inside the `com.packt.chapter9` package. This file will contain both the route and the app to run it:

```
package com.packt.chapter9

import akka.actor.{ActorRef, ActorSystem, Props}
import akka.http.scaladsl.server.HttpApp
import akka.http.scaladsl.server.Directives._
import akka.http.scaladsl.settings.ServerSettings
import com.typesafe.config.ConfigFactory
import akka.pattern.ask
import akka.util.Timeout

import scala.concurrent.duration._

class HandlingExceptionsServer(someActor: ActorRef)
 extends HttpApp with RouteExceptionHandler {
  implicit val timeout = Timeout(500 millis)

  val route =
    handleExceptions(routeExceptionHandler) {
      path("divide") {
```

```scala
                parameters('a.as[Int], 'b.as[Int]) { (a, b) =>
                  complete {
                    val result = a / b
                    s"Result is: $result"
                  }
                }
              } ~
                path("futureTimingOut") {
                  onSuccess(someActor ? "Something") {
                    case _ => complete("Actor finished processing.")
                  }
                }
            }

        }

    object HandlingExceptionsApplication extends App {
      val unresponsiveActor =
        ActorSystem().actorOf(Props[UnresponsiveActor])
      new HandlingExceptionsServer(
        unresponsiveActor).startServer(
          "0.0.0.0", 8088, ServerSettings(ConfigFactory.load))
    }
```

4. Once the code is ready, run the application in either IntelliJ or the command line:

```
hveiga$ sbt "runMain
com.packt.chapter9.HandlingExceptionsApplication"
[info] Running com.packt.chapter9.HandlingExceptionsApplication
Press RETURN to stop...
[INFO] [HandlingExceptionsServer-akka.actor.default-dispatcher-3]
[akka.actor.ActorSystemImpl(HandlingExceptionsServer)] Server
online at http://0:0:0:0:0:0:0:0:8088/
```

5. Send some requests with your preferred HTTP Client to test it out:

```
hveiga$ curl -X GET http://localhost:8088/divide?a=20&b=10
Result is: 2
hveiga$ curl -X GET http://localhost:8088/divide?a=20&b=0
You values are incorrect. Probably b needs to be different from 0
hveiga$ curl -X GET http://localhost:8088/futureTimingOut
Internal actor is not responding within 500 millis
```

How it works...

In this recipe, you learned to handle exceptions in routes to better customize the behavior of your application. This is achieved thanks to ExceptionHandler. ExceptionHandler expects PartialFunction[Throwable, Route] where you define what to do for each Throwable case. In our case, we returned a 400 response in the case of ArithmeticException and a 503 response in the case of AskTimeoutException. ArithmeticException is thrown when you call the URI /divide with parameter b set to 0. AskTimeoutException is thrown when you call the URI /futureTimingOut since this endpoint expects a message back from the actor; however, your actor ignores all the messages, and therefore, does not respond. This is only for demonstration purposes; it is always better to use onComplete instead of onSuccess where you can match Failure as well.

In order to use this exception handler in our route, we have two approaches: the explicit approach using handleExceptions(), as done in our case, or the implicit approach. You can define an implicit ExceptionHandler, where you can instantiate your route. It will be used automatically as well. The advantage of the explicit approach is that you can have multiple exception handlers for different parts of your route if your use case requires it.

It is worth mentioning that it is also possible to use all the directives in the exception handler. This is helpful if you want to extract valuable information such as the URI or HTTP method and act differently depending on the values.

Uploading a file using Akka HTTP

Another common use of REST APIs is to transfer files. This seems an easy task at first; however, it gets complicated when files become large. Most times it is not possible to store an entire file inside an HTTP request if the file is large. The HTTP protocol provides a special Content-Type for this purpose, named multipart/form-data. When using this Content-Type, the file gets sent in parts (known as body parts). Akka HTTP provides a functionality to receive these parts and put the file together on the server side. Moreover, it allows you to run some functionality as the parts are reaching the server to speed up processing in case it is required. This is known as the streaming approach.

In this recipe, we will create a REST API that is able to receive text files in both the approaches-regular and streaming. Also, we will create a client that will upload the file to the server using the Akka HTTP Client API.

Getting ready

To step through this recipe, we need to import the `Hello-Akka` project and the required Akka HTTP dependency we added in the previous recipe.

How to do it...

For this recipe, perform the following steps:

1. First, create the server portion of the recipe. Create a file named `UploadingFileServerApplication.scala` inside the `com.packt.chapter9` package. The content should be as follows:

```scala
package com.packt.chapter9

import akka.http.scaladsl.model.Multipart
import akka.http.scaladsl.server.Directives._
import akka.http.scaladsl.server.HttpApp
import akka.http.scaladsl.settings.ServerSettings
import akka.stream.scaladsl.Framing
import akka.util.ByteString
import com.typesafe.config.ConfigFactory

import scala.concurrent.duration._

object UploadingFileServer extends HttpApp {
  val route =
    extractRequestContext { ctx =>
      implicit val materializer = ctx.materializer
      implicit val ec = ctx.executionContext

      path("regularupload") {
        entity(as[Multipart.FormData]) { formData =>
          val partsFuture = formData.parts.mapAsync(1) {
            b => b.toStrict(2.seconds).map(
              _.entity.data.utf8String)
          }.runFold(List.empty[String])(_ :+ _)

          onSuccess(partsFuture) { allParts =>
            complete {
              val wholeFile = allParts.mkString
              s"Regular upload: submitted file has
              ${wholeFile.split("n").size} lines"
            }
          }
        }
```

```
              }
        } ~
          path("streamupload") {
            entity(as[Multipart.FormData]) { formData =>
              val linesFuture = formData.parts.mapAsync(1)
              { b =>
                b.entity.dataBytes
                  .via(Framing.delimiter(ByteString("n"),
                    1024, allowTruncation = true))
                  .map(_ => 1)
                  .runReduce(_ + _)
              }.runReduce(_ + _)

              onSuccess(linesFuture) { lines =>
                complete {
                  s"Stream upload: submitted file
                    has $lines lines"
                }
              }
            }
          }
        }
    }

    object UploadingFileServerApplication extends App {
      UploadingFileServer.startServer("0.0.0.0", 8088,
        ServerSettings(ConfigFactory.load))
    }
```

2. Second, create the client portion. Create a file named
   UploadingFileClient.scala inside com.packt.chapter9. This class will
   trigger two requests to the two different endpoints of our server:

```
    package com.packt.chapter9

    import java.nio.file.Paths

    import akka.actor.ActorSystem
    import akka.http.scaladsl.Http
    import akka.http.scaladsl.model.HttpMethods._
    import akka.http.scaladsl.model._
    import akka.stream.ActorMaterializer

    import scala.concurrent.Future
    import scala.concurrent.duration._
    import scala.util.{Failure, Success}

    object UploadingFileClient extends App {
```

```
implicit val system = ActorSystem()
implicit val materializer = ActorMaterializer()
import system.dispatcher

val http = Http()
val entity = Multipart.FormData.fromPath(
  "file",
  ContentTypes.`text/plain(UTF-8)`,
  Paths.get("./src/main/resources/testfile.txt")
).toEntity()
val uris = Seq(
  "http://localhost:8088/regularupload",
  "http://localhost:8088/streamupload"
)
val requests = uris.map(uri => HttpRequest(
  POST, uri, Nil, entity))

Future.traverse(requests)(http.singleRequest(_))
andThen {
  case Success(responses) => responses.foreach(response =>
    response.entity.toStrict(5 seconds).map(
      _.data.utf8String).andThen {
      case Success(content) => println(s"Response:
      $content")
        case _ =>
    })
    case Failure(e) => println(s"request failed $e")
  }
}
```

3. Once the code is ready, create a test file to test it out. Create a plain text file inside `src/main/resources`, named `testfile.txt`, with the following content:

```
HELLO WORLD AKKA HTTP!
HELLO WORLD AKKA HTTP!
HELLO WORLD AKKA HTTP!
HELLO WORLD AKKA HTTP!
```

4. Then run the server code in either IntelliJ or the command line:

```
hveiga$ sbt "runMain
com.packt.chapter9.UploadingFileServerApplication"
[info] Running com.packt.chapter9.UploadingFileServerApplication
Press RETURN to stop...
[INFO] [UploadingFileServer-akka.actor.default-dispatcher-2]
[akka.actor.ActorSystemImpl(UploadingFileServer)] Server online
at http://0:0:0:0:0:0:0:0:8088/
```

5. Finally, run the client code to make it work in either IntelliJ or the command line:

```
hveiga$ sbt "runMain com.packt.chapter9.UploadingFileClient"
[info] Running com.packt.chapter9.UploadingFileClient
Response: Regular upload: submitted file has 4 lines
Response: Stream upload: submitted file has 4 lines
```

How it works...

In this recipe, you learned to deal with multipart requests at both server side and client side to transfer files. In this example, we posted a file to a server and returned the number of lines. On the client side, we used the Request-level API to trigger both the requests. The request entity is populated because of `Multipart.FormData`. This class is responsible for defining a `multipart/form-data` request and chunking your file into different parts.

On the server side, we had two different routes. The first route, namely `regularupload`, used the `entity(as[Multipart.FormData])` directive to understand this is a multipart file that is being transferred. This yielded an instance of `formData` where the different parts of the files were streamed. Therefore, `formData.parts` is a stream that we transform to end up with `List[String]` representing the string content of each part. Once all this is done, we counted how many lines we had in the file and returned it, thanks to the `onSuccess` and `complete` directives.

The second route, namely `streamupload`, did something similar. It used the same directive to get the `formData.parts` stream. This time we used `Framing.delimiter(ByteString("n"), 1024`, and `true` in our stream. This helper flow chunks your incoming body parts into different elements as they are coming to the stream based on a delimiter (in this case, a new line character). Then, we simply mapped the line to one and reduced it so it would end up with the total number of lines.

Both the approaches do the same job; however, the procedure is different. While the first one needs to load all the contents of the file in the memory to do something with it later, the second one needs to count the lines as new body parts come into the stream. Therefore, the second approach is not only faster, but it also has a smaller memory footprint.

Routing DSL provides two directives to upload files--`uploadedFile` and `fileUpload`. These directives do something analogous to what we have seen in this recipe.

Building JSON support with Akka HTTP

As seen in the previous recipes, Akka HTTP has great integration for marshaling and unmarshaling. This is especially true if we want to serialize and deserialize JSON entities. Akka HTTP was initially developed under a different project named `Spray`. `Spray` had similar modules as Akka HTTP does. However, `Spray` had a JSON serialization library called `spray-json`. This module was not ported to Akka HTTP and stayed `spray-json`. This was because the Akka team did not want to own a serialization library, but provide means to integrate any marshaling library into Akka HTTP.

In this recipe, we will see how to easily integrate spray-json into our application to serialize and deserialize classes into and from JSON.

Getting ready

To step through this recipe, we need to import the `Hello-Akka` project and the required Akka HTTP dependency we added in the previous recipe. Also, we will include the required `spray-json` dependency.

How to do it...

For this recipe, perform the following steps:

1. Get the required dependencies.
2. Edit the `build.sbt` file and add the `akka-http-spray-json` dependency as follows:

   ```
   libraryDependencies += "com.typesafe.akka" %
     "akka-http-spray-json_2.11" % "10.0.5"
   ```

3. Now create a file named `OrderModel.scala` in the `com.packt.chapter9` package. This file will contain the case classes we are going to use. Also, it will include the trait to do the marshaling and unmarshaling automatically. The content should be as follows:

   ```
   package com.packt.chapter9

   import akka.http.scaladsl.marshallers
     .sprayjson.SprayJsonSupport
   import spray.json.DefaultJsonProtocol
   ```

```
case class Item(id: Int, quantity: Int, unitPrice: Double,
 percentageDiscount: Option[Double])
case class Order(id: String, timestamp: Long, items:
List[Item], deliveryPrice: Double,
 metadata: Map[String, String])
case class GrandTotal(id: String, amount: Double)

trait OrderJsonSupport extends SprayJsonSupport with
DefaultJsonProtocol {
  implicit val itemFormat = jsonFormat4(Item)
  implicit val orderFormat = jsonFormat5(Order)
  implicit val grandTotalFormat = jsonFormat2(GrandTotal)
}
```

4. Then, define your route and app. Create a file named
   `OrderCalculatorJsonApplication.scala` inside
   the `com.packt.chapter9` package. The `HttpApp` class will need to mix in your
   `OrderJsonSupport` trait:

```
package com.packt.chapter9

import akka.http.scaladsl.server.Directives._
import akka.http.scaladsl.server.HttpApp
import akka.http.scaladsl.settings.ServerSettings
import com.typesafe.config.ConfigFactory

import scala.util.Random._

object OrderCalculatorJsonServer extends HttpApp
with OrderJsonSupport {
val route =
    path("calculateGrandTotal" ~ Slash.?) {
      post {
        entity(as[Order]) { order =>
          complete {
            calculateGrandTotal(order)
          }
        }
      }
    } ~
      path("randomOrder") {
        get {
          complete {
generateRandomOrder()
          }
        }
```

```
    }

  private def calculateGrandTotal(o: Order) = {
    val amount = o.items.map(
      i => i.percentageDiscount.getOrElse(1.0d)
        * i.unitPrice * i.quantity).sum + o.deliveryPrice
          GrandTotal(o.id, amount)
  }

  private def generateRandomOrder(): Order = {
    val items = (0 to nextInt(5)).map(i => {
      Item(i, nextInt(100), 100 * nextDouble(),
        if (nextBoolean()) Some(nextDouble()) else None)
      }).toList
      Order(nextString(4), System.currentTimeMillis(),
        items, 100 * nextDouble(), Map("notes" -> "random"))
  }
}

object OrderCalculatorJsonServerApplication
extends App {
  OrderCalculatorJsonServer.startServer("0.0.0.0", 8088,
    ServerSettings(ConfigFactory.load))
}
```

5. Once the entire code is ready, run the server in either IntelliJ or the command line:

```
hveiga$ sbt "runMain
com.packt.chapter9.OrderCalculatorJsonServerApplication"
[info] Running
com.packt.chapter9.OrderCalculatorServerApplication
Press RETURN to stop...
[INFO] [OrderCalculatorServer-akka.actor.default-dispatcher-3]
[akka.actor.ActorSystemImpl(OrderCalculatorServer)] Server online
at http://0:0:0:0:0:0:0:0:8088/
```

6. Then, use the `randomOrder` endpoint to generate a random order:

```
hveiga$ curl -X GET http://localhost:8088/randomOrder
{"deliveryPrice":95.3433758801223,"timestamp":1488135061123,
 "items":
[{"id":0,"quantity":42,"unitPrice":65.01159569545462,
  "percentageDiscount":0.14585908649640444},
 {"id":1,"quantity":7,"unitPrice":27.047124705161696,
  "percentageDiscount":0.06400701658372476},
 {"id":2,"quantity":76,"unitPrice":24.028733083343724,
  "percentageDiscount":0.9906003213266685},
```

```
{"id":3,"quantity":18,"unitPrice":88.77181117560474,
 "percentageDiscount":0.8203117015522584},
{"id":4,"quantity":15,"unitPrice":29.73662623732769}],
 "id":"randomId","metadata":{"notes":"random"}}
```

7. Finally, use the `calculateGrandTotal` endpoint:

```
hveiga$ curl -X POST -H "Content-Type: application/json" --data"
{"deliveryPrice":95.3433758801223,"timestamp":1488135061123,
 "items":
[{"id":0,"quantity":42,"unitPrice":65.01159569545462,
 "percentageDiscount":0.14585908649640444},
 {"id":1,"quantity":7,"unitPrice":27.047124705161696,
 "percentageDiscount":0.06400701658372476},
 {"id":2,"quantity":76,"unitPrice":24.028733083343724,
 "percentageDiscount":0.9906003213266685},
 {"id":3,"quantity":18,"unitPrice":88.77181117560474,
 "percentageDiscount":0.8203117015522584},
 {"id":4,"quantity":15,"unitPrice":29.73662623732769}],
 "id":"randomId","metadata":{"notes":"random"}}"
http://localhost:8088/calculateGrandTotal
{"id":"randomId","amount":4071.565724845945}
```

How it works...

In this recipe, you learned how to easily marshal and unmarshal your case classes to and from JSON, using `spray-json` and `akka-http-spray-json`. As we can see in the definition of our route, just by calling `entity(as[Order])`, the route knows how to format the incoming JSON object into an `Order` object. The same happens when you return either an `Order` or `GrandTotal` object in the `complete` block.

The route looks for an implicitly defined marshaler to achieve this purpose. This functionality is brought through our `OrderJsonSupport` trait, thanks to `SprayJsonSupport`. `SprayJsonSupport` checks whether there is any implicitly defined JSON formatter for your type and uses it to do the serializing. In our case, we had three implicitly defined JSON formatters--`itemFormat`, `orderFormat`, and `grandTotalFormat`. `Spray-json` has formatters for the most common objects, such as `String`, `Int`, `Long`, `List`, and `Map`; however, it needs to be defined for your types. Keep in mind that if your type uses another custom type, it is required to also have the formatter in the scope. In our example, this happened with `Item` and `Order`. An `Order` class contains a list of `Item`, so we need to provide a way for formatting these items to let `Spray-json` do the task.

itemFormat, orderFormat, and grandTotalFormat use the jsonFormat helper method to provide the formatting. The number after jsonFormat just represents how many attributes the case class has. In some scenarios, it might be required for your to serialize the way in a more complicated fashion. This can also be achieved with Spray-json by writing your own formatter (also named JSON protocol) by extending DefaultJsonProtocol and implementing read() and write().

When running the code, we can randomly generate Order by calling the randomOrder endpoint and then using this order to calculate the grand total by calling the caculateGrandTotal endpoint. It is required to set the header Content-Type: application/json to do this POST operation or the route will reject your request. This happens because the marshaler expects this type to deserialize the incoming payload.

 Spray-json has great customization capabilities to do as much as your want. Refer to its GitHub repository to learn more: https://github.com /spray/spray-json.

XML support with Akka HTTP

As seen in the previous recipes, Akka HTTP has great integration for marshaling and unmarshaling. In the previous recipe, we saw how Akka HTTP can easily marshall and unmarshall JSON, thanks to Spray-json. The same is true with XML, thanks to Scala XML. Scala XML is a library that was initially part of the core Scala libraries but was later separated. Scala XML has an idiomatic API to write XML directly in your Scala code.

In this recipe, we will see how to easily integrate scala-xml dependency into our application to serialize and deserialize classes into and from XML.

Getting ready

To step through this recipe, we need to import the Hello-Akka project and the required Akka HTTP dependency we added in the previous recipe. Also, we will include the required scala-xml dependency.

How to do it...

For this recipe, perform the following steps:

1. Get the required dependencies.
2. Edit the `build.sbt` file and add the `akka-http-xml` dependency as follows:

```
libraryDependencies += "com.typesafe.akka" %
  "akka-http-xml_2.11" % "10.0.5"
```

3. Now create a file named `OrderModel.scala` in the `com.packt.chapter9` package. This file will contain the case classes you are going to use. If you did the previous recipe, the model classes will be the same. Also, it will include the trait to do the marshaling and unmarshaling automatically. The content should be as follows:

```
package com.packt.chapter9

import akka.http.scaladsl.marshallers.xml.ScalaXmlSupport
import scala.xml._

case class Item(id: Int, quantity: Int, unitPrice: Double,
  percentageDiscount: Option[Double])

case class Order(id: String, timestamp: Long, items:
  List[Item], deliveryPrice: Double, metadata: Map[String,
  String])

case class GrandTotal(id: String, amount: Double)

trait OrderXmlSupport extends ScalaXmlSupport {
  implicit def grandTotalToXML(g: GrandTotal): NodeSeq =
    <grandTotal><id>{g.id}</id><amount>{g.amount}</amount>
    </grandTotal>

  implicit def orderToXML(o: Order): NodeSeq =
    <order>
      <id>{o.id}</id>
      <timestamp>{o.timestamp}</timestamp>
      <deliveryPrice>{o.deliveryPrice}</deliveryPrice>
      <items>{o.items.map(itemToXML)}</items>
      <metadata>{o.metadata.map(keyValueToXML)}</metadata>
    </order>

  implicit def orderFromXML(xmlOrder: NodeSeq): Order = {
```

```scala
    val id = (xmlOrder  "id").text
    val timestamp = (xmlOrder  "timestamp").text.toLong
    val deliveryPrice = (xmlOrder
      "deliveryPrice").text.toDouble
    val items = (xmlOrder  "item").map(
      itemFromXML).toList
    val metadata = keyValueFromXML(xmlOrder  "metadata")
    Order(id, timestamp, items,
    deliveryPrice, metadata)
  }

  private def keyValueFromXML(xml: NodeSeq) = {
    xml.flatMap {
      case e: Elem => e.child
      case _ => NodeSeq.Empty
    }.map(x => x.label -> x.text).toMap
  }

  private def keyValueToXML(kv: (String, String)) =
    Elem(null, kv._1, Null, TopScope, false, Text(kv._2))

  private def itemFromXML(xmlItem: NodeSeq): Item = {
    val id = (xmlItem  "id").text.toInt
    val quantity = (xmlItem  "quantity").text.toInt
    val unitPrice = (xmlItem  "unitPrice").text.toDouble
    val percentageDiscount =
      if ((xmlItem  "percentageDiscount").isEmpty) None
      else Some((xmlItem
        "percentageDiscount").text.toDouble)

    Item(id, quantity, unitPrice, percentageDiscount)
  }

  private def itemToXML(i: Item) =
    <item>
      <id>{i.id}</id>
      <quantity>{i.quantity}</quantity>
      <unitPrice>{i.unitPrice}</unitPrice>
      {if (i.percentageDiscount.isDefined)
        <percentageDiscount>{i.percentageDiscount.get}
        </percentageDiscount>}
    </item>
  }
```

4. Then, define your route and app. Create a file named
   `OrderCalculatorXmlApplication.scala` inside
   the `com.packt.chapter9` package. The `HttpApp` class will need to mix in
   `OrderXmlSupport`:

```scala
package com.packt.chapter9

import akka.http.scaladsl.server.Directives._
import akka.http.scaladsl.server.HttpApp
import akka.http.scaladsl.settings.ServerSettings
import com.typesafe.config.ConfigFactory

import scala.util.Random._
import scala.xml.NodeSeq

object OrderCalculatorXMLServer extends
 HttpApp with OrderXmlSupport {

  val route =
    path("calculateGrandTotal" ~ Slash.?) {
      post {
        entity(as[NodeSeq]) { xmlOrder =>
          complete {
            calculateGrandTotal(xmlOrder)
          }
        }
      }
    } ~
      path("randomOrder") {
        get {
          complete {
            generateRandomOrder()
          }
        }
      }

  private def calculateGrandTotal(
    o: Order) : NodeSeq = {
    val amount = o.items.map(i =>
      i.percentageDiscount.getOrElse(1.0d)
        * i.unitPrice * i.quantity).sum + o.deliveryPrice
      GrandTotal(o.id, amount)
  }

  private def generateRandomOrder(): NodeSeq = {
    val items = (0 to nextInt(5)).map(i => {
      Item(i, nextInt(100), 100 * nextDouble(),
```

```
            if (nextBoolean()) Some(nextDouble())
              else None)
        }).toList
        Order(nextString(4), System.currentTimeMillis(),
          items, 100 * nextDouble(), Map("notes" -> "random"))
      }
    }

    object OrderCalculatorXMLServerApplication extends App {
      OrderCalculatorXMLServer.startServer("0.0.0.0", 8088,
        ServerSettings(ConfigFactory.load))
    }
```

5. Once the entire code is ready, run the server in either IntelliJ or the command line:

```
hveiga$ sbt "runMain
com.packt.chapter9.OrderCalculatorXMLServerApplication"
[info] Running
com.packt.chapter9.OrderCalculatorXMLServerApplication
Press RETURN to stop...
[INFO] [OrderCalculatorXMLServer-akka.actor.default-dispatcher-2]
[akka.actor.ActorSystemImpl(OrderCalculatorXMLServer)] Server
online at http://0:0:0:0:0:0:0:0:8088/
```

6. Then, use the `randomOrder` endpoint to generate a random order:

```
hveiga$ curl -X GET http://localhost:8088/randomOrder
<order><id>randomId</id><timestamp>1488154717323</timestamp>
<deliveryPrice>11.151244656534509</deliveryPrice>
<items><item><id>0</id><quantity>79</quantity>
<unitPrice>31.787820959521483</unitPrice>
<percentageDiscount>0.10558164031712036
</percentageDiscount></item><item>
<id>1</id><quantity>94</quantity>
<unitPrice>0.37387730640470185</unitPrice>
<percentageDiscount>0.09391514717571126
</percentageDiscount></item><item>
<id>2</id><quantity>70</quantity>
<unitPrice>29.414102463994286</unitPrice>
<percentageDiscount>0.5866072707110512
</percentageDiscount></item><item><id>3</id>
<quantity>84</quantity><unitPrice>67.24909246700179
</unitPrice></item></items><metadata>
<notes>random</notes></metadata></order>
```

7. Finally, use the `calculateGrandTotal` endpoint:

```
hveiga$ curl -X POST -H "Content-Type: application/xml" --data "
<order>
<id>randomId</id><timestamp>1488154717323</timestamp>
<deliveryPrice>11.151244656534509</deliveryPrice><items><item>
<id>0</id>
<quantity>79</quantity><unitPrice>31.787820959521483</unitPrice>
<percentageDiscount>0.10558164031712036</percentageDiscount>
</item>
<item><id>1</id><quantity>94</quantity>
<unitPrice>0.37387730640470185</unitPrice>
<percentageDiscount>0.09391514717571126
</percentageDiscount>
</item><item><id>2</id><quantity>70</quantity>
<unitPrice>29.414102463994286</unitPrice>
<percentageDiscount>0.5866072707110512
</percentageDiscount>
</item><item><id>3</id><quantity>84</quantity>
<unitPrice>67.24909246700179</unitPrice></item></items><metadata>
<notes>random</notes></metadata></order>" http://localhost:8088
/calculateGrandTotal
<grandTotal><id>randomId</id>
<amount>11.151244656534509</amount></grandTotal>
```

How it works...

In this recipe, you learned how to marshal and unmarshal Scala classes into and from XML. For this purpose, we used both Scala XML and `akka-http-xml`. Unlike the approach with `spray-json`, this time we had to code the marshalers and unmarshalers ourselves. It is possible to use other Scala XML tools, such as scalaxb, to generate code that creates these marshallers for you; however, this is outside the scope of this recipe.

The `ScalaXmlSupport` trait has functionality to transform objects from `NodeSeq` to XML and from XML to `NodeSeq`. This is the reason why we needed to provide code to transform the `NodeSeq` instances into our `Order` and `GrandTotal` objects. To achieve this seamlessly, we defined implicit conversion through the `grandTotalToXML`, `orderToXML`, and `orderFromXML` methods in our `OrderXmlSupport` trait that we mixed in our route. Then, we forced the use of these implicit conversations by imposing the return type of `calculateGrandTotal` and `generateRandomOrder` to NodeSeq. Therefore, the conversion Order/GrandTotal > NodeSeq > XML happens automatically.

This approach is a bit more tedious than using `spray-json`, but it provides the same functionality.

 To learn more about scalaxb, visit `http://scalaxb.org/`.

10
Understanding Various Akka patterns

In this chapter, we will cover the following recipes:

- The Master Slave work pulling pattern
- Ordered termination of actors
- Shutdown patterns in Akka
- Scheduling periodic messages to an actor
- Throttling of messages while sending them to an actor
- Balancing workload across actors
- The aggregator pattern
- The CountDownLatch pattern
- Finite-state machine
- The pausable actor pattern
- Enveloping actor

Introduction

Throughout the previous chapters of the book, we have looked at how actors behave and how we can easily create distributed, concurrent and failure-tolerant applications by combining them. Also, actors can be used to create more complex libraries. Two good examples are Akka Streams and Akka HTTP. However, many other use cases require the use of actors themselves.

In this chapter, we will go through different actor pattern recipes to showcase useful common scenarios. We will learn important concepts in order to prevent mailbox message overflow using a Master Slave work pattern, pulling and balancing the workload across a set of actors. We will revisit how to stop children actors in an orderly manner by creating and an elegant way to identify when all actors in an actor system are stopped to terminate it, which might be handy in dynamic environments.

We will also explain the convenient API Akka provided to easily create Finite State Machines just by providing a set of states and events. Moreover, we will learn different enterprise integration patterns, such as Aggregator actor, Pausable actor, or Enveloping actor.

The Master Slave work pulling pattern

We have seen how Akka actors behave: each actor is able to process one message at a time and the rest of the messages get enqueued into the mailbox. If the code inside a given actor takes time, it's likely that the messages sent to that actor will pile up in the mailbox. If the mailbox type is unbounded, this could lead to an out-of-memory error. If it is bounded, it will probably drop messages when it reaches the maximum size.

To have better control over this kind of scenario, we can use the Master Slave work pulling pattern. This pattern lets a master actor control how many slaves can do work and distribute it among them. It only pushes work tasks to them when they are ready. Therefore, it is possible to manage the behavior of your system when all slaves are busy doing work. For example, we could slow the consuming of data in case we are receiving messages from a message broker. This pattern is a primitive kind of back pressure mechanism. For a more sophisticated back pressure method, we could use Akka Streams directly, which provides built-in back pressure across all stages of the stream.

The Master Slave work pulling pattern has been heavily used by the industry to concurrently process independent tasks. This pattern is especially important in Akka since it is possible to seamlessly run slaves in different JVMs thanks to Akka Remote or Akka Cluster. In this recipe, we will explain how to achieve this pattern with actors and what is recommended in order to have a scalable system without any single point of failure.

Getting ready

To step through this recipe, we need to import te Hello-Akka project, which will include a bare Scala sbt project that brings the Akka dependency.

How to do it…

For this recipe, we need to perform the following steps:

1. Let's start with the master actor. This actor will keep a registry of worker actors and a queue of pending tasks. Create a file named `MasterWorkPulling.scala` inside the `com.packt.chapter10` package. The content should look like this:

    ```scala
    package com.packt.chapter10

    import akka.actor.{Actor, ActorLogging, ActorRef, Terminated}
    import com.packt.chapter10.WorkerWorkPulling._
    import com.packt.chapter10.MasterWorkPulling._
    import scala.collection.mutable

    object MasterWorkPulling {
      case object JoinWorker
      case object DeregisterWorker
    }
    ```

2. Additionally, let's define the master actor in the same `MasterWorkPulling.scala` file:

    ```scala
    class MasterWorkPulling(maxQueueSize: Int) extends Actor with
    ActorLogging {
        val workers = mutable.Map.empty[ActorRef, WorkerState]
        val pendingWork = mutable.Queue.empty[Work]

        def receive = {
          case JoinWorker =>
            workers += sender -> Idle
            context.watch(sender)
            log.info(s"New worker registered [$sender]")
          case Terminated(actorRef) => workers -= actorRef
          case DeregisterWorker => workers -= sender
          case PullWork if pendingWork.nonEmpty =>
            log.info(s"Idle worker asking for work. Setting [$sender]
              to [Working] state")
            sender ! pendingWork.dequeue
            workers += sender -> Working
          case PullWork =>
            log.info(s"Idle worker asking for work but no work
              available. Setting [$sender] to [Idle] state")
            workers += sender -> Idle
          case work : Work if pendingWork.size > maxQueueSize =>
            log.info(s"Work received but max pending work tasks
              reached. Rejecting [$work]")
    ```

```
        sender ! RejectWork(work)
   case work : Work =>
     pendingWork.enqueue(work)
     workers.find(_._2 == Idle) match {
       case Some((worker, _)) =>
         val nextWork = pendingWork.dequeue
         worker ! nextWork
         workers += worker -> Working
         log.info(s"Work received and found idle worker.
            Submitting [$nextWork] to [$worker]")
       case None =>
         log.info(s"Work received and no idle worker found.
            Adding to pending work tasks queue.")
     }
   }
 }
}
```

3. Now let's continue with the Worker actor. To simulate work, we will randomly
   sleep a few seconds. Create a file named `WorkerWorkPulling.scala` inside
   package `com.packt.chapter10` with the following code:

```
package com.packt.chapter10

import akka.actor.{Actor, ActorLogging, ActorRef}
import com.packt.chapter10.MasterWorkPulling.{DeregisterWorker,
JoinWorker}
import scala.util.Random

object WorkerWorkPulling {
  trait WorkerState
  case object Idle extends WorkerState
  case object Working extends WorkerState

  case object PullWork
  case class Work(workId: Int, originalSender: ActorRef)
  case class WorkDone(work: Work)
  case class RejectWork(work: Work)
}

class WorkerWorkPulling(master: ActorRef) extends Actor with
ActorLogging {
  import WorkerWorkPulling._
  override def preStart() = master ! JoinWorker
  override def postStop() = master ! DeregisterWorker

  def receive = {
    case work : Work =>
      val millis = Random.nextInt(5) * 1000
```

```
log.info(s"Sleeping for [$millis] millis to simulate
  work.")
Thread.sleep(millis)
work.originalSender ! WorkDone(work)
master ! PullWork
      }
   }
```

4. To run this pattern, we will create a generator actor that will schedule the message to be sent to the master actor. Create a file named GeneratorWorkPulling.scala in the com.packt.chapter10 package. The actor code should be as follows:

```
package com.packt.chapter10

import akka.actor.{Actor, ActorLogging, ActorRef}
import com.packt.chapter10.WorkerWorkPulling.{RejectWork, Work,
WorkDone}
import scala.concurrent.duration._
import scala.util.Random

object GeneratorWorkPulling {
  case object GenerateWork
}

class GeneratorWorkPulling(master: ActorRef) extends Actor with
ActorLogging {
  import GeneratorWorkPulling._
  import context._

  override def preStart() = context.system.scheduler.schedule(1
    second, 1 seconds, self, GenerateWork)

  def receive = {
    case GenerateWork => master ! Work(Random.nextInt(1000),
      self)
    case WorkDone(work) => log.info(s"Work done
      [${work.workId}]")
    case RejectWork(work) => log.info(s"Work rejected
      [${work.workId}]")
  }
}
```

5. At last, let's create our app to test it out. Create a file named
   `WorkPullingApp.scala` inside package `com.packt.chapter10` with the
   following code:

```scala
package com.packt.chapter10

import akka.actor.{ActorSystem, Props}

object WorkPullingApp extends App {
  val actorSystem = ActorSystem()
  val master =
    actorSystem.actorOf(Props(classOf[MasterWorkPulling], 2),
    "master")
  val worker1 =
    actorSystem.actorOf(Props(classOf[WorkerWorkPulling],
    master), "worker1")
  val worker2 =
    actorSystem.actorOf(Props(classOf[WorkerWorkPulling],
    master), "worker2")
    actorSystem.actorOf(Props(classOf[GeneratorWorkPulling],
    master), "generator")
}
```

6. Now let's run the code in either IntelliJ or the command line and analyze the logs:

```
hveiga$ sbt "runMain com.packt.chapter10.WorkPullingApp"
[info] Running com.packt.chapter10.WorkPullingApp
[akka://default/user/master] New worker registered
[Actor[worker2]]
[akka://default/user/master] New worker registered
[Actor[worker1]]
[akka://default/user/worker2] Sleeping for [1000] millis to
simulate work.
[akka://default/user/master] Work received and found idle worker.
Submitting [Work(731,Actor[generator])] to [Actor[worker2]]
[akka://default/user/master] Work received and found idle worker.
Submitting [Work(515,Actor[generator])] to [Actor[worker1]]
[akka://default/user/worker1] Sleeping for [0] millis to simulate
work.
[akka://default/user/master] Idle worker asking for work but no
work available. Setting [Actor[worker1]] to [Idle] state
[akka://default/user/generator] Work done [515]
[akka://default/user/generator] Work done [731]
...
[akka://default/user/master] Work received and no idle worker
found. Adding to pending work tasks queue.
[akka://default/user/master] Work received but max pending work
```

```
tasks reached. Rejecting [Work(341,Actor[generator])]
[akka://default/user/generator] Work rejected [341]
...
```

How it works...

In this recipe, we learned how to use the Master-Worker (or Slave) work pulling pattern. This pattern is usually applied to gain control over the flow of incoming messages to be able to distribute the load more evenly and act when it is not possible to process more work.

In this particular example, the `MasterWorkPulling` actor controls the flow of messages. First, when a new worker joins, it registers it into its internal registry, where it keeps track of which workers are busy and which ones are idle. Also, it starts *watching* them in case they are no longer alive. The master actor also holds a queue of the pending work tasks. This is to maintain a buffer of pending work items instead of directly rejecting work when all workers are busy. Every time new work comes to this actor, it first checks whether we are already maxed out of pending processing tasks. If that is the case, it just responds the sender actor with a `RejectWork` message. In other scenarios, you might not want to reject the work task but do some other action. These actions might be throttling a consumer, informing an autoscaling group that more workers are required, or just signaling an upstream system that all workers are busy. If we have room for pending processing tasks, we check whether there is any idle worker. If there is, we enqueue the incoming work, dequeue the next work item, send it to the worker and set the worker as *Working*. Otherwise, we simply add the work to the end of the queue.

The Worker actor is responsible for a few tasks. On startup, it needs to inform the master actor it is ready to do work. This happens by sending the `JoinWorker` case object to the master. After that, it just waits for work to come. Once it receives work, it does the processing (in our case, it randomly sleeps for some seconds), and then it sends the `workDone` message to the original sender and finally, it sends a message to the master advising that it is free to do more processing. We could have sent the `workDone` message to the master actor and this one to the original sender, but that seems like an unnecessary step.

Finally, we have the Generator actor that simply sends a Work message every 2 seconds to the master actor. This one also logs when a work item has been rejected or done. This actor is just a test actor to demonstrate how the pattern works. If we look at the logs carefully, we can see the workers getting registered. After that, they start processing work as messages come. Eventually, we can see that when the pending work queue is full, the master actor rejects some work messages.

This pattern also works well if we use Akka remote or Akka cluster, where you could create remote actors in different JVMs or machines. We could scale the total number of workers up or down depending on the rate of incoming work messages.

Ordered termination of actors

Actors are usually deployed in hierarchies. This layout brings flexibility to the actor system as well as other features, such as separation of concerns (where an actor will only care about the business logic and the parent would deal with the error handling through the supervision strategy). This layout also has repercussions when stopping actors. When a given actor is terminated, then all children actors of that given actor will also get terminated in a non-deterministic way. However, this default behavior might not always be the desired behavior for your use case. This might be the case when shutting down actors connecting to external services.

In this recipe, we will cover how to do ordered termination of actors to cover scenarios where some actors need to terminate before others. To demonstrate this, we will create a `ServicesManager` actor that will act as the parent of different `ServiceHandler` actors that need to terminate in an order. However, the real parent will be another actor called `OrderedKiller`.

Getting ready

To step through this recipe, we need to import the `Hello-Akka` project; all other prerequisites are the same as earlier.

How to do it...

For this recipe, we need to perform the following steps:

1. Let's start with the worker actors. These actors are the children that you want to terminate in order. Create a file named `ServiceHandler.scala` inside package `com.packt.chapter10` with the following content:

```
package com.packt.chapter10

import akka.actor.{Actor, ActorLogging}

class ServiceHandler extends Actor with ActorLogging {
```

```
    def receive = Actor.ignoringBehavior
    override def preStart() = log.info(s"${self.path.name} is
      running")
    override def postStop() = log.info(s"${self.path.name} has
      stopped")
}
```

2. Second, let's create the `ServicesManager` actor. This actor will act as the parent of the workers but it will receive the children from the real actor parent. Create a file named `ServicesManager.scala` inside package `com.packt.chapter10`. The code should look like this:

```
package com.packt.chapter10

import akka.actor.{Actor, ActorLogging, ActorRef}
import scala.concurrent.duration._

class ServicesManager(childrenCreator: ActorRef) extends Actor
with ActorLogging {
  import OrderedKiller._
  import context._

  override def preStart() = {
    log.info("Asking for my children")
    childrenCreator ! GetChildren(self)
  }

  def waiting: Receive = {
    case Children(kids) =>
      log.info("Children received")
      context.become(initialized(kids))
      context.system.scheduler.scheduleOnce(1 second, self,
        "something")
  }

  def initialized(kids: Iterable[ActorRef]) : Receive = {
    case _ => log.info(s"I have been happily initialized with
      my kids: ${kids.map(_.path.name)}")
  }

  def receive = waiting
  override def postStop() = log.info(s"${self.path.name} has
    stopped")
}
```

3. Afterward, we create the abstract class, OrderedKiller. This class will hold all the logic to orderly kill some actors. Create a file named OrderedKiller.scala inside the com.packt.chapter10 package. The content should look like this:

```scala
package com.packt.chapter10

import akka.actor.{Actor, ActorLogging, ActorRef, Terminated}
import akka.pattern._
import scala.concurrent.duration._
import scala.concurrent.Future

object OrderedKiller {
  case object AllChildrenStopped
  case class GetChildren(parentActor: ActorRef)
  case class Children(children: Iterable[ActorRef])
}

abstract class OrderedKiller extends Actor with ActorLogging {
  import OrderedKiller._
  import context._

  def killChildrenOrderly(orderedChildren: List[ActorRef]):
    Future[Any] = {
      orderedChildren.foldLeft(Future(AllChildrenStopped))(
      (p, child) => p.flatMap(_ => gracefulStop(child, 2
      seconds).map(_ => AllChildrenStopped))
    )
  }

  def noChildrenRegistered: Receive = {
    case GetChildren(parentActor) =>
      watch(parentActor)
      parentActor ! Children(children)
      become(childrenRegistered(parentActor))
  }

  def childrenRegistered(to: ActorRef): Receive = {
    case GetChildren(parentActor) if sender == to =>
      parentActor ! Children(children)
    case Terminated(`to`) =>
      killChildrenOrderly(orderChildren(children)) pipeTo self
    case AllChildrenStopped => stop(self)
  }

  def orderChildren(unorderedChildren: Iterable[ActorRef]) :
List[ActorRef]
  def receive = noChildrenRegistered
```

```
    }
```

4. Then let's create the actor that will extend `OrderedKiller`. Create a file named `ServiceHandlersCreator.scala` inside the `com.packt.chapter10` package. This actor will be responsible for creating all children actors. The code looks like this:

```scala
package com.packt.chapter10

import akka.actor.{ActorRef, Props}

class ServiceHandlersCreator extends OrderedKiller {
  override def preStart() = {
    context.actorOf(Props[ServiceHandler], "DatabaseHandler1")
    context.actorOf(Props[ServiceHandler], "DatabaseHandler2")
    context.actorOf(Props[ServiceHandler],
    "ExternalSOAPHandler")
    context.actorOf(Props[ServiceHandler],
    "ExternalRESTHandler")
  }

  def orderChildren(unorderedChildren: Iterable[ActorRef]) = {
    val result = unorderedChildren.toList.sortBy(_.path.name)
    log.info(s"Killing order is ${result.map(_.path.name)}")
    result
  }
}
```

5. Finally, let's create a small app to demonstrate the behavior of this pattern. Create a file named `OrderedTerminationApp.scala` inside the `com.packt.chapter10` package:

```scala
package com.packt.chapter10

import akka.actor.{ActorSystem, Props}
import scala.concurrent.duration._
import scala.concurrent.Await

object OrderedTerminationApp extends App {
  val actorSystem = ActorSystem()
  val orderedKiller =
actorSystem.actorOf(Props[ServiceHandlersCreator],
  "serviceHandlersCreator")
  val manager =
    actorSystem.actorOf(Props(classOf[ServicesManager],
    orderedKiller), "servicesManager")
  Thread.sleep(2000)
```

```
        actorSystem.stop(manager)
        Await.ready(actorSystem.terminate(), 2.seconds)
    }
```

6. After all the code is ready, let's run the application in either IntelliJ or the command line:

```
hveiga$ sbt "runMain com.packt.chapter10.OrderedTerminationApp"
[info] Running com.packt.chapter10.OrderedTerminationApp
[akka://default/user/servicesManager] Asking for my children
[akka://default/user/serviceHandlersCreator/ExternalSOAPHandler]
ExternalSOAPHandler is running
[akka://default/user/serviceHandlersCreator/DatabaseHandler2]
DatabaseHandler2 is running
[akka://default/user/serviceHandlersCreator/DatabaseHandler1]
DatabaseHandler1 is running
[akka://default/user/serviceHandlersCreator/ExternalRESTHandler]
ExternalRESTHandler is running
[akka://default/user/servicesManager] Children received
[akka://default/user/servicesManager] I have been happily
initialized with my kids: List(DatabaseHandler1,
DatabaseHandler2, ExternalRESTHandler, ExternalSOAPHandler)
...
[akka://default/user/servicesManager] servicesManager has stopped
[akka://default/user/serviceHandlersCreator] Killing order is
List(DatabaseHandler1, DatabaseHandler2, ExternalRESTHandler,
ExternalSOAPHandler)
[akka://default/user/serviceHandlersCreator/DatabaseHandler1]
DatabaseHandler1 has stopped
[akka://default/user/serviceHandlersCreator/DatabaseHandler2]
DatabaseHandler2 has stopped
[akka://default/user/serviceHandlersCreator/ExternalRESTHandler]
ExternalRESTHandler has stopped
[akka://default/user/serviceHandlersCreator/ExternalSOAPHandler]
ExternalSOAPHandler has stopped
```

How it works...

In this recipe, we looked at how to stop children actor in a deterministic way. The pattern relies on having a surrogate actor that creates the children actors instead of the actual actor. In this example, `ServicesManager` should be the one creating all the different `ServiceHandler` actors. However, in order to achieve the ordered termination, we create a third intermediate actor named `ServiceHandlersCreator`. This actor instantiates the children actors. When the `ServicesManager` actor starts, it tells `ServiceHandlersCreator` to get him his children. Then, `ServiceHandlersCreator` does two things: starts watching for `ServicesManager` in case of an actor termination and sends the children list to `ServicesManager`. Afterward, `ServicesManager` changes its behavior to initialized (kids: `Iterable[ActorRef]`), where it behaves as expected and has a reference to the children actors.

Once `ServicesManager` is stopped, `ServiceHandlersCreator` gets notified with a `Terminated` message. Then, it proceeds to orderly stop the children actors. In this example, we are just ordering the children actors alphabetically; however, the order method can be implemented with any logic to cover any scenario. After that, it uses `foldLeft` to traverse the list of ordered children actors and the `gracefulStop` pattern to stop them. This pattern is included in Akka and allows you to pass an actorRef and a timeout to stop and actor. It returns a `Future[Boolean]` type, signaling whether the stopping was successful or not. We map those Futures to a `Future[AllChildrenStopped]` and finally use the Akka pipe pattern to pipe the result of Future for the same actor. Once the actor receives an `AllChildrenStopped` message, it stops itself.

In this recipe, we use various built-in Akka patterns, such `asgracefulStop` and pipe, and it's a good example of the saying in computer science that a problem can be solved by adding another layer of indirection. In our case, this new layer of indirection is the actor `ServiceHandlersCreator`.

Shutdown patterns in Akka

By default, once an actor system is initialized, it stays alive until it is shut down explicitly. At first, it might seem easy to understand when to terminate an actor system, for example, if all mailboxes are empty and there is no actor processing a message for a given period of time. However, in Akka, things are more complex than that. It could be that there is a Future being processed and taking some time to complete. It could also happen an actor sent a message to a remote actor and it's waiting for the response in a remote/cluster environment.

There are different options to decide when an actor system is ready to be terminated. In this recipe, we will introduce the concept of reaper. Reaper will be an actor watching all other actors within the actor system. Only when all those actors are stopped will it proceed with the system shutdown.

Getting ready

To step through this recipe, we need to import the `Hello-Akka` project; all other prerequisites are the same as earlier.

How to do it...

For this recipe, we need to perform the following steps:

1. Let's start with the reaper actor. This actor registers actorRefs from other actors and holds it in a set. Create a file named `Reaper.scala` inside package `com.packt.chapter10`. The code should look like this:

```scala
package com.packt.chapter10

import akka.actor.{Actor, ActorLogging, ActorRef, Terminated}
import scala.collection.mutable

object Reaper {
  case class WatchMe(ref: ActorRef)
}

class Reaper extends Actor with ActorLogging {
  import Reaper._
  val watched = mutable.Set.empty[ActorRef]

  def allActorsTerminated() = {
    log.info("All actors terminated. Proceeding to shutdown
    system.")
    context.system.terminate()
  }

  def receive = {
    case WatchMe(ref) =>
      log.info(s"Registering ${ref.path.name}.")
      context.watch(ref)
      watched += ref
    case Terminated(ref) =>
```

```
        log.info(s"Terminated ${ref.path.name}")
        watched -= ref
        if (watched.isEmpty) allActorsTerminated()
    }

    override def preStart() = log.info(s"${elf.path.name} is
    running")
}
```

2. Second, let's create a trait to make all our actors aware of the reaper actor automatically. This trait will implement the `preStart` method to message the reaper actor when a new actor gets created. We will also provide another method to allow other commands in `preStart`. Create a file named `ReaperAwareActor.scala` inside the `com.packt.chapter10` package with the following content:

```
package com.packt.chapter10

import akka.actor.Actor
import com.packt.chapter10.Reaper.WatchMe

trait ReaperAwareActor extends Actor {
  override final def preStart() = {
    registerReaper()
    preStartPostRegistration()
  }

  private def registerReaper() =
    context.actorSelection("/user/Reaper") ! WatchMe(self)
  def preStartPostRegistration() : Unit = ()
}
```

3. Now let's create a worker actor that will simulate an actor that performs some processing. Create a file named `ShutdownPatternWorker.scala` inside the `com.packt.chapter10` package. The code should be as follows:

```
package com.packt.chapter10

import akka.actor.ActorLogging

class ShutdownPatternWorker extends ReaperAwareActor with
ActorLogging {
  def receive = { case e : Exception => throw e }
  override def preStartPostRegistration() =
    log.info(s"${self.path.name} is running")
  override def postStop() = log.info("${self.path.name} has
```

       stopped")
    }

4. In the same way, let's create a master actor that will also create some children actors. This is to demonstrate that this will also work in actor hierarchies. Create a file named `ShutdownPatternMaster.scala` inside the `com.packt.chapter10` package with the following code:

```scala
package com.packt.chapter10

import akka.actor.{Actor, ActorLogging, Props}
import scala.concurrent.duration._

class ShutdownPatternMaster extends ReaperAwareActor with
ActorLogging {
  import context.dispatcher

  val receive = Actor.emptyBehavior
  override def postStop() = log.info(s"${self.path.name} has
  stopped")

  override def preStartPostRegistration() = {
    val worker1 = context.actorOf(Props[ShutdownPatternWorker],
    "worker1")
    context.actorOf(Props[ShutdownPatternWorker], "worker2")
    context.system.scheduler.scheduleOnce(2 second, worker1,
    new Exception("something went wrong"))
    log.info(s"${self.path.name} is running")
  }
}
```

5. Finally, let's create an app to test it out. Create a file named `ShutdownPatternApp.scala` inside the `com.packt.chapter10` package with the following content:

```scala
package com.packt.chapter10

import akka.actor.{ActorSystem, PoisonPill, Props}
import scala.concurrent.duration._

object ShutdownPatternApp extends App {
  val actorSystem = ActorSystem()
  import actorSystem.dispatcher
  val reaper = actorSystem.actorOf(Props[Reaper], "Reaper")
  val worker =
    actorSystem.actorOf(Props[ShutdownPatternWorker], "worker")
  val master =
```

```
actorSystem.actorOf(Props[ShutdownPatternMaster], "master")
actorSystem.scheduler.scheduleOnce(3 seconds, worker,
PoisonPill)
actorSystem.scheduler.scheduleOnce(5 seconds, master,
PoisonPill)
}
```

6. Once all the code is ready, let's run it in either IntelliJ or the command line:

```
hveiga$ sbt "runMain com.packt.chapter10.ShutdownPatternApp"
[info] Running com.packt.chapter10.ShutdownPatternApp
[akka://default/user/Reaper] Registering worker.
[akka://default/user/Reaper] Registering master.
[akka://default/user/Reaper] Registering worker1.
[akka://default/user/Reaper] Registering worker2.
[[akka://default/user/master/worker1] something went wrong
java.lang.Exception: something went wrong
...
[akka://default/user/Reaper] Registering worker1.
[akka://default/user/Reaper] Terminated worker
[akka://default/user/Reaper] Terminated worker1
[akka://default/user/Reaper] Terminated worker2
[akka://default/user/Reaper] Terminated master
[akka://default/user/Reaper] All actors terminated. Proceeding to
shutdown system.
[success] Total time: 9 s
```

How it works...

In this recipe, we covered how to create a shutdown pattern to terminate an actor system once all actors are terminated. To achieve this, we create another actor called reaper that watches all other actors and holds their actorRefs. Once all actors are terminated, it proceeds to terminate the actor system. To make this intuitive, we create a helper trait named ReaperAwareActor that overrides the preStart method to send a message to the reaper with the actorRef. We do this using actorSelection. This has a few requirements:

- You need to know the actor path of the reaper actor. In this example, it has been hardcoded to /user/Reaper.

- You need to create the reaper actor **before** any of the other actors.

These implications can bring complications to some use cases, but they can be overcome with a more complex solution. For example, the reaper actor name can be retrieved from the configuration. This allows us to be consistent everywhere we use this value. Regarding the creation of the reaper before all other actors, we have different options. One option could be to resolve `actorSelection` in order to make sure the reaper actor exists. Another solution could be to have the `ReaperAwareActor` trait implement two receive behaviors, where the initial one will periodically try to register the actor in the reaper. We can confirm this using the ask pattern. Once registered, the actor would use `context.become` to change the behavior to the desired one.

Inside the master actor, we send an exception message to a worker actor, and this one throws the exception. We do this to demonstrate that even when the actor gets restarted by the default supervision strategy, the actor ref does not change and, therefore, when the message gets sent to the reaper actor again, the reaper actor already has it. Another point worth mentioning is that we are using `PoisonPill` messages to terminate actors. This is a better way than calling `context.stop()` since it allows the remaining messages in the mailboxes to be processed.

In the logs, we can see that once all actors have been terminated; the reaper then proceeds to terminate the actor system and the Java process terminates with success.

Scheduling periodic messages to an actor

Scheduling messages is another common task in Akka. Akka brings a built-in scheduler that lets you schedule messages to be sent to actors either once or periodically. While the name of the component is "scheduler", the actual implementation performs delayed delivery of messages to actors. That is why some people argue that it probably should have been called "deferrer" or "delayer". Moreover, it only allows you to schedule messages to be delivered from the moment you call the method. This lets you schedule things to happen within a given duration or every so often. However, it does not allow you to schedule things in a more standard way, for example, sending this message to this actor every day at midnight.

That is why we are also going to see an open source project that integrates the quartz scheduler into Akka. This extension brings all the functionality of a true scheduler such as Quartz into the actor world.

Getting ready

To step through this recipe, we need to import the `Hello-Akka` project, all other prerequisites are the same as earlier. Also, we will define the required dependency to bring the Akka Quartz Scheduler extension.

How to do it...

For this recipe, we need to perform the following steps:

1. We need to bring the required dependencies.
2. Edit the `build.sbt` file and add the Akka Stream dependency, as follows:

```
libraryDependencies += "com.enragedginger" % "akka-quartz-
scheduler_2.11" % "1.6.0-akka-2.4.x"
```

3. Let's create an actor that will use the built-in scheduler. Create a file named `MessageAkkaScheduler.scala` inside the `com.packt.chapter10` package. The content should look like this:

```
package com.packt.chapter10

import akka.actor.{Actor, ActorLogging, Cancellable}
import scala.concurrent.duration._

object MessageAkkaScheduler {
  case object JustOne
  case object Every2Seconds
}

class MessageAkkaScheduler extends Actor with ActorLogging {
  import MessageAkkaScheduler._
  import context.dispatcher
  var scheduleCancellable : Cancellable = _

  override def preStart() = {
    context.system.scheduler.scheduleOnce(2 seconds, self,
    JustOne)
    scheduleCancellable = context.system.scheduler.schedule(2
    seconds, 1 second, self, Every2Seconds)
  }

  override def postStop() = scheduleCancellable.cancel()
  def receive = { case x => log.info(s"Received $x") }
}
```

4. Then, let's create another actor that will use the quartz scheduler. Create a file named `MessageQuartzScheduler.scala` inside the `com.packt.chapter10` package with the following content:

```scala
package com.packt.chapter10

import akka.actor.{Actor, ActorLogging}
import com.typesafe.akka.extension.quartz
.QuartzSchedulerExtension

object MessageQuartzScheduler {
  case object Every2Seconds
}

class MessageQuartzScheduler extends Actor with ActorLogging {
  import MessageQuartzScheduler._
  override def preStart() =
    QuartzSchedulerExtension(context.system)
    .schedule("Every2Seconds", self, Every2Seconds)
  override def postStop() =
    QuartzSchedulerExtension(context.system)
    .cancelJob("Every2Seconds")
  def receive = { case x => log.info(s"Received $x") }
}
```

5. Finally, let's create an app to run the code. This time, we will also pass the configuration when instantiating the actor system. Create a file named `SchedulingMessagesApp.scala` inside the `com.packt.chapter10` package. The code would be as follows:

```scala
package com.packt.chapter10

import akka.actor.{ActorSystem, Props}
import com.typesafe.config.ConfigFactory

object SchedulingMessagesApp extends App {
  val c = """akka.quartz.schedules.Every2Seconds.expression =
    "*/2 * * ? * *""""
  val actorSystem = ActorSystem("scheduling",
    ConfigFactory.parseString(c))
  actorSystem.actorOf(Props[MessageAkkaScheduler],
    "MessageAkkaScheduler")
  actorSystem.actorOf(Props[MessageQuartzScheduler],
    "MessageQuartzScheduler")
  Thread.sleep(10000)
  actorSystem.terminate()
}
```

6. After all the code is ready, let's run it in either IntelliJ or the command line:

```
hveiga$ sbt "runMain com.packt.chapter10.SchedulingMessagesApp"
[info] Running com.packt.chapter10.SchedulingMessagesApp
[20:14:19.767] [[QuartzScheduler~scheduling]] Setting up
scheduled job 'Every2Second', with
'com.typesafe.akka.extension.quartz.QuartzCronSchedule@4f7da7ba'
[20:14:20.018] [akka://scheduling/user/MessageQuartzScheduler]
Received EverySecond
[20:14:21.732] [akka://scheduling/user/MessageAkkaScheduler]
Received JustOne
[20:14:21.732] [akka://scheduling/user/MessageAkkaScheduler]
Received EverySecond
[20:14:22.004] [akka://scheduling/user/MessageQuartzScheduler]
Received EverySecond
...
[20:14:28.005] [akka://scheduling/user/MessageQuartzScheduler]
Received EverySecond
[20:14:28.730] [akka://scheduling/user/MessageAkkaScheduler]
Received EverySecond
[20:14:29.718] [[QuartzScheduler~scheduling]] Cancelling Quartz
Job 'Every2Second'
[success] Total time: 13 s
```

How it works...

In this recipe, we covered how to schedule messages within an actor system. Through the actor MessageAkkaScheduler, we can see how the actor system provides a built-in scheduler. This scheduler lets you schedule messages to be sent after a given duration through the scheduleOnce method or periodically with an initial delay using the method schedule. We can also see how the scheduler returns an instance of Cancellable. This allows you to cancel the delivery of messages in case your use case requires it. Another good point to mention is that the scheduler needs execution content in order to execute these tasks. We are importing context.dispatcher for this purpose. This allows the scheduler to use the same dispatcher as your actor system.

In `MessageQuartzScheduler`, we cover how to use the quartz scheduler extension. The `QuartzSchedulerExtension` class allows you to schedule message to be delivered to a given actor. The actual schedule gets defined in the Akka configuration, and they are referenced by name. In this example, we define a schedule named `Every2Second` in `SchedulingMessagesApp` and pass the configuration when we create the actor system. The quartz scheduler uses Cron expressions to understand when it needs to trigger. For example, to send every 2 seconds, we use the `*/2 * * ? * *` expression. If `QuartzSchedulerExtension` cannot find a schedule matching the given name, it will throw an exception. As in the Akka scheduler, it is possible to cancel this running schedule by calling `QuartzSchedulerExtension.cancelJob()`.

> You can learn more about Cron expressions at `http://www.quartz-scheduler.org/documentation/quartz-2.x/tutorials/crontrigger.html`.

Throttling of messages while sending them to an actor

There are some scenarios where you need to limit the rate at which you are sending some messages. For example, this happens when we need to use an external service. This service might have a threshold upon which you get blocked, or it becomes a pay-as-you-go utility. Akka provides a timer-based throttler as part of the `akka-contrib` module to achieve this kind of behavior.

In this recipe, we will revisit how to configure and use the timer-based throttler and provide an explanation of what the implications are.

Getting ready

To step through this recipe, we need to import the `Hello-Akka` project; all other prerequisites are the same as earlier. Also, we will define the required dependency to bring the Akka Contrib module.

How to do it...

For this recipe, we need to perform the following steps:

1. We need to bring the required dependencies.

2. Edit `build.sbt` file and add the Akka Stream dependency, as follows:

   ```
   libraryDependencies += "com.typesafe.akka" % "akka-
   contrib_2.11" % "2.4.4"
   ```

3. To begin with, lets create a receiver actor. This actor's only task will be to log a statement when it has received a message. Create a file named `EasyToOverwhelmReceiver.scala` inside the `com.packt.chapter10` package. The content should look like this:

   ```scala
   package com.packt.chapter10

   import akka.actor.{Actor, ActorLogging}

   class EasyToOverwhelmReceiver extends Actor with ActorLogging {
   def receive = { case x => log.info(s"Received $x") }
   }
   ```

4. Then, let's create an actor that will send the messages we want to throttle. Create a file named `ReallyFastSender.scala` inside the the `com.packt.chapter10` package. The code will be as follows:

   ```scala
   package com.packt.chapter10

   import akka.actor.{Actor, ActorLogging, ActorRef}
   import scala.concurrent.duration._
   import scala.util.Random

   object ReallyFastSender {
     case object Tick
     case class ReallyImportantMessage(i: Int)
   }

   class ReallyFastSender(nextActor: ActorRef) extends Actor with
   ActorLogging {
     import ReallyFastSender._
     import context.dispatcher
     override def preStart() = context.system.scheduler.schedule(2
     second, 200 millis, self, Tick)

     def receive = {
   ```

```
    case Tick =>
      val msg = ReallyImportantMessage(Random.nextInt(100))
      log.info(s"Sending $msg")
      nextActor ! msg
  }
}
```

5. Finally, let's create the app to run it where we will define the throttler. Create a file named `ThrottlingApp.scala` inside the `com.packt.chapter10` package. The content should be like this:

```
package com.packt.chapter10

import akka.actor.{ActorSystem, Props}
import akka.contrib.throttle.Throttler._
import akka.contrib.throttle.TimerBasedThrottler
import scala.concurrent.duration._

object ThrottlingApp extends App {
  val actorSystem = ActorSystem()
  val throttler =
    actorSystem.actorOf(Props(classOf[TimerBasedThrottler], 2
    msgsPer 1.second))
  val easyToOverwhelmReceiver =
    actorSystem.actorOf(Props[EasyToOverwhelmReceiver],
    "receiver")
    throttler ! SetTarget(Some(easyToOverwhelmReceiver))
    actorSystem.actorOf(Props(classOf[ReallyFastSender],
    throttler), "sender")
}
```

6. Once all the code is ready, let's run it either in IntelliJ or the command line. This app will not stop by itself, so you can terminate it manually at your convenience:

```
hveiga$ sbt "runMain com.packt.chapter10.ThrottlingApp"
[info] Running com.packt.chapter10.ThrottlingApp
[21:53:57.351] [akka://default/user/sender] Sending
ReallyImportantMessage(16)
[21:53:57.357] [akka://default/user/receiver] Received
ReallyImportantMessage(16)
[21:53:57.540] [akka://default/user/sender] Sending
ReallyImportantMessage(52)
[21:53:57.541] [akka://default/user/receiver] Received
ReallyImportantMessage(52)
[21:53:57.739] [akka://default/user/sender] Sending
ReallyImportantMessage(38)
[21:53:57.941] [akka://default/user/sender] Sending
```

```
ReallyImportantMessage(53)
[21:53:58.382] [akka://default/user/receiver] Received
ReallyImportantMessage(38)
[21:53:58.383] [akka://default/user/receiver] Received
ReallyImportantMessage(53)
[21:53:58.540] [akka://default/user/sender] Sending
ReallyImportantMessage(92)
[21:53:58.741] [akka://default/user/sender] Sending
ReallyImportantMessage(26)
```

How it works...

In this recipe, we covered how to use a throttler actor to control the rate of the message coming out. Akka provides a timer-based throttler in the `akka-contrib` module that helps you control the rate by passing a `Rate` object. In our example, we are implicitly defining our rate of two messages per second by giving `2 msgsPer 1.second` when creating the throttler actor. After instantiating, we need to initialize the throttler by setting the target actor. In our case, we do this by sending a message to the throttler with the message `SetTarget`. To verify that all is working as expected, we run the application and then we can see that for any given second, there are only two messages received.

Meanwhile, this implementation throttles messages to the desired rate, and it also brings some complications. By default, all messages are queued in an internal queue inside the throttler. This means that all messages will be stored and it environments with millions of messages per second, this solution might lead to an out-of-memory error. Moreover, this implementation does not support persistence. If your actor dies, you will not be able to recover the messages that were waiting in the internal queue. Another interesting point to mention is the weakness of the throttling. Since they are based on a timer, there could be scenarios where you are sending more than what's excepted depending on when your timer triggers. Finally, messages are not delivered spread evenly in time but rather together when the timer triggers. This can also cause unexpected behaviors.

The Akka team recommends that you move to a more robust solution rather than using the time-based throttler. The solution is to migrate to Akka Streams and use the out-of-the-box throttler.

 Find more information about the Akka Streams throttler at `http://doc.akka.io/docs/akka/current/scala/stream/stages-overview.html#throttle`.

Balancing workload across actors

Often, you may want to ensure that all your worker actors are processing roughly the same number of messages. Akka provides a couple of interesting approaches to achieve this behavior. The first one is using a balancing dispatcher. This dispatcher is backed by `ExecutorService` where a group of actors shares the same mailbox. The dispatcher will try to redistribute work from busy actors to idle actors. This dispatcher can be easily used by implementing `BalancingPool`, as we will see in this recipe.

The second option is using `SmallestMailboxRouter`. When sending a message, this type of router would try to route the message to the actor with the mailbox with fewer messages. In this recipe, we will look at how to configure our actors to use either of these approaches.

Getting ready

To step through this recipe, we need to import the `Hello-Akka` project; all other prerequisites are the same as earlier.

How it works...

For this recipe, we need to perform the following steps:

1. First, create a file named `BalancedWorker.scala` inside the `com.packt.chapter10` package. This file will contain an actor that will be simulated for processing. The content should look like this:

```scala
package com.packt.chapter10

import akka.actor.{Actor, ActorLogging}

object BalancedWorker {
  case class WorkTask(id: Int)
}

class BalancedWorker extends Actor with ActorLogging {
  import BalancedWorker._

  def receive = {
    case WorkTask(id) =>
      log.info(s"[$id] Sleeping for 1000 milliseconds.")
      Thread.sleep(1000)
```

```
        }
    }
```

2. Second, let's create a file with two apps. The first one will use the balancing dispatcher approach using `BalancingPool`. The second one will use the smallest mailbox router approach using `SmallestMailboxPool`. Create a file named `BalancingWorkApp.scala` inside the `com.packt.chapter10` package. The code is as follows:

```scala
package com.packt.chapter10

import akka.actor.{ActorSystem, Props}
import akka.routing.{BalancingPool, SmallestMailboxPool}
import com.packt.chapter10.BalancedWorker.WorkTask
import scala.concurrent.duration._
import scala.util.Random

object BalancingDispatcherApp extends App {
  val actorSystem = ActorSystem()
  val workerPool =
    actorSystem.actorOf(Props[BalancedWorker].
    withRouter(BalancingPool(4)),"workers")
  import actorSystem.dispatcher
  actorSystem.scheduler.schedule(1 second, 200 millis)
  (sendTask)
  def sendTask : Unit = workerPool !
    WorkTask(Random.nextInt(10000))
}

object SmallestMailboxRouterApp extends App {
  val actorSystem = ActorSystem()
  val workerPool =
    actorSystem.actorOf(Props[BalancedWorker].
    withRouter(SmallestMailboxPool(4)),"workers")
  import actorSystem.dispatcher
  actorSystem.scheduler.schedule(1 second, 200 millis)
  (sendTask)
  def sendTask() : Unit = workerPool !
    WorkTask(Random.nextInt(10000))
}
```

3. Once the code is ready, let's run the two different apps and analyze the logs. First, let's run `BalancingDispatcherApp` in either IntelliJ or the command line:

```
hveiga$ sbt "runMain com.packt.chapter10.BalancingDispatcherApp"
[info] Running com.packt.chapter10.BalancingDispatcherApp
[akka://default/user/workers/$a] [6920] Sleeping for 1000
```

```
milliseconds.
[akka://default/user/workers/$b] [4051] Sleeping for 1000
milliseconds.
[akka://default/user/workers/$d] [9] Sleeping for 1000
milliseconds.
[akka://default/user/workers/$c] [5623] Sleeping for 1000
milliseconds.
[akka://default/user/workers/$a] [9806] Sleeping for 1000
milliseconds.
[akka://default/user/workers/$b] [3888] Sleeping for 1000
milliseconds.
[akka://default/user/workers/$d] [9338] Sleeping for 1000
milliseconds.
[akka://default/user/workers/$c] [5259] Sleeping for 1000
milliseconds.
[akka://default/user/workers/$a] [8054] Sleeping for 1000
milliseconds.
. . .
```

4. Finally, run `SmallestMailboxRouterApp` in either IntelliJ or the command line:

```
hveiga$ sbt "runMain
com.packt.chapter10.SmallestMailboxRouterApp"
[info] Running com.packt.chapter10.SmallestMailboxRouterApp
[akka://default/user/workers/$a] [5534] Sleeping for 1000
milliseconds.
[akka://default/user/workers/$b] [4581] Sleeping for 1000
milliseconds.
[akka://default/user/workers/$c] [5318] Sleeping for 1000
milliseconds.
[akka://default/user/workers/$d] [9493] Sleeping for 1000
milliseconds.
[akka://default/user/workers/$a] [2934] Sleeping for 1000
milliseconds.
[akka://default/user/workers/$b] [8072] Sleeping for 1000
milliseconds.
[akka://default/user/workers/$c] [3817] Sleeping for 1000
milliseconds.
[akka://default/user/workers/$d] [4976] Sleeping for 1000
milliseconds.
[akka://default/user/workers/$a] [7379] Sleeping for 1000
milliseconds.
. . .
```

How it works...

In this recipe, we covered how to distribute messages evenly to a pool of actors using two different approaches. Both are similar; however, they do not behave exactly the same. The balancing dispatcher tries to distribute the messages as evenly as possible. This happens thanks to having only one mailbox that is shared among all the routee actors. In the logs, when we execute `BalancingDispatcherApp`, we can see how the messages are getting processed: all actors from `$a` to `$e` get a message before any of them get a second message. Then, we see the actors processing messages using the `$a -> $b -> $d -> $c` pattern and then starting with `$a` again. We should not worry about not getting an alphabetical sequence since all routees are identical.

The `SmallestMailboxRouter` approach is comparable; however, a few other rules apply when using a `SmallestMailboxPool` router. We mentioned earlier that an incoming message would end up in the mailbox with fewer number of messages. However, the selection of the routee happens in the following order:

1. Select **any** idle routee that has a mailbox with no messages
2. Select **any** routee with empty mailbox
3. Select the routee with the fewest messages in its mailbox
4. Select **any** remote routee (remote actors are considered the lowest priority since their mailbox size is unknown)

This is the reason why we do not see the same kind of actor sequence processing the messages in the `SmallestMailboxRouterApp` logs. At some point, there might be multiple actors with empty mailboxes or idle actors with empty mailboxes; then, the algorithm will pick any of those actors. Therefore, some actors **might** be processing more messages than others.

Even if these two approaches are great to distribute work across a group of routee actors, neither of the solutions provide a back pressure mechanism or any control to prevent mailbox overflow. This could lead to out-of-memory errors or unexpected dropping of messages. To overcome these problems, we can use a different pattern, such as Master Slave work pulling pattern, which we revisited at the beginning of this chapter and which allows you to control how much work a worker does.

The aggregator pattern

The aggregator pattern is mainly used to collect data from different sources, package that data together, and then proceed to do something with the aggregated outcome. A good example is retrieving account balances from multiple accounts. Once you have all the required information, you package and deliver it together to, for example, a mobile device or an API.

In this recipe, we will look at how to use the Aggregator trait, which provides the means to achieve the behavior we explained in the previous paragraphs. The Aggregator trait is also part of the akka-contrib module. To demonstrate this, we will create a social network feed aggregator. This aggregator actor will ask other actors for the latest posts in various social networks from a given user. Since accessing the real APIs of social networks is out of the scope of this recipe, we will just simulate it using some other actors.

Getting ready

To step through this recipe, we need to import the Hello-Akka project; all other prerequisites are the same as earlier. Also, we will define the required dependency to bring the akka-contrib module.

How to do it…

For this recipe, we need to perform the following steps:

1. We need to bring the required dependencies.
2. Edit the build.sbt file and add Akka Stream dependency, as follows:

```
libraryDependencies += "com.typesafe.akka" % "akka-
contrib_2.11" % "2.4.4"
```

3. To begin with, let's create an actor that simulates getting latest posts from a social network. Create a file named SocialMediaHandler.scala inside the com.packt.chapter10 package. The content should look like this:

```
package com.packt.chapter10

import akka.actor.{Actor, ActorLogging}
import com.packt.chapter10.SocialMediaAggregator.
{GetLatestPosts, LatestPostResult, Post}
import scala.util.Random
```

```
class SocialMediaHandler(socialMedia: String) extends Actor
with ActorLogging {
  def receive = {
    case GetLatestPosts(id) =>
      Thread.sleep(Random.nextInt(4) * 100)
      val posts = (0 to Random.nextInt(2)).map(_ => Post("some
        title", "some content"))
      sender ! LatestPostResult(socialMedia, posts)
  }
}
```

4. Then, let's create the aggregator actor and the messages that will be used to communicate with other actors. Create a file named SocialMediaAggregator.scala inside the com.packt.chapter10 package. The code to define the messages should be as follows:

```
package com.packt.chapter10

import akka.actor.{Actor, ActorLogging, ActorRef, PoisonPill}
import akka.contrib.pattern.Aggregator
import scala.collection.mutable
import scala.concurrent.duration._

object SocialMediaAggregator {
  case object GetPosts
  case object ReturnPosts
  case class StartFetching(userId: String, period:
  FiniteDuration)
  case class StopFetching(userId: String)
  case class GetLatestPosts(userId: String)
  case class Post(title: String, content: String)
  case class LatestPostResult(socialNetwork: String, posts:
  Seq[Post])
  case class Report(list: List[LatestPostResult])
}
```

5. Additionally, we can create the aggregator actor in the same SocialMediaAggregator.scala file:

```
class SocialMediaAggregator(handlers: List[ActorRef]) extends
Actor with Aggregator with ActorLogging {
  import SocialMediaAggregator._
  import context._
  val initBehavior : Receive = {
    case StartFetching(id, period) =>
      log.info(s"Fetching latest posts for $id")
      new LatestPostsAggregator(sender, id, period)
```

```
  }
  expectOnce(initBehavior)

  class LatestPostsAggregator(originalSender: ActorRef, userId:
  String, period: FiniteDuration) {
    val latestPosts =
      mutable.ArrayBuffer.empty[LatestPostResult]
    val returnPostCancel =
      context.system.scheduler.schedule(1.second, period, self,
      ReturnPosts)
    val getPostsCancel =
      context.system.scheduler.schedule(0.seconds, 400 millis,
      self, GetPosts)

    val behavior : Receive = {
      case GetPosts => handlers.foreach(_ !
      GetLatestPosts(userId))
      case lpr : LatestPostResult => latestPosts += lpr
      case ReturnPosts =>
        originalSender ! Report(latestPosts.toList)
        latestPosts.clear()
      case StopFetching(id) =>
        log.info(s"Stopping latest posts fetching for $id")
        returnPostCancel.cancel()
        getPostsCancel.cancel()
        context.system.scheduler.scheduleOnce(5 seconds, self,
        PoisonPill)
    }
    expect(behavior)
  }
}
```

6. Afterward, let's create an actor that will ask `SocialMediaAggregator` to aggregate the data and, once ready, it will send back the combined data. Create a file named `SocialMediaStalker.scala` inside the `com.package.chapter10` package. The content should be as follows:

```
package com.packt.chapter10

import akka.actor.{Actor, ActorLogging, ActorRef,
ReceiveTimeout}
import com.packt.chapter10.SocialMediaAggregator.{Report,
StartFetching, StopFetching}
import scala.collection.mutable
import scala.concurrent.duration._

class SocialMediaStalker(aggregator: ActorRef, userId: String)
```

```
extends Actor with ActorLogging {
  import context.dispatcher
  context.setReceiveTimeout(10 seconds)
  val counts = mutable.Map.empty[String,
    Int].withDefaultValue(0)

  override def preStart() = {
    log.info("Politely asking to aggregate")
    aggregator ! StartFetching(userId, 1 second)
    context.system.scheduler.scheduleOnce(5 second, aggregator,
    StopFetching(userId))
  }
  override def postStop() = log.info(s"Stopping. Overall counts
    for $userId: $counts")

  def receive = {
    case Report(list) =>
      val stats =
        list.groupBy(_.socialNetwork).
        mapValues(_.map(_.posts.size).sum)
      log.info(s"New report: $stats")
      stats.foreach(kv => counts += kv._1 -> (counts(kv._1) +
      kv._2))
    case ReceiveTimeout => context.stop(self)
  }
}
```

7. Finally, let's create an app to run the example. Create a file named `AggregatorPatternApp.scala` inside the `com.packt.chapter10` package with the following code:

```
package com.packt.chapter10

import akka.actor.{ActorSystem, Props}

object AggregatorPatternApp extends App {
  val actorSystem = ActorSystem()
  val tHandler =
    actorSystem.actorOf(Props(classOf[SocialMediaHandler],
    "Twitter"), "twitterHandler")
  val fHandler =
    actorSystem.actorOf(Props(classOf[SocialMediaHandler],
    "Facebook"), "facebookHandler")
  val lHandler =
    actorSystem.actorOf(Props(classOf[SocialMediaHandler],
    "LinkedIn"), "linkedInHandler")
  val handlers = List(tHandler, fHandler, lHandler)
  val aggregator =
```

```
        actorSystem.actorOf(Props(classOf[SocialMediaAggregator],
          handlers), "aggregator")
      actorSystem.actorOf(Props(classOf[SocialMediaStalker],
        aggregator, "stalker"), "stalker")
    }
```

8. Once all the code is ready, let's run it on either IntelliJ or the command line:

```
hveiga$ sbt "runMain com.packt.chapter10.AggregatorPatternApp"
[info] Running com.packt.chapter10.AggregatorPatternApp
[akka://default/user/stalker] Politely asking to aggregate
[akka://default/user/aggregator] Fetching latest posts for
stalker
[akka://default/user/stalker] New report: Map(Twitter -> 3,
LinkedIn -> 3, Facebook -> 3)
...
[akka://default/user/stalker] New report: Map(Twitter -> 4,
LinkedIn -> 4, Facebook -> 6)
[akka://default/user/aggregator] Stopping latest posts fetching
for stalker
[akka://default/user/stalker] New report: Map(Twitter -> 5,
LinkedIn -> 4, Facebook -> 4)
[akka://default/user/stalker] Stopping. Overall counts for
stalker: Map(Twitter -> 18, LinkedIn -> 20, Facebook -> 19)
```

How it works...

In this recipe, we covered how to use the aggregator pattern. This pattern is commonly used to aggregate data from different locations and package the result as a single data unit. In our case, we aggregate posts from different social networks, we get results for a period of time, and then we log a small report for it.

The SocialMediaHandler actors are responsible for simulating access to the different social networks. When they get a GetLatestPosts message, they generate a random number of posts and send them back. The SocialMediaStalker actor is responsible for asking the aggregator to get some data from those social networks and once it's done, it logs a report of the number of posts per social network there are.

The interesting portion of this recipe relies on the `SocialMediaAggregator` actor. As we can see, this actor class also mixes in the `Aggregator` trait. This trait brings in some methods that we can use to specify the behavior of our aggregation. These methods are `expectOnce`, `expect`, and `unexpect`. All of them take a `Receive` object, which basically means `PartialFunction[Any,Unit]` that represents what to do with the incoming messages. These methods stack the given `Receive` objects to understand and allow you to perform similar operations as become/unbecome. The `expect` and `expectOnce` methods return a handler that you can later use in unexpect to remove a given behavior from the stack. In our example, we start using `expectOnce`. The `expectOnce` method uses a `Receive` object only once and then removes it from the behavior stack. After receiving a `StartFetching` message, we create an inner class and call expect(behavior). From that point, behavior is the `Receive` object that will handle the incoming messages. It's in this behavior that the actual aggregation occurs. We first tell all the handlers to go to `GetLatestPosts`. Every time we receive `LatestPostResult`, we append it to our `ArrayBuffer`. Once the scheduler sends a `ReturnPosts` message, we send the report to the original sender. It is required to keep the reference of the original sender in this scenario. At some point, `SocialMediaStalker` sends a `StopFetching` message. Then, we proceed to cancel all schedulers and schedule a `PoisonPill` message to happen in the future in order to process the remaining results.

Even though we have not shown it in this example, it is possible to do some behavior chaining by calling `expect`, `expectOne`, and `unexpect` multiple times with different behaviors to cover other scenarios where, for example, the aggregator actor needs to remain alive. It is strongly recommended that you do not override the `receive` method since the trait is handling it by itself and you might be breaking some functionality.

The CountDownLatch pattern

Another pattern we can easily implement using Akka is CountDownLatch. The basic behavior of a latch is to wait until the count has reached zero in order to allow another action to happen. This is normally referred to as "to open the gate". The idea is to have some processing tasks running in other threads or services and wait until all of them have been completed. This pattern has multiple use cases. For example, it can be used to aggregate some elements into a single unit similarly in order to have what we implemented in the previous recipe, *The aggregator pattern*.

In this recipe, we will demonstrate how to create a `CountDownLatch` actor and use it to wait until some other processing tasks are happening in other actors. We will implement two approaches: `Future` and `Await`.

Getting ready

To step through this recipe, we need to import the `Hello-Akka` project; all other prerequisites are the same as earlier.

How to do it...

For this recipe, we need to perform the following steps:

1. To begin with, let's create CountDownLatch. We will have three pieces for this: a Scala object to create one, a Scala class that holds the methods to interact with it, and finally, an actor that does the thread-safe counting. Create a file named `CountDownLatch.scala` inside the `com.packt.chapter10` package and let's start with the Scala object and Scala class:

```scala
package com.packt.chapter10

import akka.Done
import akka.actor.{Actor, ActorLogging, ActorRef, ActorSystem,
Props}
import scala.concurrent.{Await, Future, Promise}
import scala.concurrent.duration._
import com.packt.chapter10.CountDownLatch._

object CountDownLatch {
  case object CountDown

  def apply(count:Int)(implicit actorSystem: ActorSystem) = {
    val promise = Promise[Done]()
    val props = Props(classOf[CountDownLatchActor], count,
      promise)
    val countDownLatchActor = actorSystem.actorOf(props,
      "countDownLatchActor")
    new CountDownLatch(countDownLatchActor, promise)
  }
}

class CountDownLatch(private val actor: ActorRef, private val
promise: Promise[Done]) {
  def countDown() = actor ! CountDown
  def await() : Unit = Await.result(promise.future, 10 minutes)
  val result : Future[Done] = promise.future
}
```

2. After that, in the same file, let's create the actor:

```
class CountDownLatchActor(count: Int, promise: Promise[Done])
extends Actor with ActorLogging {
  var remaining = count

  def receive = {
    case CountDown if remaining - 1  == 0 =>
      log.info("Counting down")
      promise.success(Done)
      log.info("Gate opened")
      context.stop(self)
    case CountDown =>
      log.info("Counting down")
      remaining -= 1
  }
}
```

3. Then, let's create an actor that will simulate some processing and signal the latch. Create a file named CountDownLatchWorker.scala inside the com.packt.chapter10 package. The content should look like this:

```
package com.packt.chapter10

import akka.actor.{Actor, ActorLogging}
import scala.util.Random

class CountDownLatchWorker(countDownLatch: CountDownLatch)
extends Actor with ActorLogging {
  override def preStart() = {
    val millis = Random.nextInt(5) * 100
    log.info(s"Sleeping $millis millis")
    Thread.sleep(millis)
    countDownLatch.countDown()
  }
  def receive = Actor.ignoringBehavior
}
```

4. Finally, let's create the app to run the example. Create a file named CoundDownLatchApp.scala inside the com.packt.chapter10 package with the following content:

```
package com.packt.chapter10

import akka.actor.{ActorSystem, Props}
import akka.routing.RoundRobinPool
```

```
object CountDownLatchApp extends App {
  implicit val actorSystem = ActorSystem()
  import actorSystem._
  val routeesToSetUp = 2
  val countDownLatch = CountDownLatch(routeesToSetUp)
  actorSystem.actorOf(Props(classOf[CountDownLatchWorker],
  countDownLatch)
    .withRouter(RoundRobinPool(routeesToSetUp)), "workers")

  //Future based solution
  countDownLatch.result.onSuccess { case _ => log.info("Future
  completed successfully") }

  //Await based solution, you can do something else after latch
  //is open
  countDownLatch.await()
  actorSystem.terminate()
}
```

5. Once all the code is ready, let's run the app in either IntelliJ or the command line:

```
hveiga$ sbt "runMain com.packt.chapter10.CountDownLatchApp"
[info] Running com.packt.chapter10.CountDownLatchApp
[akka://default/user/workers/$a] Sleeping 0 millis
[akka://default/user/workers/$b] Sleeping 200 millis
[akka://default/user/countDownLatchActor] Counting down
[akka://default/user/countDownLatchActor] Counting down
[akka://default/user/countDownLatchActor] Gate opened
[akka.actor.ActorSystemImpl(default)] Future completed
successfully
[success] Total time: 4 s
```

How it works...

In this recipe, we covered how to develop CountDownLatch by leveraging Akka actors. We start by creating a CountDownLatch object, where you pass the count and, implicitly, an actor system. This object is responsible for instantiating the CountDownLatchActor class, creating Promise[Done], and returning a new instance of the CountDownLatch class. This instance is what we give to other resources to count down. It also provides an await method to block until the latch is open or a result value to signal that through an asynchronous instance of the type Future[Done].

In this particular example, we give the `CountDownLatch` instance to the 2 `CountDownLatchWorker` instances. These instances call `countDown()` once they are done in the `preStart()` method. Therefore, we can see two statements in the logs announcing "Counting Down" and then "Gate opened" indicating that the latch has reached the desired count. Once that happens, the latch is open and the `await()` method no longer blocks. The same way, `Future[Done]` completes with success and we can see the "Future-based solution completed successfully" log.

To accomplish the future-based variant of CountDownLatch, we have used `Promise[Done]`. A `Promise` approach is similar to `Future`; however, it is possible to write to it. That is exactly what we do inside `CountDownLatchActor` by calling `promise.success(Done)` when the count reaches 0.

Finite-state machine

Another way of defining how your actors behave is using a finite-state machine. This is a well-known method to create machines in digital circuits that work as well for Akka actors. An FSM can be described as a set of relations of this form:

State(S) x Event(E) -> Actions (A), State(S')

We can interpret these relations by saying that if we are in state *S* and an event *E* comes, then we will perform actions *A* and change our state to *S'*. Akka FSM brings some APIs to easily achieve these relations by defining different behaviors using the `when` function. This feature can fit several use cases, such as example aggregation of values.

In this recipe, we will explore how to use Akka FSM by implementing a simple traffic light. We will also look at how we can perform action between transitions by providing a partial function to `onTransition`.

Getting ready

To step through this recipe, we need to import the `Hello-Akka` project; all other prerequisites are the same as earlier.

How to do it...

For this recipe, we need to perform the following steps:

1. To begin with, let's create the `ChangeSubscriber` actor. This actor will receive a message every time a transition happens between states. Create a file named `FSMChangeSubscriber.scala` inside the `com.packt.chapter10` package. This actor will only log every time it receives a message:

    ```scala
    package com.packt.chapter10

    import akka.actor.{Actor, ActorLogging}
    import com.packt.chapter10.TrafficLightFSM.ReportChange

    class FSMChangeSubscriber extends Actor with ActorLogging {
      def receive = { case ReportChange(s, d) => log.info(s"Change
        detected to [$s] at [$d]") }
    }
    ```

2. Second, let's create our model classes that will define the states, the data in each state, and the events that this actor can receive. Later, we will define the traffic light actor that will extend FSM. Create a file named `TrafficLightsFSM.scala` inside the `com.packt.chapter10` package with the following content:

    ```scala
    package com.packt.chapter10

    import java.util.Date
    import akka.actor.{Actor, ActorLogging, ActorRef, FSM}
    import TrafficLightFSM._
    import scala.concurrent.duration._

    object TrafficLightFSM {
      sealed trait TrafficLightState
      case object Green extends TrafficLightState
      case object Yellow extends TrafficLightState
      case object Red extends TrafficLightState

      sealed trait Data
      case class Countdown(i: Int) extends Data

      //Events
      case object Tick
      case class ReportChange(to: TrafficLightState, date: Date)
    }
    ```

3. In the same file, let's create the actual FSM actor:

```scala
class TrafficLightFSM(target: ActorRef) extends Actor with
ActorLogging with FSM[TrafficLightState, Data]{
  import context.dispatcher

  trafficLightState(Green, Yellow, 2)
  trafficLightState(Yellow, Red, 4)
  trafficLightState(Red, Green, 8)
  startWith(Green, Countdown(8))

  initialize()
  scheduleTick()

  onTransition {
    case Green -> Yellow => target ! ReportChange(Yellow, new
    Date())
    case Yellow -> Red => target ! ReportChange(Red, new
    Date())
    case Red -> Green => target ! ReportChange(Green, new
    Date())
  }

  private def scheduleTick() =
    context.system.scheduler.scheduleOnce(1 second, self, Tick)

  private def trafficLightState(
    trafficLightState: TrafficLightState,
    nextTrafficLightState: TrafficLightState,
    totalSecondsNextState: Int) = {
      when(trafficLightState) {
      case Event(Tick, Countdown(i)) if i != 0 =>
      scheduleTick()
        log.info(s"Current state [$trafficLightState].
        Countdown: [$i].")
        stay using Countdown(i - 1)
      case Event(Tick, Countdown(i)) if i == 0 =>
        scheduleTick()
        log.info(s"Changing from $trafficLightState to
        $nextTrafficLightState.")
        goto(nextTrafficLightState) using
        Countdown(totalSecondsNextState)
    }
  }
}
```

4. Finally, create an app to run the code. Create a file named `FSMApp.scala` inside the `com.packt.chapter10` package. The code should look like this:

```scala
package com.packt.chapter10

import akka.actor.{ActorSystem, Props}

object FSMApp extends App {
  val actorSystem = ActorSystem()
  val changeSubscriber =
    actorSystem.actorOf(Props[FSMChangeSubscriber],
    "FSMChangeSubscriber")
    actorSystem.actorOf(Props(classOf[TrafficLightFSM],
    changeSubscriber), "trafficLight")
}
```

5. Once all the code is done, let's run the app in either IntelliJ or the command line:

```
hveiga$ sbt "runMain com.packt.chapter10.FSMApp"
[info] Running com.packt.chapter10.FSMApp
[akka://default/user/trafficLight] Current state [Green].
Countdown: [8].
...
[akka://default/user/trafficLight] Current state [Green].
Countdown: [1].
[akka://default/user/trafficLight] Changing from Green to Yellow.
[akka://default/user/FSMChangeSubscriber] Changed detected to
[Yellow] at [16:46:16]
[akka://default/user/trafficLight] Current state [Yellow].
Countdown: [2].
[akka://default/user/trafficLight] Current state [Yellow].
Countdown: [1].
[akka://default/user/trafficLight] Changing from Yellow to Red.
[akka://default/user/FSMChangeSubscriber] Change detected to
[Red] at [16:46:19]
[akka://default/user/trafficLight] Current state [Red].
Countdown: [4].
...
[akka://default/user/trafficLight] Current state [Red].
Countdown: [1].
[akka://default/user/trafficLight] Changing from Red to Green.
...
```

How it works...

In this recipe, we covered how to take advantage of the FSM capabilities that Akka provides. To bring this functionality, we mix in the `FSM[S, D]` trait, where S represents the super type of the possible states and D represents the super type of the possible data values. In our case, we define a trait `TrafficLightState` trait, which is extended by `Green`, `Yellow`, and `Red`. For data, we just have `Countdown`, which we use to count down to change to the next state. The next thing we do is define our states. We do this by calling the `when` method. This happens inside `trafficLightState` since the code for the three states is pretty similar and we don't want to repeat ourselves.

When defining a state, you need to provide a partial function with all possible events that the state can receive. An event will have an instance of the incoming message (`Tick`, in our example) and the event data (`Countdown`, in our example). We can see how if we receive a tick and the countdown is not zero, we just stay using the countdown minus 1. It is stay using what allow us to remain in the same state instead of changing. However, when the count reaches zero, we use `goto()` using to move to a different state with some initial data. After defining our three states, we call `startWith` to set an initial state for our machine, and afterward, we initialize and schedule the first tick to be sent.

It is also possible to do actions when your actor is transitioning from one state to another. We can achieve that by implementing `onTransition`. In this particular function, you provide the transition and what actions to run in that case. In our example, we just notify another actor about that change by sending a `ReportChange` message.

In some scenarios, it is a possibility that some messages sent to your FSM actor will not be handled by the current state (or any state at all). We can implement the `whenUnhandled` function to account for those cases.

The pausable actor pattern

Another common pattern among all enterprise integration patterns is to have a pausable entity. In the case of Akka, we might want to do this in order to make sure that an actor has finished processing one message before receiving another. We can easily create another actor to accomplish this thanks to two features: become/unbecome and stash/unstash. Become/unbecome lets us change the behavior of an actor at runtime. Stash/unstash lets us save messages in an internal queue to later put them back into the mailbox. Then, this new actor will act as a proxy in front of your actor to deliver messages one by one only.

Getting ready

To step through this recipe, we need to import the `Hello-Akka` project; all other prerequisites are the same as earlier.

How to do it...

For this recipe, we need to perform the following steps:

1. To begin with, let's create the `HardWorker` actor. This actor wants to receive a new message only after finishing processing a previous one. It will randomly sleep for a few milliseconds to simulate some processing. Create a file named `HardWorker.scala` inside the `com.packt.chapter10` package. The content should look like this:

   ```scala
   package com.packt.chapter10

   import akka.actor.{Actor, ActorLogging}
   import com.packt.chapter10.PausableActor.{Ready, Work}
   import scala.util.Random

   class HardWorker extends Actor with ActorLogging {
     def receive = {
       case Work(id) =>
         Thread.sleep(Random.nextInt(3) * 1000)
         log.info(s"Work [$id] finished.")
         sender ! Ready
     }
   }
   ```

2. Then, let's create our pausable actor. Create a file named `PausableActor.scala` inside the `com.packt.chapter10` package with the following code:

   ```scala
   package com.packt.chapter10

   import akka.actor.{Actor, ActorLogging, ActorRef, Stash}
   import com.packt.chapter10.PausableActor.{Ready, Work}

   object PausableActor {
     case class Work(id: Int)
     case object Ready
   }

   class PausableActor(target: ActorRef) extends Actor with
   ```

```
ActorLogging with Stash {
  def receive = {
    case work: Work =>
      target ! work
      log.info(s"Received Work [${work.id}]. Sending and
      pausing.")
      context.become(pausedBehavior, discardOld = false)
  }

  def pausedBehavior : Receive = {
    case work: Work => stash()
    case Ready if sender == target =>
      log.info(s"[${target.path.name}] is ready again.")
      context.unbecome()
      unstashAll()
    case Ready => log.info(s"Discarding [Ready] from other
    actor different from ${target.path.name}")
  }
}
```

3. Finally, create an app to run the code. Create a file named
   PausableActorApp.scala inside the com.packt.chapter10 package with the
   following content:

```
package com.packt.chapter10

import akka.actor.{ActorSystem, Props}
import com.packt.chapter10.PausableActor.Work

object PausableActorApp extends App {
  val actorSystem = ActorSystem()
  val hardWorker = actorSystem.actorOf(Props[HardWorker],
  "hardWorker")
  val pausableHardWorker =
    actorSystem.actorOf(Props(classOf[PausableActor],
    hardWorker), "pausableActor")
  (1 to 100).foreach { i => pausableHardWorker ! Work(i) }
}
```

4. Once all the code is ready, let's run our app in either IntelliJ or the command line:

```
hveiga$ sbt "runMain com.packt.chapter10.PausableActorApp"
[info] Running com.packt.chapter10.PausableActorApp
[akka://default/user/pausableActor] Received Work [1]. Sending
and pausing.
[akka://default/user/hardWorker] Work [1] finished.
[akka://default/user/pausableActor] [hardWorker] is ready again.
[akka://default/user/pausableActor] Received Work [2]. Sending
```

```
and pausing.
[akka://default/user/hardWorker] Work [2] finished.
[akka://default/user/pausableActor] [hardWorker] is ready again.
...
```

How it works...

In this recipe, we covered how to create a pausable actor that is able to send messages one by one to another actor. We have developed `PausableActor` with two different behaviors to achieve this purpose. The regular behavior receives a `Work` message, sends it to the target actor, and calls `context.become` to change the behavior to `pausedBehavior`. Once the actor's behavior is `pausedBehavior`, it no longer sends the `Work` message to the target actor, but it calls `stash()` to save it for later processing. Only when the target actor sends back a `Ready` message does `PausableActor` call `context.unbecome` to come back to the previous behavior. It also calls `unstashAll()` to put back all messages in the mailbox. These messages come back to the mailbox in the same other they came to the actor while it was in `pausedBehavior`. Note that we are checking whether the target actor is the one sending the `Ready` message in order to make sure no other actor tries to change the behavior. If any other actor different from the target actor sends a `Ready` message, the actor will still remain in `pausedBehavior`.

If we analyze the logs, we can see how the `HardWorker` actor processes messages one by one in order. It also receives a new message from the pausable actor once it is ready. Finally, it is important to mention that the `Stash` trait must be mixed into the `Actor` trait before any trait/class that overrides the `preRestart` callback.

Enveloping actor

It is easy to find scenarios where our messages need additional information or metadata to do some extra tasks, for example, when you need a correlation ID or a timestamp to track when things were created or tagged. Other frameworks, such as Apache Camel, use an envelope that contains the actual message, some headers, and some attachments. This envelope is called **Exchange** in the Apache Camel world. Unlike Apache Camel, Akka does not provide an out-of-the-box envelope implementation of this kind. Since actors exchange messages of the type `Any` (different from null), we can indeed create our own implementation of an envelope, where we can add additional knowledge about the message we are sending around.

In this recipe, we will define our own envelope, which will have capabilities to hold the additional knowledge in a headers map. Also, we will create an actor that will turn any message into an envelope.

Getting ready

To step through this recipe, we need to import the Hello-Akka project; all other prerequisites are the same as earlier.

How to do it...

For this recipe, we need to perform the following steps:

1. To begin with, let's create the receiver actor. This actor will only log whatever it receives. Create a file named EnvelopReceive.scala inside the com.packt.chapter10 package. The content should be as follows:

```scala
package com.packt.chapter10

import akka.actor.{Actor, ActorLogging}

class EnvelopeReceiver extends Actor with ActorLogging {
  def receive = { case x => log.info(s"Received [$x]") }
}
```

2. Second, let's create the enveloping actor and define the Envelop case class. Create a file named EnvelopingActor.scala inside the com.packt.chapter10 package. The code should look like this:

```scala
package com.packt.chapter10

import akka.actor.{Actor, ActorRef}
import com.packt.chapter10.Envelope._

object Envelope {
  type Headers = Map[String, Any]
  case class Envelope[T](msg: T, headers: Headers = Map.empty)
}

class EnvelopingActor(nextActor: ActorRef, addHeaders: Any)
extends Actor {
  def this(nextActor: ActorRef) = this(nextActor, _ => Map())
  def receive = { case msg => nextActor ! new Envelope(msg,
```

```
                        addHeaders(msg)) }
         }
```

3. Finally, create a small app to run the test. Create a file named
   `EnvelopingActorApp.scala` inside the `com.packt.chapter10` package with
   the following object:

```scala
package com.packt.chapter10

import java.util.UUID
import akka.actor.{ActorSystem, Props}

object EnvelopingActorApp extends App {
  val actorSystem = ActorSystem()
  val envelopReceived =
    actorSystem.actorOf(Props[EnvelopeReceiver], "receiver")
  val envelopingActor =
    actorSystem.actorOf(Props(classOf[EnvelopingActor],
    envelopReceived, headers _))
    envelopingActor ! "Hello!"
  def headers(msg: Any) = Map("t" ->
    System.currentTimeMillis(), "cId" ->
    UUID.randomUUID().toString)
}
```

4. Once the code is all done, run the application in either IntelliJ or the command
   line:

```
hveiga$ sbt "runMain com.packt.chapter10.EnvelopingActorApp"
[info] Running com.packt.chapter10.EnvelopingActorApp
[akka://default/user/receiver] Received [Envelope(Hello!,Map(t ->
1489551681040, cId -> 22a262b3-f02e-4ae5-9745-14183b40a806))]
```

How it works...

In this recipe, we covered how to create an `Envelop` case class where we can add additional
information about a given message. In this particular example, the `Envelope` case class
holds the message of type `Any` and a map of headers of type `String` to `Any`. The addition of
this header happens in `EnvelopingActor`. This actor takes two parameters: the target actor
where we will send the envelope and a function from `Any` to `Headers` that is used to
generate the headers for a given message. When it receives a message, it calls the
`addHeaders` function to create the headers and adds those to the envelope. Once the
envelope is ready, it gets sent to the target actor.

In the `EnvelopingActorApp` object, we can see that we are defining the function `headers`. This function is indeed a function from `Any` to `Headers` (since `Headers` is an alias for `Map[String,Any]`). Then, we use it when calling `actorOf` to create our `EnvelopingActor` class. Note that we are passing the function and that's why we need to partially define it using `headers _`. After running the code, we can see how `EnvelopeReceiver` class prints out the envelop it received with the message `Hello!`.

11
Microservices with Lagom

In this chapter, we will cover the following recipes:

- Installing Lagom and creating a Lagom project
- Understanding the service locator
- Understanding service descriptors
- Implementing Lagom services
- Consuming services
- Testing services
- Writing persistent and clustered services
- Running Lagom in production
- Integrating with Akka

Introduction

Architectures based on microservices are becoming more popular than classical monolithic ones. Traditional monolithic architectures have been popular for decades. Although this paradigm has worked well for many years, they cause problems that are hard to solve, such as scalability and maintainability. These problems became exponentially harder in the modern Internet, where millions of people or devices need to use remote services.

Large companies, such as Google, Netflix, Amazon, or Nike, have spent years transforming their architectures into a new architectural paradigm that brings advantages such as scalability and separation of concerns. In general terms, a microservice is a service that is responsible only for one task. Each microservice is supposed to have an isolated data store (or even no data store), and the data in the data store can only be accessed through the service API. This setup allows developers to use different data stores for each microservice as long as they exchange information through their APIs. Also, it lets each service scale independently and reduces coupling.

Similar to actors, one microservice is no microservice; they come in systems. A microservice architecture contains multiple microservices that talk to each other. For instance, Amazon.com uses a microservices architecture. Every time you visit Amazon.com, multiple calls to hundreds of microservices are made to compile the website you see in your browser.

Lagom is an opinionated microservices framework built on top of Akka and Play. It uses these two mature and popular frameworks as the foundation to process incoming API calls. We will learn how to use Lagom in the following recipes to create microservices that can exchange data and store it in their private data stores.

Installing Lagom and creating a Lagom project

Lagom heavily relies on the Scala build tool (also known as sbt) as the primary tool to install, create, build, configure, and run Lagom projects. While it is possible to use other build tools to do that, we will stick to sbt during this and the following recipes. In this recipe, we will look at how to create a Lagom project from scratch using the provided hello-world project. This project brings in two sample modules that use Kafka and Cassandra behind the scenes to manage the persistence layer.

Once we have our Hello-world sample project, we will extend it adding a new endpoint in one of the modules, and finally, we will use sbt to run all microservices. Afterward, we will use the curl command to access all our modules through REST calls.

Getting ready

To start with the hello world Lagom project, we need two have preinstalled two tools. Visit their respective websites to download and install them if they are not available in your system:

- **sbt 0.13.5 (or higher)**: https://www.scala-sbt.org/download.html
- **Java 8 (or higher)**: https://java.com/en/download/

Before moving forward, ensure your system has both tools ready to be used by going to the console and running this:

```
hveiga$ sbt sbtVersion
[info] 0.13.13
hveiga$ java -version
java version "1.8.0_60"
```

Once those two are installed, we can proceed.

How to do it...

For this recipe, we need to perform the following steps:

1. Let's start cloning the hello world project. Open a terminal console and navigate to the directory where you want the project to be cloned to. Once there, run the following command to clone the project from Giter8:

   ```
   sbt new lagom/lagom-scala.g8
   ```

2. While cloning the project, sbt will ask for a few parameters to configure the project. Enter the following values:

   ```
   name [Hello]: akkacookbook
   organization [com.example]: com.packt.chapter11
   version [1.0-SNAPSHOT]: 1.0-SNAPSHOT
   lagom_version [1.3.1]: 1.3.1
   Template applied in ./akkacookbook
   ```

3. At this point, we have our project ready to be opened in IntelliJ. To do that, open IntelliJ, navigate to menu **File | Open...**, and select the newly created `build.sbt` file that lives inside the `akkacookbook` directory. We can see that our project consists of four different modules: `akkacookbook-api`, `akkacookbook-impl`, `akkacookbook-stream-api`, and `akkacookbook-stream-impl`.

4. Open the `AkkacookbookService` trait that lives inside the `akkacookbook-api` module. We need to modify this file to add a new endpoint to this service. To do that, add a third `pathCall` identifier inside the descriptor method. The resulting code of the trait should look like this:

```
trait AkkacookbookService extends Service {
  def hello(id: String): ServiceCall[NotUsed, String]
  def useGreeting(id: String): ServiceCall[GreetingMessage,
  Done]
  def healthCheck() : ServiceCall[NotUsed, Done]

  override final def descriptor = {
    import Service._
    named("akkacookbook").withCalls(
      pathCall("/api/hello/:id", hello _),
      pathCall("/api/hello/:id", useGreeting _),
      pathCall("/api/healthcheck", healthCheck)
    ).withAutoAcl(true)
  }
}
```

5. Once the API descriptor definition is done, we need to create the implementation for it. This needs to happen in the `akkacoobook-impl` module. Open the `AkkacookbookServiceImpl` abstract class. We should see that there is a compilation error because we now need to implement the `healthCheck()` method. We will return an `akka.Done` object so the REST call returns `200 OK` to indicate that the service is running:

```
package com.packt.chapter11.akkacookbook.impl

import akka.Done
import com.lightbend.lagom.scaladsl.api.ServiceCall
import com.lightbend.lagom.scaladsl.persistence
.PersistentEntityRegistry
import com.packt.chapter11.akkacookbook.api.AkkacookbookService
import scala.concurrent.Future

class AkkacookbookServiceImpl(per: PersistentEntityRegistry)
extends AkkacookbookService {
  override def healthCheck() = ServiceCall( _ =>
```

```
    Future.successful(Done))
  override def hello(id: String) = ServiceCall { _ =>
    val ref = per.refFor[AkkacookbookEntity](id)
    ref.ask(Hello(id, None))
  }
  override def useGreeting(id: String) =
  ServiceCall { request =>
    val ref = per.refFor[AkkacookbookEntity](id)
    ref.ask(UseGreetingMessage(request.message))
  }
}
```

6. With all the code ready, let's run and test our services. Open a terminal console and run `sbt runAll`.

7. To do that, we need to have an Internet connection. After a long log of compiling, downloading, and starting services, we should see `[info] (Services started, press enter to stop and go back to the console...)` to indicate that we are ready to test our services. To start with, open your favorite browser and go to `http://localhost:9000/`. You should see a list of available services, with their HTTP methods and endpoints:

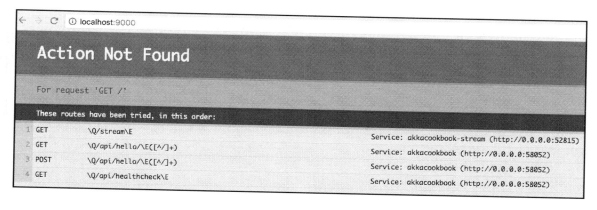

8. Finally, let's run some curl commands to test our services:

```
hveiga$ curl -v -X GET http://localhost:9000/api/hello/hveiga
...
< HTTP/1.1 200 OK
Hello Lagom!, hveiga!
hveiga$ curl -v -H "Content-Type: application/json" -X POST -d
'{"message":"Hello Lagom!"}'
http://localhost:9000/api/hello/hveiga
...
< HTTP/1.1 200 OK
hveiga$ curl -v -X GET http://localhost:9000/api/healthcheck
...
< HTTP/1.1 200 OK
```

How it works...

In this recipe, we covered our first Lagom project. We explored how each service is structured, consisting of two different modules. First, there is a module that defines the API of the service by characterizing the `descriptor` method. Second, there is a module that provides the implementation for that particular API. Note that each API module can define multiple endpoints. For instance, the `akkacookbook-api` API module defines three different endpoints by making three calls to `pathCall` inside the `descriptor` method. Each of these path calls need to return an instance of `ServiceCall[Request,Response]`.

The `ServiceCall` is the class that allows the application understand the type of the request and response for a given call. Lagom will automatically use the available serializers to transform the incoming/outgoing data from/to the required types. Lagom provides built-in JSON serialization thanks to the Play JSON library. If other formats are required, it is possible to create a different registry with custom serializers. If you need to do a `GET` call, you can use the helper Akka object, `NotUsed`. Moreover, if the calls do not need to return any data, you can use the helper Akka object `Done`. Since Lagom is natively asynchronous, you need to return `Future` as the response when implementing your `ServiceCall` class. A good example is our `heathCheck` path call, which returns only `Future(Done)`.

Once we have all the code ready, we run `sbt runAll`. This command starts all the required services, including `ServiceLocator`, the service gateway, an embedded Cassandra instance, and your services that we can easily test by issuing `curl` commands. We will cover all these other pieces in the upcoming recipes.

Understanding the service locator

In an environment full of dynamic components, it is important to have a registry where services can register themselves and discover other services at runtime. This registry needs to maintain an updated list of available services. The ServiceLocator is the API that Lagom provides as the query mechanism to achieve these tasks. The actual implementation behind the ServiceLocator API can be chosen depending on the use case. There are plenty of technologies that provide Service Registry capabilities, such as Apache Zookeeper, Consul, or ConductR.

When running Lagom in development, the framework provides an in-memory service locator where all services get registered when we run sbt runAll. Although this might be sufficient for development environments, when running services in production, this will not be enough since your services would be running remotely. In this recipe, we will explain how the service locator API works and how to add external services to it. In the *Running Lagom in production* recipe, we will explain how to use a service discovery mechanism different from the in-memory one.

Getting ready

To step through this recipe, we need to import the Lagom Akkacoobook project that we created in the initial recipe of this chapter; all other prerequisites are the same as earlier.

How to do it...

For this recipe, we need to perform the following steps:

1. Open the build.sbt file and add the following statement at the end of the file:

   ```
   lagomUnmanagedServices in ThisBuild := Map("login" ->
   "http://localhost:8888")
   ```

2. Now we will modify our AkkacookbookServiceImpl.scala class in the akkacookbook-impl module in order to have the service locator as the class parameter. We will use it to query the service registry and print out where our external service is running. The code should be as follows:

   ```
   package com.packt.chapter11.akkacookbook.impl

   import akka.Done
   import com.lightbend.lagom.scaladsl.api.{ServiceCall,
   ```

```
ServiceLocator}
import com.lightbend.lagom.scaladsl.persistence
.PersistentEntityRegistry
import com.packt.chapter11.akkacookbook.api.AkkacookbookService
import scala.concurrent.{Await, ExecutionContext, Future}
import scala.concurrent.duration._

class AkkacookbookServiceImpl(per: PersistentEntityRegistry,
serviceLocator: ServiceLocator)
(implicit ex: ExecutionContext) extends AkkacookbookService {

  override def healthCheck() = ServiceCall { _ =>
    Await.result(serviceLocator.locate("login"), 2 seconds)
    match {
      case Some(serviceUri) => println(s"Service found at:
      [$serviceUri]")
      case None => println("Service not found")
    }
    Future.successful(Done)
  }
  override def hello(id: String) = ServiceCall { _ =>
    val ref = per.refFor[AkkacookbookEntity](id)
    ref.ask(Hello(id, None))
  }
  override def useGreeting(id: String)=ServiceCall { request =>
    val ref = per.refFor[AkkacookbookEntity](id)
    ref.ask(UseGreetingMessage(request.message))
  }
}
```

3. With all code ready to go, we can run our Lagom application by executing sbt
   runAll.

4. Once all services have been successfully started, access
   http://localhost:9000/api/healthcheck either in your browser or call
   executing curl -X GET http://localhost:9000/api/healthcheck and
   check the standard output of your application. It should have printed this:

```
...
[info] Service akkacookbook-impl listening for HTTP on
0:0:0:0:0:0:0:0:58052
[info] Service akkacookbook-stream-impl listening for HTTP on
0:0:0:0:0:0:0:0:52815
[info] (Services started, press enter to stop and go back to the
console...)
Service found at: [http://localhost:8888]
```

How it works...

In this recipe, we covered what `ServiceLocator` is, how to access it, and how to use it. In this particular example, we modified our `AkkacookbookServiceImpl` class to have the service locator as a class parameter. Lagom understands that you need it in your service and injects it using dependency injection. The `ServiceLocator` is only a trait and its implementation should not be relevant for the services. This trait contains two main calls:

- The `locate()` call to look up a service in the registry by name
- The `doWithService()` call to look up a service in the registry and interact with it

We use `locate()` to query the registry and print out where is the service running. Since we explicitly stated that our login service would be running in `http://localhost:8888/`, we get the same value when printing out the completion of `Future`. While this works well for external services, Lagom provides a more elegant way of discovering other Lagom services, which we will review in the *Consuming services* recipe.

Understanding service descriptors

Lagom strictly separates the API definition from its actual implementation. This brings some advantages, such as separation of concerns, easy understanding of the contract of a service, the possibility to have multiple implementations for a given API and straightforward communication between services by just importing the API module. This separation occurs by having different modules at the project level.

The service descriptor is the main piece in the API module. It describes what the different endpoints of your service are. This happens by describing each endpoint with a call identifier. These call identifiers characterize the endpoint name as well as the expected request and response types through the `ServiceCall` definition. Moreover, the call identifier tells which underlying transport network protocol should be used. In this recipe, we will explain the different available call identifiers and service calls and explain the automatic **Access Control List (ACL)** Lagom provides.

Getting ready

To step through this recipe, we need to import the `Lagom Akkacoobook` project that we created in the initial recipe of this chapter; all other prerequisites are the same as earlier.

How to do it...

For this recipe, we need to perform the following steps:

1. We are going to modify the current `AkkacookbookService` API to showcase all possible call identifiers. For this purpose, we will turn it into a simple `StringUtils` as a service API. Open the `AkkacookbookService.scala` file that lives inside the `akkacookservice-api` module and modify the code to look like this:

```scala
import com.lightbend.lagom.scaladsl.api.transport.Method
trait AkkacookbookService extends Service {
  def toUppercase: ServiceCall[String, String]
  def toLowercase: ServiceCall[String, String]
  def isEmpty(str: String): ServiceCall[NotUsed, Boolean]
  def areEqual(str1: String, str2: String) :
  ServiceCall[NotUsed, Boolean]

  override final def descriptor = {
    import Service._
    named("stringutils").withCalls(
      call(toUppercase),
      namedCall("toLowercase", toLowercase),
      pathCall("/isEmpty/:str", isEmpty _),
      restCall(Method.GET, "/areEqual/:one/another/:other",
      areEqual _)
    ).withAutoAcl(true)
  }
}
```

2. With the API changes ready, we need to implement them in the `akkacoobookservice-impl` module. Open the `AkkacookbookServiceImpl.scala` file and provide a simple implementation of these methods:

```scala
class AkkacookbookServiceImpl extends AkkacookbookService {
  override def toUppercase = ServiceCall { x =>
    Future.successful(x.toUpperCase) }
  override def toLowercase = ServiceCall { x =>
    Future.successful(x.toLowerCase) }
  override def isEmpty(str: String) = ServiceCall { _ =>
    Future.successful(str.isEmpty) }
  override def areEqual(str1: String, str2: String) =
    ServiceCall { _ => Future.successful(str1 == str2) }
}
```

3. Once all the code is ready, run it and test it out with our browser. Run `sbt runAll` to start all the services.

4. We can access the service gateway to take a look at the all available routes:

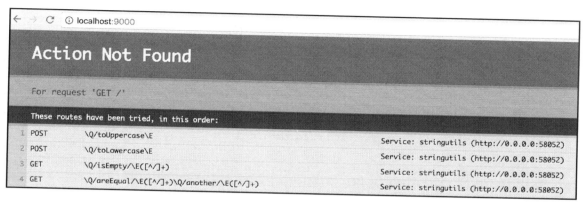

5. Once that's ready, we can run a few `curl` commands to test the endpoints out:

```
hveiga$ curl -X POST -H "Content-Type: text/plain" --data
"UPPERCASE" http://localhost:9000/toLowercase
uppercase
hveiga$ curl -X POST -H "Content-Type: text/plain" --data
"lowercase" http://localhost:9000/toUppercase
LOWERCASE
hveiga$ curl -X GET http://localhost:9000/isEmpty/notEmpty
false
hveiga$ curl -X GET
http://localhost:9000/areEqual/something/another/somethingElse
false
```

How it works

In this recipe, we covered how to use the different call identifiers to define a service descriptor. We are using four identifiers:

- `call()`: This is just an alias for `namedCall()`, where the name of the provided function is used, in this case, `toUppercase`.
- `namedCall()`: This is used for named identifiers where you cannot match parameters.

- `pathCall()`: This is used for named identifiers where you can match parameters and use them in your service calls.
- `restCall()`: This is used for named identifiers where you can match parameters and also enforce the REST method to be matched.

For all these, we pass a function that returns a `ServiceCall[Request,Response]` type. It is based on the types of `Request` and `Response` and how the service infers the REST methods to use for each of the calls (except if we use `restCall()`, where we can enforce it). After defining the calls of the API, we use `withAutoAcl(true)`. ACL stands for Access Control List and defines a list of permissions for a given object. AutoACL lets services access your service and also allows the service gateway to redirect the requests to the real services. That explains why it is possible to access a service through the default port 9000 (where the service gateway listens) even if services are running in other ephemeral ports. Lagom lets you have more fine-grained access control for your service descriptor by providing the desired permission to the `withAcls()` method.

In an environment with several microservices, it is important to only share the definition of your API. You should not let others know about any details of the implementation. Occasionally, developers rely on details of the internal implementation, which can turn into severe integration issues whenever internal implementations change or evolve.

Implementing Lagom services

As we have explained through the previous recipes, services in Lagom have two modules: the API module responsible for defining the contract of the service and the implementation module where we develop the logic behind the API calls. Lagom is asynchronous by default. This means that multiple incoming requests will be served concurrently. Lagom leverages Akka and Play to provide a powerful and resilient engine to run your services. Every service implementation contains at least three components: the service loader, the service application, and the service implementation.

In this recipe, we will review these three components by creating a token service implementation and explain the responsibilities and duties for each of them.

Getting ready

To step through this recipe, we need to import the Lagom Akkacoobook project that we created in the initial recipe of this chapter; all other prerequisites are the same as earlier.

How to do it...

For this recipe, we need to perform the following steps:

1. First, we need to define the two new modules in our `build.sbt`. Open `build.sbt` and add the following modules at the end of the file:

```
lazy val `token-api` = (project in file("token-api"))
  .settings(
    libraryDependencies ++= Seq(
      lagomScaladslApi
    )
  )
lazy val `token-impl` = (project in file("token-impl"))
  .enablePlugins(LagomScala)
  .settings(
    libraryDependencies ++= Seq(
      lagomScaladslPersistenceCassandra,
      lagomScaladslTestKit,
      macwire,
      scalaTest
    )
  )
  .settings(lagomForkedTestSettings: _*)
  .dependsOn(`token-api`)
```

2. Second, we need to add the `token-api` and `token-impl` modules to the aggregate of the project. In `build.sbt`, update the following to list our two new modules as well:

```
lazy val `akkacookbook` = (project in
file(".")).aggregate(`akkacookbook-api`, `akkacookbook-impl`,
`token-api`,`token-impl`)
```

3. Once we are done with `build.sbt`, save the file and run `sbt compile`. This will generate the new folder structure necessary to implement the new service.

4. Let's start with the API module. Open the `token-api` module and create a package named `com.packt.chapter11.token.api` inside the `src/main/scala` directory.

5. Create a file named `Messages.scala` inside the `com.packt.chapter11.token.api` package. This file will contain all requests and results to interact with your service:

```scala
package com.packt.chapter11.token.api

import play.api.libs.json.{Format, Json}

case class RetrieveTokenRequest(clientId: String, clientSecret:
String)
case class RetrieveTokenResult(successful: Boolean, token:
Option[String] = None)
case class ValidateTokenRequest(clientId: String, token: String)
case class ValidateTokenResult(successful: Boolean)

object RetrieveTokenRequest {
  implicit val retrieveTokenRequestFormat:
  Format[RetrieveTokenRequest] =
    Json.format[RetrieveTokenRequest]
}
object RetrieveTokenResult {
  implicit val retrieveTokenResultFormat:
  Format[RetrieveTokenResult] = Json.format[RetrieveTokenResult]
}
object ValidateTokenRequest {
  implicit val validateTokenRequestFormat:
  Format[ValidateTokenRequest] =
  Json.format[ValidateTokenRequest]
}
object ValidateTokenResult {
  implicit val validateTokenResultFormat:
  Format[ValidateTokenResult] = Json.format[ValidateTokenResult]
}
```

6. Create a file named `TokenService.scala` inside the `com.packt.chapter11.token.api` package. This file will define our service. The code should look like this:

```scala
package com.packt.chapter11.token.api

import com.lightbend.lagom.scaladsl.api.{Service, ServiceCall}

trait TokenService extends Service {
```

```
def retrieveToken: ServiceCall[RetrieveTokenRequest,
  RetrieveTokenResult]
def validateToken: ServiceCall[ValidateTokenRequest,
  ValidateTokenResult]

override final def descriptor = {
  import Service._
  named("token").withCalls(
    pathCall("/token/retrieve", retrieveToken),
    pathCall("/token/validate", validateToken)
  ).withAutoAcl(true)
}
}
```

7. Once we are done with the API, let's move to the implementation. Open the `token-impl` module and create a package named `com.packt.chapter11.token.impl` inside the `src/main/scala` directory.

8. Create a file named `TokenServiceImpl.scala` inside the `com.packt.chapter11.token.impl` package. This file will contain the actual implementation of our service. The content should be as follows:

```
package com.packt.chapter11.token.impl

import java.util.UUID
import com.lightbend.lagom.scaladsl.api.ServiceCall
import com.packt.chapter11.token.api._
import scala.concurrent.{ExecutionContext, Future}

class TokenServiceImpl(implicit val ec: ExecutionContext) extends
TokenService {
  val permittedIds = Map("123456" -> "in9ne0dfka","678901" ->
    "0923nsnx00")
  var tokenStore = Map.empty[String, String]

  override def retrieveToken: ServiceCall[RetrieveTokenRequest,
  RetrieveTokenResult] = ServiceCall {
    request => Future {
      permittedIds.get(request.clientId) match {
        case Some(secret) if secret == request.clientSecret =>
          val token = UUID.randomUUID().toString
          tokenStore += request.clientId -> token
          RetrieveTokenResult(true, Some(token))
        case _ => RetrieveTokenResult(false)
      }
    }
  }
}
```

```
      override def validateToken: ServiceCall[ValidateTokenRequest,
    ValidateTokenResult] = ServiceCall {
      request => Future {
        tokenStore.get(request.clientId) match {
          case Some(token) if token == request.token =>
          ValidateTokenResult(true)
          case _ => ValidateTokenResult(false)
        }
      }
    }
  }
```

9. Afterward, we need to create our service loader. Create a file named
   `TokenLoader.scala` inside the `com.packt.chapter11.token.impl` package.
   This file needs to contain the following code:

```scala
package com.packt.chapter11.token.impl

import com.lightbend.lagom.scaladsl.api.ServiceLocator
import com.lightbend.lagom.scaladsl.api.
ServiceLocator.NoServiceLocator
import com.lightbend.lagom.scaladsl.devmode
.LagomDevModeComponents
import com.lightbend.lagom.scaladsl.server._
import com.packt.chapter11.token.api.TokenService
import com.softwaremill.macwire._
import play.api.libs.ws.ahc.AhcWSComponents

class TokenLoader extends LagomApplicationLoader {
  override def load(context: LagomApplicationContext):
  LagomApplication =
    new TokenApplication(context) { override def serviceLocator:
      ServiceLocator = NoServiceLocator }
  override def loadDevMode(context: LagomApplicationContext):
  LagomApplication =
    new TokenApplication(context) with LagomDevModeComponents
  override def describeServices =
  List(readDescriptor[TokenService])
}

abstract class TokenApplication(context: LagomApplicationContext)
  extends LagomApplication(context) with AhcWSComponents {
  override lazy val lagomServer = LagomServer.forServices(
    bindService[TokenService].to(wire[TokenServiceImpl])
  )
}
```

10. Finally, we need to let know Lagom where our service loader is. This is achieved through the `application.conf` file. Create a file named `application.conf` inside the `src/main/resources` in the module `token-impl` directory. The content should be as follows:

```
play.application.loader =
com.packt.chapter11.token.impl.TokenLoader
```

How it works...

In this recipe, we covered how service implementation is done for Lagom services. In this particular example, we create a simple token service that authenticates a user and provides a token. Then, the token can be validated. This service is not backed by any database and it's only for demonstration purposes. To begin with, we define our modules in our `build.sbt` file and add them to the aggregate of the project definition. Once the directory structure gets created, we define our API module. The API module defines both the service interface as well as the messages that are exchanged by this service. In this case, the service calls defined are `retrieveToken` and `validateToken` inside the `TokenService` file. We can see that both calls have their own request and result case classes. Also, these case classes have their JSON serializers to automatically translate them from and to JSON.

The implementation module is composed of the service implementation, the service loader, and the Lagom application. The service implementation gets defined inside `TokenServiceImpl`. The `retrieveToken` service call takes `clientId` and `clientSecret` and returns a token if the ID and secret are a match. The `validateToken` service call checks whether the token is already in memory and returns the result. The lagom application is defined in the `TokenApplication` abstract class, which extends `LagomApplication`. This class represents an instance of one or more services that get bound to their APIs by calling `LagomServer.forServices`. Keep in mind that it is perfectly possible to have a Lagom application representing more than one service. Finally, the service loader is responsible for loading and describing your Lagom application. In our case, `TokenLoader` is our service loader. The `TokenLoader` extends `LagomApplicationLoader`, which is basically a wrapper of Play `ApplicationLoader`. It's the service loader in the component that defines which service locator to use in order to register your services and discover other services. It provides the `load()` method to achieve this. In production, this call would be used to inject your production service locator. It is also possible to optionally override the `loadDevMode()` method if you want to have a different service locator in the development mode. To ease the development of microservices with Lagom, the framework provides `LagomDevModeComponents`. This object brings in the in-memory service locator, which is the one used when we run `sbt runAll`.

Finally, the way the framework finds the service loader is through `application.conf`, which brings in the fully qualified name of the loader class.

Consuming services

A microservices architecture is formed by multiple different microservices that communicate with each other to work together and achieve a task. For example, your architecture could have an `authentication` microservice responsible for authorizing and authenticating users. Other services would use the `authentication` microservice to check the permissions of the user making the request. So, the rest of the services would need to communicate with the `authentication` service before proceeding with any other task. Lagom provides an elegant mechanism to locate an external service (through the Service Locator) and interact with it by knowing its API module.

In this recipe, we will look at how we can communicate with other Lagom services without the need to manually create a REST client, a serialization framework, or any other elements.

Getting ready

To step through this recipe, we need to import the Lagom Akkacoobook project that we created in the initial recipe of this chapter; all other prerequisites are the same as earlier. We will make use of the token service we created in the previous recipe, *Implementing Lagom services*.

How to do it...

For this recipe, we need to perform the following steps:

1. First, we need to define the new two modules in our `build.sbt` file. Open `build.sbt` and add the following modules at the end of the file:

```
lazy val `consumer-api` = (project in file("consumer-api"))
  .settings(
    libraryDependencies ++= Seq(
      lagomScaladslApi
    )
  )
lazy val `consumer-impl` = (project in file("consumer-impl"))
  .enablePlugins(LagomScala)
  .settings(
```

```
        libraryDependencies ++= Seq(
          lagomScaladslPersistenceCassandra,
          lagomScaladslTestKit,
          macwire,
          scalaTest
        )
      )
      .settings(lagomForkedTestSettings: _*)
      .dependsOn(`consumer-api`,`token-api`)
```

2. Second, we need to add both modules `consumer-api` and `consumer-impl` to the aggregate of the project. In `build.sbt`, update the following to list our two new modules as well:

```
lazy val `akkacookbook` = (project in
file(".")).aggregate(`akkacookbook-api`, `akkacookbook-impl`,
`token-api`,`token-impl`, `consumer-api`, `consumer-impl`)
```

3. Once we are done with `build.sbt`, save the file and run `sbt compile`. This will generate the new folder structure necessary to implement the new service.

4. Let's start with the API module. Open the `consumer-api` module and create a package named `com.packt.chapter11.consumer.api` inside the `src/main/scala` directory.

5. Create a file named `Messages.scala` inside the `com.packt.chapter11.consumer.api` package. This file will contain all the requests and results to interact with your service:

```
package com.packt.chapter11.consumer.api

import play.api.libs.json.{Format, Json}

case class ConsumeRequest(clientId: String, token: String,
message: String)
object ConsumeRequest {
  implicit val consumeRequestFormat: Format[ConsumeRequest] =
  Json.format[ConsumeRequest]
}
```

6. Create a file named `ConsumerService.scala` inside the `com.packt.chapter11.consumer.api` package. This file will define our service. The code should look like this:

```
package com.packt.chapter11.consumer.api

import com.lightbend.lagom.scaladsl.api.{Service, ServiceCall}

trait ConsumerService extends Service {
  def consume: ServiceCall[ConsumeRequest, Boolean]

  override final def descriptor = {
    import Service._
    named("consume").withCalls(
      pathCall("/api/consume", consume)
    ).withAutoAcl(true)
  }
}
```

7. Once we are done with the API, let's move on to the implementation. Open the `consumer-impl` module and create a package named `com.packt.chapter11.consumer.impl` inside the `src/main/scala` directory.

8. Create a file named `ConsumerServiceImpl.scala` inside the `com.packt.chapter11.consumer.impl` package. This file will contain the actual implementation of our service. The content should be as follows:

```
package com.packt.chapter11.consumer.impl

import com.lightbend.lagom.scaladsl.api.ServiceCall
import com.packt.chapter11.consumer.api.ConsumerService
import com.packt.chapter11.token.api.{TokenService,
ValidateTokenRequest}
import scala.concurrent.ExecutionContext

class ConsumerServiceImpl(tService: TokenService)(implicit ec:
ExecutionContext) extends ConsumerService {
  override def consume = ServiceCall { request =>
    val validateTokenRequest =
    ValidateTokenRequest(request.clientId, request.token)
    tService.validateToken.invoke(validateTokenRequest)
    .map(_.successful)
  }
}
```

9. Afterward, we need to create our service loader and application. Create a file named `ConsumerLoader.scala` inside the `com.packt.chapter11.consumer.impl` package. This file needs to contain the following code:

```scala
package com.packt.chapter11.consumer.impl

import com.lightbend.lagom.scaladsl.api.ServiceLocator
import com.lightbend.lagom.scaladsl.api
.ServiceLocator.NoServiceLocator
import com.lightbend.lagom.scaladsl.devmode
.LagomDevModeComponents
import com.lightbend.lagom.scaladsl
.server.{LagomApplication, LagomApplicationContext,
LagomApplicationLoader, LagomServer}
import com.packt.chapter11.consumer.api.ConsumerService
import com.packt.chapter11.token.api.TokenService
import com.softwaremill.macwire.wire
import play.api.libs.ws.ahc.AhcWSComponents

class ConsumerLoader extends LagomApplicationLoader {
  override def load(context: LagomApplicationContext):
  LagomApplication =
    new ConsumerApplication(context) { override def
    serviceLocator: ServiceLocator = NoServiceLocator }
  override def loadDevMode(context: LagomApplicationContext):
  LagomApplication =
    new ConsumerApplication(context) with LagomDevModeComponents
    override def describeServices =
    List(readDescriptor[ConsumerService])
}

abstract class ConsumerApplication(context:
LagomApplicationContext)
  extends LagomApplication(context) with AhcWSComponents {
  override lazy val lagomServer = LagomServer.forServices(
    bindService[ConsumerService].to(wire[ConsumerServiceImpl])
  )
  lazy val tokenService = serviceClient.implement[TokenService]
}
```

10. Finally, we need to let Lagom know where our service loader is. This is achieved through the `application.conf` file. Create a file named `application.conf` inside the `src/main/resources` directory in the `consumer-impl` module. The content should be as follows:

```
play.application.loader =
com.packt.chapter11.consumer.impl.ConsumerLoader
```

11. Once all the code is ready, let's run all our services by executing `sbt runAll`.

12. Wait until all the services are started and then run the following command to test it out:

```
hveiga$ curl -d '{"clientId":"some-invalid-
clientId","token":"some-invalid-token","message":""}'
http://localhost:9000/api/consume
false
hveiga$ curl -d '{"clientId":"123456","clientSecret":"something-
wrong"}' http://localhost:9000/token/retrieve
{"successful":false}
hveiga$ curl -d
'{"clientId":"123456","clientSecret":"in9ne0dfka"}'
http://localhost:9000/token/retrieve
{"successful":true,"token":"ee34ee95-f908-4b03-b6e5-
8e0b46b2f4bf"}
hveiga$ curl -d '{"clientId":"123456","token":"ee34ee95-f908-
4b03-b6e5-8e0b46b2f4bf","message":""}'
http://localhost:9000/api/consume
true
```

How it works...

In this recipe, we covered how service consumption from another service is done within a Lagom service. To demonstrate this behavior, we have created a new service named consumer. To start, we create the API and implementation modules in `build.sbt`. The consumer service will be using the token service, which is why we add the `token-api` module as a dependency in the implementation module (`consumer-impl`). Once that is ready, we develop our API module. This service takes `ConsumeRequest` and returns a Boolean. The desired behavior is to use the token service when the consumer service receives a request and return true if the token is valid and false if it's not.

In order to use the token service in `ConsumerServiceImpl`, we just add a class parameter that gives us a reference to the service. This reference has all calls the API provides and an `invoke()` method to use it, which returns `Future`. Every time `ConsumerServiceImpl` receives `ConsumeRequest`, a new `ValidateTokenRequest` case class gets created and the token service gets invoked. We can see in the logs that in order to correctly use the consumer service, we need to retrieve a token from the token service using a valid `clientId` and `clientSecret`. After that, you provide the token in `ConsumeRequest` when calling the consumer service. Finally, the way Lagom injects the token service into the consumer service is by defining it in the `ConsumerApplication` class. We can do that by calling `Client.implement[TokenService]` service. This call internally uses the service locator to locate a service that implements the `TokenService` interface.

As we have seen, just by using the `serviceClient` and adding a class parameter with the type of service we want to use, we are able to seamlessly interact with other Lagom services where serialization and network communication is taken care of.

Testing services

Testing is always a crucial element in any software project. Untested code usually ends up turning into problematic code. In a large microservice architectures, a single service could be used by tens of others. Pushing untested code that might break other services is not what you want in your architecture. Lagom provides comprehensive testing support to make sure your services behave as expected before promoting them to staging or production environments. In this recipe, we will look at how to test a single Lagom service with the help of Scala test.

Getting ready

To step through this recipe, we need to import the Lagom Akkacoobook project that we created in the initial recipe of this chapter; all other prerequisites are the same as before. We will make use of the token service we created in the previous recipe, *Implementing Lagom services*.

How to do it...

For this recipe, we need to perform the following steps:

1. First, create a package named `com.packt.chapter11.token.impl` inside the `src/test/scala` directory in the `token-impl` module.

2. Second, create a file named `TokenServiceSpec.scala` inside `com.packt.chapter11.token.impl` in `src/test/scala`. This class will hold our service tests. The skeleton of the class should look like this:

```scala
package com.packt.chapter11.token.impl

import com.lightbend.lagom.scaladsl.server.LocalServiceLocator
import com.lightbend.lagom.scaladsl.testkit.ServiceTest
import com.packt.chapter11.token.api._
import org.scalatest.{AsyncWordSpec, BeforeAndAfterAll, Matchers}

class TokenServiceSpec extends AsyncWordSpec with Matchers with
BeforeAndAfterAll {
  lazy val server =
    ServiceTest.startServer(ServiceTest.defaultSetup) { ctx =>
    new TokenApplication(ctx) with LocalServiceLocator
  }
  lazy val serviceClient =
    server.serviceClient.implement[TokenService]

  "The token service" should {
    //tests go here
  }

  override protected def beforeAll() = server
  override protected def afterAll() = server.stop()
}
```

3. Now let's add one test for token retrieval from the service. Add the following piece of code inside The `token service should`:

```scala
"return a token if clientId and clientSecret are correct" in {
  val retrieveTokenRequest = RetrieveTokenRequest("123456",
  "in9ne0dfka")
  serviceClient.retrieveToken.invoke(retrieveTokenRequest).map {
  response =>
    response.successful shouldBe true
    response.token should not be 'empty
  }
}
```

4. Additionally, let's add a second test for the token validator from the service. Add the following piece of code inside `The token service should`:

```
"validate a valid token" in {
  val retrieveTokenRequest = RetrieveTokenRequest("123456",
  "in9ne0dfka")
  serviceClient.retrieveToken.invoke(retrieveTokenRequest)
  .flatMap { retrieveResponse =>
    val validateTokenRequest = ValidateTokenRequest("123456",
    retrieveResponse.token.get)
    serviceClient.validateToken.invoke(validateTokenRequest).map
    { validateResponse =>
      validateResponse shouldBe ValidateTokenResult(true)
    }
  }
}
```

5. Once we have our new tests, let's run them in order to make sure they pass. Run `sbt` in the console. Afterward, change to the `token-impl` module by executing `project token-impl`. Finally, run `test` and wait for the result:

```
[info] Run completed in 3 seconds, 574 milliseconds.
[info] Total number of tests run: 2
[info] Suites: completed 1, aborted 0
[info] Tests: succeeded 2, failed 0, canceled 0, ignored 0,
pending 0
[info] All tests passed.
```

How it works...

In this recipe, we covered how to create unit tests for our services. In this particular example, we are testing our token service with two tests: one for the `retrieveToken` call and the other one for the `validateToken` call. In order to create an instance of our service, we use the `ServiceTest` helper class. This class manages all internals to bring up a server running your service in memory. By default, `ServiceTest` does not support using persistence, clustering, or pubsub. If they are required for your use case, they need to be enabled by updating the provided `Setup` object. With our service running, we need something to access it and use it. We can achieve that thanks to the service client. It's the server that provides the service client. The remaining thing to interact with the service is to provide the service client with the type of service in the `implement` method (`TokenService`, in this example).

Once we have our service client, we start with our tests. First, we test the token retrieval. We instantiate a `RetrieveTokenRequest` object with the appropriate `clientId` and `clientSecret` values. We use the service client to invoke the `retrieveToken` call and then we map the `Future` response to assert that the result is the expected one. Since we are using `AsyncWordSpec`, every test excepts to return `Future`. Similarly, we test the token validation. This time, we need to make two calls to the service: to retrieve a token and to validate it. That's why we are using `flatMap` in the primary call to `turnFuture[Future[_]]` into a single `Future[_]`. Finally, we run our tests using `sbt` and confirm that our service is working as expected.

The `ServiceTest` is only valid for testing one service at a time. While this might seem sufficient, there might be a scenario where you need to involve multiple services in a test. This feature is currently being developed and will be available in a future release of Lagom.

Writing persistent and clustered services

Another advantage of using Lagom is the ease of having persistent and cluster services. Persistent and clustered services are possible thanks to Akka persistence, Akka cluster, and Akka cluster sharding. Traditionally, developers have used the well-known CRUD operations to implement persistence for their data. Lagom, however, adopts event sourcing and **Command Query Responsibility Segregation (CQRS)** as the techniques to implement persistence. Event sourcing and CQRS is a pattern to achieve persistence by storing state changes as historical events instead of the actual modified state. These changes are immutable and only get appended to the data store, which improves the write performance. There is no modification of the stored data. This brings in a new set of advantages, such as the possibility to restore state just by executing the ordered list of changes or having a complete log about what happened in the lifetime of an object and not just the latest state of an object.

Lagom defines `PersistentEntity` as a uniquely identifiable entity that can be persisted using Event Sourcing and CQRS. Each instance has a stable identifier, and for a given ID, there will be only one instance of the entity (basically same as for Akka cluster sharding). The framework takes care of distributing the instances across all nodes of the cluster. Apache Cassandra is the data store used by Lagom by default. Lagom also provides clustered services that can connect to each other using Akka Cluster.

In this recipe, we are going to create a trip service that will start, track, and end trips similar to what happened with the popular ride-share companies. This service will use the persistence APIs to persist information about these trips.

Getting ready

To step through this recipe, we need to import the Lagom Akkacoobook project that we created in the initial recipe of this chapter; all other prerequisites are the same as earlier.

How to do it...

For this recipe, we need to perform the following steps:

1. First, we need to define the new two modules in our `build.sbt` file. Open `build.sbt` and add the following modules at the end of the file:

```
lazy val `trip-api` = (project in file("trip-api"))
  .settings(
    libraryDependencies ++= Seq(
      lagomScaladslApi
    )
  )
lazy val `trip-impl` = (project in file("trip-impl"))
  .enablePlugins(LagomScala)
  .settings(
    libraryDependencies ++= Seq(
      lagomScaladslPersistenceCassandra,
      lagomScaladslTestKit,
      macwire,
      scalaTest
    )
  )
  .settings(lagomForkedTestSettings: _*)
  .dependsOn(`trip-api`)
```

2. Second, we need to add both to the aggregate of the project. In `build.sbt`, update the following to list our two new modules as well:

```
lazy val `akkacookbook` = (project in
file(".")).aggregate(`akkacookbook-api`, `akkacookbook-impl`,
`token-api`,`token-impl`, `consumer-api`, `consumer-impl`,
`trip-api`, `trip-impl`)
```

3. Once we are done with `build.sbt`, save the file and run `sbt compile`. This will generate the new folder structure necessary to implement the new service.

4. Let's start with the API module. Open the `trip-api` module and create a package named `com.packt.chapter11.trip.api` inside the `src/main/scala` directory.

5. Create a file named `Messages.scala` inside the `com.packt.chapter11.trip.api` package. This file will contain all the requests and results required to interact with your service:

```scala
package com.packt.chapter11.trip.api

import play.api.libs.json.{Format, Json}

case class ReportLocation(latitude: Double, longitude: Double)
object ReportLocation {
  implicit val reportLocationRequestFormat:
  Format[ReportLocation] = Json.format[ReportLocation]
}
```

6. Create a file named `TripService.scala` inside the `com.packt.chapter11.trip.api` package. This file will define our service. The code should look like this:

```scala
package com.packt.chapter11.trip.api

import akka.{Done, NotUsed}
import com.lightbend.lagom.scaladsl.api.{Service, ServiceCall}

trait TripService extends Service {
  def startTrip(clientId: String): ServiceCall[NotUsed, Done]
  def reportLocation(clientId: String):
  ServiceCall[ReportLocation, Done]
  def endTrip(clientId: String): ServiceCall[NotUsed, Done]

  override final def descriptor = {
    import Service._
    named("trip").withCalls(
      pathCall("/trip/start/:id", startTrip _),
      pathCall("/trip/report/:id", reportLocation _),
      pathCall("/trip/end/:id", endTrip _)
    ).withAutoAcl(true)
  }
}
```

7. Once we are done with the API, let's move on to the implementation. Open the `trip-impl` module and create a package named `com.packt.chapter11.trip.impl` inside the `src/main/scala` directory.

8. Create a file named `CommandEventState.scala` inside the `com.packt.chapter11.trip.impl` package. This will contain all classes required to deal with the persistence:

```scala
package com.packt.chapter11.trip.impl

import akka.Done
import com.lightbend.lagom.scaladsl.persistence
.PersistentEntity.ReplyType
import com.packt.chapter11.trip.api.ReportLocation
import play.api.libs.json.{Format, Json}

sealed trait ClientCommand[R] extends ReplyType[R]
case object StartTrip extends ClientCommand[Done]
case object EndTrip extends ClientCommand[Done]
case class AddLocation(reportLocationRequest: ReportLocation)
extends ClientCommand[Done]
sealed trait ClientEvent
case class TripStarted(time: Long) extends ClientEvent
case class TripEnded(time: Long) extends ClientEvent
case class LocationAdded(location: Location) extends
ClientEvent
case class Location(lat: Double, lon: Double)
case class ClientState(tripInProgress: Boolean, locations:
List[Location])

object Location { implicit val format : Format[Location] =
Json.format[Location] }
object ClientState { implicit val format: Format[ClientState] =
Json.format }
object TripStarted { implicit val format: Format[TripStarted] =
Json.format }
object TripEnded { implicit val format: Format[TripEnded] =
Json.format }
object LocationAdded { implicit val format:
Format[LocationAdded] = Json.format }
object AddLocation { implicit val format: Format[AddLocation] =
Json.format }
```

9. Create a file named `ClientSerializerRegistry.scala` inside the `com.packt.chapter11.trip.impl` package. This file will hold the JSON serializer to serialize the data to and from the data store:

```scala
package com.packt.chapter11.trip.impl

import com.lightbend.lagom.scaladsl.playjson.{JsonSerializer,
JsonSerializerRegistry}
import scala.collection.immutable.Seq

object ClientSerializerRegistry extends JsonSerializerRegistry
{
  override def serializers: Seq[JsonSerializer[_]] = Seq(
    JsonSerializer[Location],
    JsonSerializer[ClientState],
    JsonSerializer[TripStarted],
    JsonSerializer[TripEnded],
    JsonSerializer[LocationAdded],
    JsonSerializer[AddLocation]
  )
}
```

10. Create a file named `ClientEntity.scala` inside the `com.packt.chapter11.trip.impl` package. This entity will represent each client and manage the commands, events, and state:

```scala
package com.packt.chapter11.trip.impl

import java.util.Date
import akka.Done
import com.lightbend.lagom.scaladsl.
persistence.PersistentEntity

class ClientEntity extends PersistentEntity {
  override type Command = ClientCommand[_]
  override type Event = ClientEvent
  override type State = ClientState
  override def initialState = ClientState(false, Nil)

  override def behavior: Behavior =
    Actions()
      .onCommand[StartTrip.type, Done] {
      case (_, ctx, state) if !state.tripInProgress =>
        ctx.thenPersist(TripStarted(new Date().getTime)) { _ =>
        ctx.reply(Done)  }
      case (_, ctx, _) =>
        ctx.invalidCommand("The trip has started already.")
```

```
        ctx.done
   }
     .onCommand[EndTrip.type, Done] {
     case (_, ctx, state) if state.tripInProgress =>
       ctx.thenPersist(TripEnded(new Date().getTime)) { _ =>
       ctx.reply(Done) }
     case (_, ctx, _)   =>
       ctx.invalidCommand("The trip has not started.")
       ctx.done
   }
     .onCommand[AddLocation, Done] {
     case (AddLocation(req), ctx, state) if
     state.tripInProgress =>
       ctx.thenPersist(LocationAdded(Location(req.latitude,
       req.longitude))) { _ => ctx.reply(Done) }
     case (_, ctx, _) =>
       ctx.invalidCommand("The trip has not started.")
       ctx.done
   }
     .onEvent {
       case (TripStarted(_), _) => ClientState(true, Nil)
       case (TripEnded(_), _) => ClientState(false, Nil)
       case (LocationAdded(loc), state) =>
       state.copy(locations = state.locations :+ loc)
   }
 }
```

11. Create a file named `TripServiceImpl.scala` inside the `com.packt.chapter11.trip.impl` package. This file will contain the actual implementation of our service. The content should be as follows:

```
package com.packt.chapter11.trip.impl

import com.lightbend.lagom.scaladsl.api.ServiceCall
import com.lightbend.lagom.scaladsl.persistence
.PersistentEntityRegistry
import com.packt.chapter11.trip.api.TripService

class TripServiceImpl(per: PersistentEntityRegistry) extends
TripService {
  override def startTrip(clientId: String) = ServiceCall { _ =>
    per.refFor[ClientEntity](clientId).ask(StartTrip)
  }
  override def reportLocation(clientId: String) = ServiceCall {
  req =>
    per.refFor[ClientEntity](clientId).ask(AddLocation(req))
  }
  override def endTrip(clientId: String) = ServiceCall { _ =>
```

```
per.refFor[ClientEntity](clientId).ask(EndTrip)
  }
}
```

12. Afterward, we need to create our service loader. Create a file named `TripLoader.scala` inside the `com.packt.chapter11.trip.impl` package. This file needs to contain the following code:

```scala
package com.packt.chapter11.trip.impl

import com.lightbend.lagom.scaladsl.api.ServiceLocator
import com.lightbend.lagom.scaladsl.api
.ServiceLocator.NoServiceLocator
import com.lightbend.lagom.scaladsl.devmode
.LagomDevModeComponents
import com.lightbend.lagom.scaladsl.persistence.
cassandra.CassandraPersistenceComponents
import com.lightbend.lagom.scaladsl.server.{LagomApplication,
LagomApplicationContext, LagomApplicationLoader, LagomServer}
import com.packt.chapter11.trip.api.TripService
import com.softwaremill.macwire.wire
import play.api.libs.ws.ahc.AhcWSComponents

class TripLoader extends LagomApplicationLoader {
  override def load(context: LagomApplicationContext):
  LagomApplication =
    new TripApplication(context) { override def serviceLocator:
      ServiceLocator = NoServiceLocator }
    override def loadDevMode(context: LagomApplicationContext):
    LagomApplication = {
      new TripApplication(context) with LagomDevModeComponents
  }
  override def describeServices =
    List(readDescriptor[TripService])
}

abstract class TripApplication(context:
LagomApplicationContext) extends LagomApplication(context) with
CassandraPersistenceComponents with AhcWSComponents {
  override lazy val lagomServer = LagomServer.forServices(
    bindService[TripService].to(wire[TripServiceImpl])
  )
  override lazy val jsonSerializerRegistry =
    ClientSerializerRegistry persistentEntityRegistry
    .register(wire[ClientEntity])
}
```

13. Finally, we need to let Lagom know where our service loader is. This is achieved through the `application.conf` file. Create a file named `application.conf` inside the `src/main/resources` directory in the `consumer-impl` module. The content should be as follows:

```
play.application.loader =
    com.packt.chapter11.trip.impl.TripLoader
```

14. Once all the code is ready, let's run all our services by executing `sbt runAll`.

15. Wait until all services have started and then run the following command to test it out:

```
hveiga$ curl http://localhost:9000/trip/end/0
{"name":"com.lightbend.lagom.scaladsl.persistence
.PersistentEntity$InvalidCommandException: The trip has not
started.","detail":"com.lightbend.lagom.scaladsl
.persistence.PersistentEntity$InvalidCommandException: The trip .
has not started.n"}
hveiga$ curl http://localhost:9000/trip/start/0
hveiga$ curl -d '{"latitude":0.1,"longitude":0.1}'
http://localhost:9000/trip/report/0
hveiga$ curl -d '{"latitude":0.2,"longitude":0.2}'
http://localhost:9000/trip/report/0
hveiga$ curl -d '{"latitude":0.3,"longitude":0.3}'
http://localhost:9000/trip/report/0
hveiga$ curl http://localhost:9000/trip/end/0
```

How it works...

In this recipe, we covered how to use the persistence layer of Lagom. We have mentioned that Lagom uses event sourcing and CQRS to implement persistence instead of a traditional approach, such as CRUD. In this particular example, we have a trip service that is able to start, collect locations, and end a trip. In order to make this service persistent, we need to define our persistent entities. We define `ClientEntity` for this purpose. `ClientEntity` extends from `PersistentEntity`, which forces us to implement a few things: the type of command, the type of event, the type of state, the initial state, and the behavior. Commands represent actions sent to this entity. In our case, we have three commands: `StartTrip`, `EndTrip`, and `AddLocation`. Events represent state changes.

In our case, we have three events: `TripStarted`, `TripEnded`, and `LocationAdded`. Events are saved in the data store in order and are responsible for updating the current state. A state is the type used to represent the entity's state. The initial state represents the state when a new entity is created, and behavior defines what to do when it receives a command or event. This is similar to the `receive` method in an Akka actor.

It's in the entity behavior that we really define how we persist our events. With the `onCommand` method, we implement what to do depending on the incoming command. We have three cases in our scenario. We use `ctx` to either persist the change and reply `Done` or call `invalidCommand` to invalidate it. We want to invalidate some of the commands, for example, when we receive `EndTrip` but the trip has not started yet. If the command is valid, we call `ctx.thenPersist` and provide an event to the method. This event gets persisted and the current state gets updated through the `onEvent` method. The `ClientEntity` gets registered in `TripApplication` by calling `persistentEntityRegistry.register(wire[ClientEntity])`. Once that is done, we can use it in our service implementation by adding the (per: `PersistentEntityRegistry`) parameter to `TripServiceImpl`. Then, in order to process and persist the incoming requests, you use the `refFor` method and provide an entity ID (in our example, the client ID) and a command.

To demonstrate how this works, we ran few curl commands to verify that if a trip has not been started, it cannot be ended. In this case, we get the error "The trip has not started.". Afterward, we start the trip, add three locations, and end the trip for the id 0. In a cluster environment, the entities would be evenly distributed across all nodes by default.

Running Lagom in production

Moving systems to production is always a hard task to achieve. A production-like system involves many non-functional requirements that we don't normally pay attention to while in the development stage. Lightbend provides a fully managed tool in its commercial product list named ConductR, which makes it easy to deploy and manage Lagom services. Although ConductR is a great tool, it is perfectly possible to run your Lagom services in a standalone mode on any other platform, such as Docker or AWS.

In this recipe, we will talk about the aspects one would need to focus on when deploying Lagom services to production.

 If you want to learn more about ConductR, visit `https://www.lightbend.com/platform/production`.

Getting ready

This recipe lists some of the aspects to keep in mind when moving a Lagom services project from development to production.

How to do it...

For this recipe, we need to perform the following steps:

1. **Service Locator**: To begin, we need to use a remote, highly available, and scalable service locator. This will bring flexibility to the deployment strategy and will help if your service belongs to an elastic auto-scaling mechanism. Good technologies for this purpose are Apache Zookeeper (`https://zookeeper.apache.org`) or HashiCorp Consul (`https://consul.io`). Jonas Bonér, CTO of Lightbend, has shared some code to use both technologies as service locator of your Lagom application on his GitHub account. You can find the code at `https://github.com/jboner?tab=repositories`.

2. **Packaging**: Secondly, we need to decide how to package and run our application. Sbt provides a useful tool named `sbt-native-packager`, which helps you package your code in your desired format (RPM, Zip, Docker, and so on). Depending on the packaging decided, you might be required to create some extra code to run the service loader of your service. It is also advisable that you use the CI/CD methodology to continuously deliver code to your services.

3. **Isolated data store**: Each of your service should have it's own data store. This data store should only be accessed through the service API.

4. **Logging**: Logging is essential in a production environment to get some feedback from the application. Lagom uses SLF4J for logging, which allows developers to decide the actual logging engine. By default, Lagom is backed by Logback as its logging implementation; however, it's also possible to use any other logging framework, such as Log4j2, to achieve this task. It is advisable that you have a log aggregator in production to query logs in a structured and fast manner. Tools such as Splunk help with this task.

5. **Metrics**: Metrics are really valuable. In a microservices environment, you need to know when a service is performing badly so you can act on it. We can only know that if we keep some metrics of latency, throughput, successful requests, and failed requests. Lightbend provides a monitoring framework in their ecosystem for this purpose.

6. **Alarms**: When things go wrong, we should get notified. It is advisable that you have some alarms based on our metrics to send notifications or run remediation steps when things are not running as expected.

How it works...

In this recipe, we covered what aspects to keep in mind when moving our services from development to a production environment. This list only intends to be a small guide of the most common points to review; however, there might be other non-functional requirements for other specific scenarios not covered by it.

Integrating with Akka

Lagom is built on top of Play and Akka, so it is not surprising that the framework provides capabilities to interact with Akka actors. This makes Lagom really interesting for Akka developers who already have developed applications. It is easy and possible to migrate your Akka applications to microservices using Lagom. Another good use case for Akka in Lagom is when using clustered services. In this case, a developer might want to use a consistent hashing group of actors in order to ensure that the data always ends in the same actor even if it was received from different instances of a given service.

In this recipe, we will explore how to access the actor system to be able to leverage all the Akka power we have been learning through the book.

Getting ready

To step through this recipe, we need to import the Lagom Akkacoobook project that we created in the initial recipe of this chapter; all other prerequisites are the same as earlier.

How to do it...

For this recipe, we need to perform the following steps:

1. First, we need to define the new two modules in our `build.sbt` file. Open `build.sbt` and add the following modules at the end of the file:

```
lazy val `akka-api` = (project in file("akka-api"))
  .settings(
    libraryDependencies ++= Seq(
      lagomScaladslApi
    )
  )
lazy val `akka-impl` = (project in file("akka-impl"))
  .enablePlugins(LagomScala)
  .settings(
    libraryDependencies ++= Seq(
      lagomScaladslPersistenceCassandra,
      lagomScaladslTestKit,
      macwire,
      scalaTest
    )
  )
  .settings(lagomForkedTestSettings: _*)
  .dependsOn(`akka-api`)
```

2. Second, we need to add both to the aggregate of the project. In `build.sbt`, update the following to list our two new modules as well:

```
lazy val `akkacookbook` = (project in
file(".")).aggregate(`akkacookbook-api`, `akkacookbook-impl`,
`token-api`,`token-impl`, `consumer-api`, `consumer-impl`,
`trip-api`, `trip-impl`,`akka-api`, `akka-impl`)
```

3. Once we are done with `build.sbt`, save the file and run `sbt compile`. This will generate the new folder structure necessary to implement the new service.

4. Let's start with the API module. Open the `akka-api` module and create a package named `com.packt.chapter11.akka.api` inside the `src/main/scala` directory.

5. Create a file named `CalculatorService.scala` inside the `com.packt.chapter11.akka.api` package. This file will define our service. The code should look like this:

```scala
package com.packt.chapter11.akka.api

import akka.NotUsed
import com.lightbend.lagom.scaladsl.api.{Service, ServiceCall}

trait CalculatorService extends Service {
  def add(one: Int, other: Int): ServiceCall[NotUsed, Int]
  def multiply(one: Int, other: Int): ServiceCall[NotUsed, Int]

  override final def descriptor = {
    import Service._
    named("calculator").withCalls(
      pathCall("/add/:one/:other", add _),
      pathCall("/multiply/:one/:other", multiply _)
    ).withAutoAcl(true)
  }
}
```

6. Once we are done with the API, let's move on to the implementation. Open the `akka-impl` module and create a package named `com.packt.chapter11.akka.impl` inside the `src/main/scala` directory.

7. Create a file named `CalculatorActor.scala` inside the `com.packt.chapter11.akka.impl` package. This actor will be responsible for the calculations:

```scala
package com.packt.chapter11.akka.impl

import akka.actor.Actor

object CalculatorActor {
  case class Sum(one: Int, another: Int)
  case class Multiply(one: Int, another: Int)
}
class CalculatorActor extends Actor {
  import CalculatorActor._
```

```
    def receive = {
      case Sum(one, another) => sender ! one + another
      case Multiply(one, another) => sender ! one * another
    }
  }
```

8. Create a file named `CalculatorServiceImpl.scala` inside the `com.packt.chapter11.akka.impl` package. This file will contain the actual implementation of our service. The content should be as follows:

```scala
package com.packt.chapter11.akka.impl

import akka.actor.{ActorSystem, Props}
import com.lightbend.lagom.scaladsl.api.ServiceCall
import com.packt.chapter11.akka.api.CalculatorService
import akka.pattern.ask
import akka.util.Timeout
import com.packt.chapter11.akka.impl.CalculatorActor.{Multiply, Sum}
import scala.concurrent.duration._
import scala.concurrent.ExecutionContext

class CalculatorServiceImpl(system: ActorSystem)
(implicit val ec: ExecutionContext) extends CalculatorService {
  implicit val timeout = Timeout(2 seconds)

  override def add(one: Int, other: Int) = ServiceCall { _ =>
    val calculatorActor = system.actorOf
    (Props[CalculatorActor]) (calculatorActor ? Sum(one,
    other)).mapTo[Int]
  }
  override def multiply(one: Int, other: Int) = ServiceCall { _
  =>
    val calculatorActor =
      system.actorOf(Props[CalculatorActor])
      (calculatorActor ? Multiply(one, other)).mapTo[Int]
  }
}
```

9. Afterward, we need to create our service loader. Create a file named `CalculatorLoader.scala` inside the `com.packt.chapter11.akka.impl` package. This file needs to contain the following code:

```scala
package com.packt.chapter11.akka.impl

import com.lightbend.lagom.scaladsl.api.ServiceLocator
import com.lightbend.lagom.scaladsl.api
.ServiceLocator.NoServiceLocator
import com.lightbend.lagom.scaladsl.devmode
.LagomDevModeComponents
import com.lightbend.lagom.scaladsl.server.{LagomApplication,
LagomApplicationContext, LagomApplicationLoader, LagomServer}
import com.packt.chapter11.akka.api.CalculatorService
import com.softwaremill.macwire.wire
import play.api.libs.ws.ahc.AhcWSComponents

class CalculatorLoader extends LagomApplicationLoader {
  override def load(context: LagomApplicationContext):
  LagomApplication =
    new CalculatorApplication(context) { override def
    serviceLocator: ServiceLocator = NoServiceLocator }
  override def loadDevMode(context: LagomApplicationContext):
  LagomApplication = {
    new CalculatorApplication(context) with
    LagomDevModeComponents
  }
  override def describeServices =
  List(readDescriptor[CalculatorService])
}

abstract class CalculatorApplication(context:
LagomApplicationContext)
extends LagomApplication(context) with AhcWSComponents {
  override lazy val lagomServer = LagomServer.forServices(
  bindService[CalculatorService].to(wire[CalculatorServiceImpl])
  )
}
```

10. Finally, we need to let know Lagom where our service loader is. This is achieved through the `application.conf` file. Create a file named `application.conf` inside the `src/main/resources` directory in the `consumer-impl` module. The content should be as follows:

```
play.application.loader =
com.packt.chapter11.akka.impl.CalculatorLoader
```

11. Once all the code is ready, let's run all our services by executing `sbt runAll`.

12. Wait until all services are started and then run the following command to test it out:

```
hveiga$ curl http://localhost:9000/add/3/5
8
hveiga$ curl http://localhost:9000/multiply/3/5
15
```

How it works

In this recipe, we explored how Lagom integrates with Akka. In this particular example, we created a simple calculator service where the actual calculations occur in an actor. The way we can use the actor system in our `CalculatorServiceImpl` class is by adding a parameter (`system: ActorSystem`). Lagom will understand that it needs to inject the instance of the actor system. Once you have the actor system reference, you can do almost anything you need with Akka, as we have seen in all the chapters in this book. In this case, we create a new actor and ask for either `Sum` or `Multiply`.

Therefore, turning already developed Akka applications into microservices can be a matter of creating a new service in front of each actor (or set of actors). Afterward, the messages previously exchanged by actors would need to be used as the messages exchanged between microservices.

Index